SEDA
STAFF AND EDUCATIONAL
DEVELOPMENT ASSOCIATION

Staff and Educational Development Series

ACADEMIC AND EDUCATIONAL DEVELOPMENT

RESEARCH, EVALUATION *and* CHANGING PRACTICE *in* HIGHER EDUCATION

Ranald Macdonald and James Wisdom

**KOGAN
PAGE**

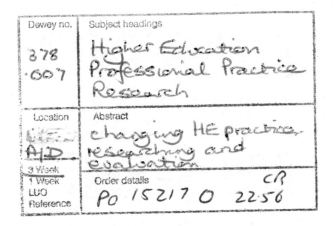

First published in 2002

Kogan Page Limited
120 Pentonville Road
London N1 9JN
UK

Stylus Publishing Inc.
22883 Quicksilver Drive
Sterling VA 20166-2012
USA

British Library Cataloguing in Publication Data

A CIP record for this book is available from the British Library.

ISBN 0 7494 3533 X

Typeset by JS Typesetting, Wellingborough, Northants
Printed and bound in Great Britain by Clays Ltd, St Ives plc

Contents

Notes on contributors

Paul Bailey is a Learning Technology Adviser within the Institute of Learning and Research Technology at the University of Bristol, responsible for the support and promotion of the use of learning technologies within the institution. He leads the EFFECTS project team which developed a national recognition scheme for staff involved in using learning technologies which is now a SEDA Award in Embedding Learning Technologies.
Paul.Bailey@bristol.ac.uk

Helen Beetham is currently a Research Fellow at the Open University and consultant on a number of national learning technology projects based at the Institute for Learning and Research Technologies, University of Bristol. Previously she was Project Officer on the EFFECTS project. She has published and presented widely on learning technologies generally and on the EFFECTS framework in particular.
H.Beetham@open.ac.uk

Paul Blackmore is Director of the Centre for Academic Practice at the University of Warwick and is responsible for leading the university's policy and strategy in academic staff development. He has 15 years' experience in professional development for staff in both higher and further education, and has developed and managed a number of accredited programmes. He has research interests in conceptualizations of professional expertise and in research based teaching and learning.
P.Blackmore@warwick.ac.uk

Jennifer Blumhof is the former Associate Director of the Hertfordshire Integrated Learning Project. She is developing the work of this project at the University of Hertfordshire in her role as Learning and Teaching Development Tutor, through regional networks, and at a national level through work with the LTSN. She is also Senior Subject Advisor for Environmental Sciences for the Subject Centre for Geography, Earth and Environmental Sciences (LTSN-GEES), with particular responsibility for working with the Committee of the Heads of Environmental Sciences (CHES). Jennifer was a member of the Benchmark Panel for Earth Sciences, Environmental Sciences and Environmental Studies. Her pedagogical interests include researching into curriculum change issues, particularly skills development

work and problem based learning. Current interests include researching into the effectiveness of fieldwork and producing teaching support guides for the Earth and Environmental Sciences academic communities.
J.R.Blumhof@herts.ac.uk

Mary Caddick is the course tutor for the Post Graduate Certificate in Learning and Teaching Architecture at the University of East London. She teaches 'creative process workshops' at Central St Martin's School of Art and is a course facilitator for the LIFT (London International Festival of Theatre) Teachers' Forum. Her work combines her training and practice in art therapy, art and design, and teaching. She is interested in how psychoanalytic thinking can inform teaching and learning.
m.f.caddick@uel.ac.uk

Maggie Challis wrote her chapter for this book while working as Educational Adviser to the Medical Postgraduate Dean at the University of Nottingham. She is now the Higher Education Manager at Ufi. Her major research and development interests have always been, and remain, adult access to education and the use of portfolios for educational planning, review and the award of credit. She has published widely in this field, particularly within the medical education press.
MChallis@ufi.com

James A Coleman has recently been appointed Professor of Language Learning and Teaching at the Open University, with a predominantly research brief. He coordinated the FDTL Residence Abroad Project (1997–2001) from Portsmouth University, and has wide experience of quality assurance and enhancement as an external examiner, TQA Subject Specialist Assessor, and member of the European Studies panel in RAE 2001. He has published on French literature, as well as several books and articles on adult language learning, and is editing *Effective Learning and Teaching in Modern Languages* in the ILT/Kogan Page series.
j.a.coleman@open.ac.uk

Grainne Conole is the director of the Institute for Learning and Research Technology at Bristol University. The Institute is a centre of excellence in the development and use of information and communication technology to support learning and research, hosting 49 projects and services and over 70 people. Her research interests include evaluation, curriculum design, online learning, portals and metadata, as well as more recent work in theory and gender. In addition to running the ILRT, she teaches Master's courses in aspects of learning technology, and is editor for the journal of the Association for Learning Technology.
grainne.conole@bristol.ac.uk

Paul Curzon is a Reader in Formal Verification at the School of Computing Science, Middlesex University. He is Convener of the Interaction Design Centre (a research group with interests including human–computer interaction, digital libraries and formalisms for interaction) and is interested in the links between interaction design and teaching and learning, including academic staff development. He led the SEDA funded virtual reading group project at Middlesex University.
p.curzon@mdx.ac.uk

Gabi Diercks-O'Brien works in the Learning Media Unit at the University of Sheffield, where high quality learning resources which include animations and video are produced. Her responsibilities include educational advice and evaluation. Much of her research interest is centred on evaluation and the experiences of students and teachers using technology, with particular emphasis on online learning. She is also interested in developments in the fields of curriculum innovation, instructional design and project management.
G.Diercks-OBrien@sheffield.ac.uk

Jacqueline A Dempster is Head of Educational Technology in the Centre for Academic Practice at the University of Warwick. She has eight years' experience in promoting and supporting educational development in the use of communications and information technologies (ICT) in higher education both at Warwick and at national levels. She currently manages three national projects in this area and is actively involved in developing national professional development opportunities for learning technologists. Her research interests include research based learning and teaching, and operational strategies for ICT implementation and support.
jay.dempster@warwick.ac.uk

Chris Foggin is the Project Associate at the University of the West of England working on the integration of technology based learning materials into the delivery of modules within the programmes at the universities of the West of England, De Montfort and Westminster. His areas of research include learning technology, programme evaluation, student learning, quality assurance and staff development.
Chris.Foggin@uwe.ac.uk

David Hall is Lecturer and University Teaching Fellow in the Department of Sociology, Social Policy and Social Work Studies at the University of Liverpool. He has been a partner in disseminating community based learning through the CoBaLT Project, and is a participant in a European project of research and development on the international Science Shop movement. His interests are in applied sociology, research and evaluation,

particularly with the voluntary sector on Merseyside, and the development and assessment of student skills and reflective learning.
djhall@liv.ac.uk

Irene Hall is a Senior Lecturer in Sociology at Liverpool Hope University College, with responsibility for developing programmes which enable students to undertake work in the community as volunteers or as researchers as part of assessment for their degrees. She is interested in researching various aspects of the voluntary sector and its relation to building civil society and developing citizenship. Higher education is emerging as a key player in this process at local levels (community regeneration) and at national and international levels. Her own research interests run from analysing one form of community group (credit unions) to developing European and transatlantic links with like-minded academics through networks and research projects.
halli@hope.ac.uk

Marianne Hall is the former Researcher for the Hertfordshire Integrated Learning Project, and is now working within the University of Hertfordshire's Learning and Teaching Development Centre to implement skills-related aspects of the university's learning and teaching strategy. Marianne also manages the Environmental Sciences 'satellite' of the Subject Centre for Geography, Earth and Environmental Sciences (LTSN-GEES), which is based at the university, including the Web site of the Committee of the Heads of Environmental Sciences (CHES). Her pedagogical interests include the development of resources for online higher education learning environments, and environmental interests include habitat conservation, organic vegetable growing and sustainable development.
m.hall@herts.ac.uk

Judith Harding is Associate Director of Learning Development in the Centre for Learning Development at Middlesex University. She works across the institution to develop contexts for discussion of learning and teaching issues, and is programme leader for the Postgraduate Certificate in Higher Education course for new lecturers. She is also an art historian interested in problems of early medieval iconography and a practising artist who writes on contemporary textiles.
J.harding@mdx.ac.uk

Peter Hartley is a National Teaching Fellow and Professor of Communication at Sheffield Hallam University. As Head of Academic Policy in the School of Cultural Studies, he is responsible for quality assurance and curriculum development across the school's portfolio: art and design, humanities, and communication, film and media. His textbooks reflect his main teaching interests: interpersonal, group and most recently organisational communication. Over the last decade he has become heavily involved in educational development. Current interests include the use of multimedia, Web and VLE technologies, applications of speech recognition software, and assessment practices in HE. One of his software projects – Interviewer – reached the finals of the European Academic Software Awards in 2000. p.hartley@shu.ac.uk

Gina Hefferan is a Senior Lecturer in the Faculty of Business at the Auckland University of Technology, New Zealand. She has extensive teaching and curriculum development experience with the implementation of problem based learning in both legal courses and integrated courses for business students. Currently she is leading the development of a problem based Advanced Contract Law paper for AUT's Bachelor of Business. She is interested in exploring the efficacy of problem based learning as a means of enhancing higher-level engagement for less academic students. She is also interested in easing the path for staff who may be adopting problem based learning for the first time. gina.hefferan@aut.ac.nz

Andrew Honeybone is the former Director of the Hertfordshire Integrated Learning Project. His interest in learning and teaching in higher education developed while he was Director of Studies in Environmental Sciences at the University of Hertfordshire and through his MA work on learning environments. Andrew is continuing his work in this field through his role as one of the University's Learning and Teaching Development Tutors. His work on skills development in higher education continues at a regional level, through the Association of Universities of the East of England, and at national level, through the Learning and Teaching Support Network. Andrew is currently undertaking a PhD at the Institute of Education, University of London. A.J.Honeybone@herts.ac.uk

Alison Kennard coordinates language learning at the Surrey Institute of Art and Design, University College, where she also teaches French and Italian. She is also coordinator of the ALLADIN project, which seeks to embed the use of ICTs into language learning for art, design and media disciplines. Particular interests include supporting the acquisition of languages for specific purposes within non-specialist provision, and learning styles and strategies employed by students of the creative disciplines. akennard@surrart.ac.uk

Juliet Laxton is a Tutor in the Centre for Language Studies at the University of Southampton where she teaches French, Italian and EAP. She also works on the TLTP ALLADIN Project, which focuses on the integration of ICT into language programmes for non-specialist learners. Through her work

for ALLADIN, Dr Laxton has developed support materials for teaching and learning languages in virtual online environments known as MOOs. Her current research interests include ICT use for non-specialist language learners, and the use of computer mediated communications for independent and collaborative language learning.
juliet.laxton@talk21.com

Shona Little is a principal lecturer in the Centre for Professional Development at the Auckland University of Technology, New Zealand. She has responsibilities for assisting with educational, research and staff development across the university. She has had a 15-year interest in the development and implementation of problem based programmes across a wide range of disciplines and has published in this area. She is particularly interested in working cooperatively with academic staff to research the effectiveness of innovative approaches to teaching and learning.
shona.little@aut.ac.nz

Ranald Macdonald is Vice-Chair of the Staff and Educational Development Association (SEDA) and mainly supports the work in networking, conferences and events, and research. As Co-Chair from 1998–2001 he also had a responsibility, together with his Co-Chair Liz Beaty, for the strategy and development of the organization as well as liaison with other organizations, including the ILT. As Associate Head: Academic Development in the Learning and Teaching Institute at Sheffield Hallam University, his main responsibility is to support schools and other departments in the development, implementation and evaluation of their learning, teaching and assessment strategies. He has been a teacher and course leader in higher education since 1984 and, more recently, an educational developer since 1994. His current research and development interests are concerned with achieving more learner focused learning, including through the use of problem based learning, and support for the implementation of innovation in learning and teaching.
R.Macdonald@shu.ac.uk

Richard Moyes, recently retired from the University of Hull (1964–99), is now a Senior Fellow of that university. He was Director of the Improve Project from 1996 to 1999. Though his research area was heterogeneous catalysis, throughout his academic career he always had an interest in chemical education. This interest was mostly expressed through active membership of the Royal Society of Chemistry, in particular through its Education Division of which he has been honorary Secretary, Treasurer (twice) and, more recently, President.
r.b.moyes@chem.hull.ac.uk

Martin Oliver is a Lecturer in the Department of Education and Professional Development at UCL. His main area of work involves action research based

secondments with academic staff from across the college. In addition, Martin is currently involved in researching and developing a Masters course in learning technology. Research interests include evaluation, curriculum design and educational theory, usually applied to examples of learning technology.
martin.oliver@ucl.ac.uk

Dave O'Reilly is Head of Research in Educational Development at the University of East London. For some years he has been the Course Leader for the MA in Learning and Teaching, and has recently published *Developing the Capable Practitioner* with Lynne Cunningham and Stan Lester. He has worked with Mary Caddick on the Architecture FDTL project, and his areas of interest are self-managed and experiential learning.
d.oreilly@uel.ac.uk

Ruth Pilkington is a Principal Lecturer in the University of Central Lancashire's Department of Languages and International Studies. Her current role is as Project Manager for the DfEE-funded Developing Learning Organisations project, focusing on developing learning cultures in HEIs and business through collaboration and exchange between arts and humanities, and small and medium sized enterprises. Her specialisms and interests are business German, German companies and management; transferable skills and CIT skills development, reflective and experiential learning, employability; simulations as learning tools. Her research interests are in reflective learning and employability; and simulations.
RMHPilkington@uclan.ac.uk

Felicity Skelton is a published short story writer who teaches creative writing and English language at Sheffield Hallam University. A book of her stories *Eating A Sandwich* is published by Smith/Doorstop, and she has had stories published in *Mslexia*, *The North*, *Sheaf* and *Sheffield Thursday*. Her previous career was as a theatre director and playwright, and words – spoken and written – have always been a passion. Her involvement in the 'Extending the Professional Writer' project was as Research Associate and co-writer of 'StoryWriter' with John Turner.

John Turner is a Senior Lecturer in English Studies at Sheffield Hallam University. He is currently leader of the Level 1 creative writing course within the department and for four years was course leader of the university's MA in Writing. He is a published poet and short story writer and has written plays for BBC Radio 4 and material for television and radio comedy shows. As a performance poet, he has made over 1,000 live performances in Britain and in Europe and around 50 television and radio appearances. He is the main author of the creative writing multimedia programmes, VerseWriter and StoryWriter.
j.turner@shu.ac.uk

John Winter is the Associate Dean in the Faculty of the Built Environment, UWE, Bristol. His current responsibilities in the faculty include postgraduate programmes, international links, teaching and learning policy and Project Director, BEATL. His present research interests in the teaching and learning area include supportive management of the process of ICT innovation in HE, and examining the potential of the Web for the enrichment of distance learning programmes, with a particular emphasis on accessibility and on educationally relevant interactivity.
John.Winter@uwe.ac.uk

James Wisdom is a higher education consultant specializing in educational development. He coordinates SEDA's publications programme, is one of the consultancy team of the Oxford Centre for Staff and Learning Development and is part of the National Coordination Team of the HEFCE's Teaching Quality Enhancement Fund. His main area of interest is the preparation of university managers to implement pedagogic change.
JamesWisdom@Compuserve.com

Introduction

1

Educational development: research, evaluation and changing practice in higher education

Ranald Macdonald

INTRODUCTION AND BACKGROUND

This book arose out of a conference organized by the Staff and Educational Development Association (SEDA) and the Society for Research into Higher Education (SRHE) Educational Development Research Network in April 1999. The conference, entitled 'Research and Practice in Educational Development(s): Exploring the links', sought to enable participants to share experiences of practice, research and policy in all types of educational developments, encompassing a variety of techniques and technologies. The conference was aimed at, and attracted, teachers in higher education, learning support staff, educational developers, academics and managers with responsibility for teaching and learning policy developments, researchers, and independent educational consultants.

A subsequent call for chapters resulted in offers from a diverse range of contexts, though with the emphasis weighted towards funded projects. The decision was taken by the editors to reflect this emphasis, with some alternative, non project-based, examples of educational development to act as a contrast.

What educational development is

Educational development is the term which has become most widely used in the UK, partly to distinguish it from staff ('faculty' in the US) development, but also to mean 'academic', 'professional' or other similar terms. What they all have in common is some notion of activities that are concerned with 'sustaining and enhancing the quality of learning and teaching within the institution' (Hounsell, 1994). Webb (1996a) chooses to use the term 'staff development', while acknowledging that 'staff development in tertiary institutions such as universities has mostly been concerned with educational development: the development of teaching and learning'.

By contrast, Baume and Baume (1994) distinguish between staff development for pedagogy – 'a matter of training teachers in certain reasonably well-defined skills, attitudes and approaches' – and educational development – 'working with people to solve their educational problems, to meet their educational challenges'. They summarize, and acknowledge that they perhaps over-simplify in the process, that 'staff development implies workshops and trainer-led content and, sometimes, client boredom or, hopefully, storage of ideas and techniques for future use. Educational development implies consultancy and client-led content, and, usually, client active participation and immediate use of what is learnt'.

In his review of the work of educational development units in the UK, Gosling (2001) summarizes a number of writers (including Moses, 1987; Hounsell, 1994; and Candy, 1996) who include all, or some combination of, the following:

1. Improvement of teaching and assessment practices, curriculum design, and learning support – including the place of information technology in learning and teaching.

2. Professional development of academic staff, or staff development.

3. Organizational and policy development within the context of higher education.

4. Learning development of students – supporting and improving effective student learning.

Gosling goes on to quote Badley (1998) and Webb (1996b) on the fact that this list offers no account of 'development', which in itself may be a contested notion and, secondly, that it offers no place for research or scholarship. So Gosling now extends his list of characteristics of educational development to include:

5. Informed debate about learning, teaching, assessment, curriculum design, and the goals of higher education.

6. Promotion of the scholarship of teaching and learning and research into higher education goals and practices.

D'Andrea and Gosling (2001) conclude that, for educational developers to be valued in their institution, they must offer something unique and that 'this value resides in being the repository of knowledge about research into learning and teaching, and about the likely impact of strategies on student learning'. So while the pragmatic and *ad hoc* approaches, for example in response to the quality agenda, are important, 'our contention is that they are not a substitute for strategic, proactive and holistic development across the institution'.

Land (2001) draws on his research to categorize the practice of educational/ academic developers as a set of orientations. These 12 orientations – managerial, political strategist, entrepreneurial, romantic, vigilant opportunist, researcher, professional competence, reflective practitioner, internal consultant, modeller-broker, interpretive-hermeneutic and discipline-specific – need to be mapped against the organizational culture in which the developer is a practitioner. Land draws on the work of Becher to identify four main patterns of organizational behaviour: hierarchical, collegial, anarchical and political. These typologies were originally defined for an institutional context. It will require further research to see whether they transfer equally to a project-based context.

RESPONSES TO A CHANGING CONTEXT

Many of the current activities of educational developers have come about as a response to a changing higher education environment at both an institutional and national level. In the UK this can be seen through the influence of the Higher Education Funding Council for England (HEFCE) and its Learning and Teaching Strategy (see below); the Quality Assurance Agency (QAA) through its subject and academic review process, codes of practice and other frameworks; and also as a result of the so-called Dearing Report: the National Committee of Inquiry into Higher Education (1997).

A key recommendation of the Dearing Committee was the establishment of a professional Institute for Learning and Teaching in Higher Education (ILT). The functions of the Institute would be 'to accredit programmes of training for higher education teachers; to commission research and development in learning and teaching process; and to stimulate innovation'. Whilst the first aim is well under way leading to the professionalization of teaching within the UK, and the HEFCE is stimulating innovation in learning and teaching through its various initiatives, the commissioning of research has sadly been neglected through the ILT. The Economic and Social Research Council's Teaching and Learning Research Programme (ESRC-TLRP) has been widened somewhat to include higher education, though to only a limited extent so far.

Many educational developers have become involved in accreditation courses for teachers in higher education, often through programmes originally recognized by the Staff and Educational Development Association (SEDA), as well as supporting bids for innovation funding in learning and teaching.

Funded initiatives

In recent years – and in particular during the latter years of the 20th and early years of the 21st centuries –the UK's higher education funding bodies have instituted various initiatives to 'promote and enhance high quality learning and teaching'. However, the precedent was set during the 1980s in response to employers' complaints that universities were not producing effective graduates equipped with the necessary skills to apply their knowledge in the workplace. The Secretary of State for Employment announced the launch of the Enterprise in Higher Education scheme late in 1987, which offered up to £1 million over five years to institutions of higher education to assist them 'to develop enterprising graduates in partnership with employers'.

Though the term 'enterprise' was met with a certain degree of suspicion and scepticism by many academics, in the financial climate of the time it did provide an incentive for many institutions to look at how to change teaching methods. The scheme was assisted by the fact that 'enterprise' could be interpreted quite widely (Sneddon and Kremer, 1994).

Enterprise in Higher Education, together with a separate discipline network funding established by the then Department for Education and Employment (DfEE), provided models of funding teaching and learning developments to be followed by, amongst others, the UK higher education funding councils' Teaching and Learning Technology Programme (TLTP) in 1992. The first two phases of TLTP spanned 1992–96 with £7.5 million a year for three years in the first phase and £3.5 million in the second, in addition to institutional contributions. The aim of the programmes was stated as being 'to make teaching and learning more productive and efficient by harnessing modern technology'. However, there was concern that the projects concentrated on production and, following an evaluation of the programme which identified the need 'to concentrate more on implementation and embedding or materials within institutions', TLTP Phase 3 made £3.5 million a year available over three years from 1998 to address these concerns.

A further initiative is the Fund for the Development of Teaching and Learning (FDTL) which was launched in 1995 by the English and Northern Ireland higher education funding councils 'to stimulate developments in teaching and learning; and to secure the widest possible involvement of institutions in the take-up and implementation of good teaching and learning practice'. Bids were only accepted from institutions which had achieved an excellent grade or a commendation in the funding council's Teaching Quality Assessment, with 15 units of assessments being eligible in Phase One and a further eight in Phase Two. An overall budget of just under £14 million was allocated to the first two phases over four years (44 projects and £8.5 million over three years in Phase One and 19 projects and £4.0 million in Phase Two, in addition to coordination costs), with additional amounts subsequently being released to cover accessibility issues, further transferability of the outcomes of the projects and some continuation activities. The projects are not allowed to include further dissemination of existing funded initiatives such as TLTP or to fund research on teaching and learning.

Following an evaluation of FDTL, the Higher Education Funding Council for England (HEFCE) consolidated its learning and teaching strategy into three strands: institutional, subject and individual. The subject strand mainly concerns this book as it funded a Phase Three of FDTL – 33 projects with a total of £6.8 million over three years – and established the Learning and Teaching Support Network (LTSN) with the specific aim of disseminating and embedding good practices.

The LTSN, which is funded by the four UK higher education funding bodies, consists of a network of 24 subject centres offering subject-specific expertise and information on learning and teaching and a Generic Centre which offers similar support across subject boundaries. Following a bidding round, the Subject Centres were established in 2000 and are based in higher education institutions throughout the UK.

The growth in educational developers and development

The initiatives outlined in the previous section all served to increase the number of educational developers in the UK, though many of the individuals involved may not have described themselves by such a term, at least not in the first instance. Project staff in FDTL and TLTP projects, those in LTSN Subject Centres and the Generic Centre, together with those working on various projects which they fund or run themselves, have all led to a significant increase in people working on educational development activities. A range of other initiatives – including widening participation, increasing the use of technology and supporting students with disabilities – have also included in their teams those who might be thought of as educational developers.

The institutional strand of the English funding council's learning and teaching strategies provided funds to institutions to develop and implement their own strategies, and much of this has resulted both in increased numbers in educational development units (Gosling, 2001) and also in the growth of staff carrying out educational development activities in academic and other central departments. Many institutions have introduced Teaching Fellowship schemes which release staff time to engage in development activities within their departments, often with support from their educational development unit.

Recent conferences organized by the UK's Staff and Educational Development Association (SEDA), and its first Summer School for educational developers in July 2001 (SEDA, 2001), have seen a significant change in those participating, with the LTSN Subject Centres, in particular, becoming well represented. Greater collaboration between the LTSN, SEDA and other organizations involved in higher education is also resulting in a further widening of those engaged in educational development activities. The chapters in this book reflect some of the widening involvement of those who would now describe themselves as 'educational developers', though it is still difficult to put a figure or scale on this as many have not yet, and may never, take up the use of the descriptor.

This growth in educational development and its accompanying practitioners is, to an extent, mirrored elsewhere in the English-speaking world and in Europe. Similar funding initiatives have been seen in some countries, as have moves to establish national educational development networks, as evidenced by the growing number of members of the International Consortium for Educational Development (ICED).

RESEARCH AND EVALUATION IN EDUCATIONAL DEVELOPMENT

Research in educational development

Research in educational development has a relatively short history, as distinct from specific research into teaching and learning, though the latter has often focused on compulsory education prior to students entering higher education. While other research into educational development has appeared over the years, the launch of the *International Journal for Academic Development* in 1996 sought to focus scholarly activity in this and closely related topics. In the journal's first editorial, Baume (1996) wrote that the journal's distinctive focus 'will thus be the processes of helping institutions, departments, course teams and individual staff to research into, reflect on and develop policy and practice about teaching, learning and other activities in support of learning. . . The journal is intended to help define, develop and extend the practice of academic development in higher education worldwide'.

Much of the research is thus focused on practice and policy and providing the evidence for change in educational development, as part of the process of change or to judge the effectiveness of that change. The emphasis has largely, but not exclusively, been on qualitative research methods, largely borrowed from social science traditions. There has also been an emphasis in some areas on action research as a way of researching changing or developing practices. 'Action research. . . may be defined as collaborative, critical enquiry by the academics themselves (rather than expert educational researchers) into their own teaching practice, into problems of student learning and into curriculum problems. It is professional development through academic course development, group reflection, action, evaluation and improved practice'(Zuber-Skerritt, 1992). Beaty, France and Gardiner (1997), in advocating action research for use by educational developers 'because it involves an experiential learning cycle that fuses research, development and evaluation into a dynamic process', describe 'consultancy style action research – CSAR – as an appropriate variant because it is based on a triangular partnership involving 'the knowledge of the educational developer, the skills and time of a social researcher and the concerns and expertise of academic staff'.

There is an extensive and growing literature on educational research methods, as a glance along the appropriate library bookshelf will show. Some of the chapters in this book demonstrate a number of these research methods in action, but it is in the use of various methods of evaluation that many concentrate. However, it is not just the methods that differ – and in fact they may demonstrate methodologies equally as rigorous as much research – but also the intentions and outcomes expected. Scott and Usher (1999) note that 'evaluators are more concerned with assessing the effectiveness, or describing the impact, of a deliberately engineered social intervention'. By contrast 'researchers do not operate with such a close relationship between themselves and the initiators of those interventions, though they may still be dealing with the effects of policy interventions, since these are an abiding feature of educational systems'. In the context of educational development, it is to evaluation that we should now turn our attention as this has been a major focus, rather than research *per se*.

Evaluation of educational development

While evaluation was once seen by many academics as a threat to academic autonomy, 'it has now come to be seen not only as a necessary adjunct to accountability, but also as an integral part of good professional practice' (Hounsell, 1999). So when developing a project or proposing an innovation in learning and teaching, the first question is often 'how will you evaluate it?'

The National Co-ordination Team (NCT) for the FDTL and TLTP produced a Project Briefing (1999) in which it links monitoring with evaluation. The reasons for monitoring and evaluation are given as being: formative evaluation to influence the future direction of the project; accountability through summative evaluation to satisfy stakeholders; and learning about teaching and learning practice and about project process, to inform future development projects. The main emphasis is therefore on whether the evaluation is formative/developmental or summative. The briefing also summarizes an evaluation strategy adapted for educational development by Baume and Baume (1995) from Nevo (1986):

1. Decide what is or are to be evaluated, and when.

2. Identify stakeholders in the project.

3. Identify stakeholders' questions and concerns.

4. Identify the criteria for judging answers to stakeholders' questions.

5. Devise and pilot the evaluation method and instruments.

6. Carry out the evaluation.

7. Report to the stakeholders.

8. Change project practice as necessary.

9. Review evaluation methods from time to time.

Evaluation is thus a dynamic process and not just something that happens at the end of a project or developmental activity. The link to monitoring enables those involved with evaluation to see it as part of the project process. As a past member of the NCT I was always conscious that project staff initially expected the summative elements of monitoring and evaluation to dominate, whereas the reality was that, on most occasions, it was the formative or developmental aspects which came to the fore – perhaps reflecting the background of the NCT members as educational developers.

There is not the space here to go into detail about evaluation methods but a useful source is the *Evaluation Cookbook* (Harvey, 1998), which was produced as part of the Learning Technology Dissemination Initiative, funded by the Scottish Higher Education Funding Council. However, most of the examples contained in this book ask themselves, in one way or another, the following questions in relation to evaluation of an educational development: Why? For whom? Of what? How? When? From whom? By whom?

The relationship between research and evaluation

Many educational researchers would question the use of both action research and evaluation as legitimate or suitably academic approaches to understanding educational developments. However, developing approaches to evaluation, partly in response to the demands of growing numbers of stakeholders for increased accountability for the spending of public funds, has meant that the line between research and evaluation has become somewhat blurred.

Chapters in this book will demonstrate a variety of approaches to evaluation, often linked to more covert research activities – the pressures of the Research Assessment Exercise in the UK are felt even within educational development projects – but still with the intention of assessing both the outcomes and process of those developments, both summatively and formatively.

CHANGES TO PRACTICE

The practices being addressed by the developments in this book are a fair reflection of the concerns being experienced in higher education throughout the world. Reduced funding in real, if not money terms; calls for greater accountability from government and electorates; moves to drive up academic standards through formalized quality assurance mechanisms; increases in participation rates in higher education with consequent entry of much more diverse students with their differing support needs; calls for much greater flexibility in provision – in terms of time, pace and place as well as the whole nature of the learning experience – to meet the needs of the more heterogeneous student population; a growing use of communications and information technology in learning, leading to the lowering of barriers between education, the commercial world and international boundaries. And all, or at least most, of these have been accompanied by the appropriate policies, strategies and/or funding initiatives.

So the changes described in the following chapters reflect a mixture of pragmatic or even opportunistic developments and more strategic approaches to change, though the latter have sometimes been with the benefit of hindsight. Change has been both internally and externally funded, has been research driven or evidence based, and the scale has varied from the local, though the institutional, to the national. In particular, the call from employers for more skilled graduates who can use their knowledge to solve problems in the real world has led to responses at many levels. Similarly, initiatives by funding bodies to encourage a more strategic approach to learning, teaching and assessment has resulted in most institutions following relatively similar approaches, though without any large scale sharing of the outcomes of these developments to date.

HOW THE CHAPTERS REFLECT THESE ELEMENTS

The chapters in this book all reflect to varying degrees the various elements described above: research, evaluation and changing practice in higher education, with the emphasis on changes to the experience of students. Further, they almost all reflect the changing agenda in the UK where the funding councils have sought to bring about improvements in learning and teaching through funded initiatives. For this reason, we invited contributions from a range of TLTP and FDTL projects which we knew offered some contrasting approaches and outcomes.

The contributions also reflect the range of contexts in which change is taking place: at departmental, institutional and national level. They also describe different discipline or subject areas, including chemistry, languages, sociology, English, law, architecture and medical education.

By way of contrast, as well as to add an international dimension to the contributions, we invited Shona Little and Gina Hefferan to provide an example of a more traditional approach to educational development where the lecturer concerned, supported by an educational developer, seeks to improve the experience of learners in their classroom. This is more within the Angelo and Cross (1993) tradition of classroom assessment or of action research.

We hope there will be something of interest in this book for all educational developers, whether they are based in teaching departments, central units, managerial positions, funded projects or national support networks. As well as brief biographies of all the authors we have, where possible, provided e-mail contacts. There will inevitably be changes in these over time but search engines make it increasingly easy to track people down – they may escape but they cannot hide! So do make contact with authors and share your own experiences of educational development: research, evaluation and changing practices in higher education.

REFERENCES

Angelo, T and Cross, P (1993) *Classroom Assessment Techniques: A handbook for college teachers*, Jossey-Bass, San Francisco

Badley, G (1998) Making a case for educational development in times of drift and shift, *Quality Assurance in Education*, **6** (2)

Baume, D (1996) Editorial, *International Journal for Academic Development*, **1** (1), pp 3–5

Baume, D and Baume, C (1994) Staff and educational development: a discussion paper, *SEDA Newsletter*, 2 (March), pp 6–9

Baume, D and Baume, C (1995) A strategy for evaluation, in *Directions in Staff Development*, ed A Brew, pp 189–202, SRHE and Open University Press, Buckingham

Beaty, E, France, L and Gardiner, P (1997) Consultancy style action research: a constructive triangle, *International Journal for Academic Development*, **2** (2), pp 83–88

Candy, P (1996) Promoting lifelong learning: academic developers and the university as a learning organisation, *International Journal for Academic Development*, **1** (1), pp 7–19

D'Andrea, V and Gosling, D (2001) Joining the dots: reconceptualizing educational development, *Active Learning in Higher Education*, **2** (1), pp 64–80

Gosling, D (2001) Educational development units in the UK – what are they doing five years on?, *International Journal for Academic Development*, **6** (1), pp 74–90

Harvey, J (ed) (1998) *Evaluation Cookbook*, Learning Technology Dissemination Initiative, Edinburgh [online] http://www.icbl.hw.ac.uk/ltdi [accessed 28 January 2002]

Hounsell, D (1994) Educational development, in *Managing the University Curriculum: Making common cause*, ed J Bocok and D Watson, pp 89–102, SRHE and Open University Press, Buckingham

Hounsell, D (1999) The evaluation of teaching, in *A Handbook for Teaching and Learning in Higher Education*, ed H Fry, S Ketteridge and S Marshall, pp 161–74, Kogan Page, London

Land, R (2001) Agency, context and change in academic development, *International Journal for Academic Development*, **6** (1), pp 4–20

Moses, I (1987) Educational development units: a cross-cultural perspective, *Higher Education*, **16**, pp 449–79

National Committee of Inquiry into Higher Education (1997) *Higher Education in the Learning Society*, HMSO, London

National Coordination Team (1999) [online] project resources at www.ncteam.ac.uk [accessed 28 January 2002]

Nevo, D (1986) The conceptualisation of educational evaluation: an analytic review of the literature, in *New Directions in Educational Evaluation*, ed E House, Falmer Press, Lewes

Scott, D and Usher, R (1999) *Researching Education: Data, methods and theory in educational enquiry*, Cassell, London

SEDA (Staff and Educational Development Association) (2001) SEDA summer school for educational developers, *Educational Developments*, **2** (3), p 20

Sneddon, I and Kremer, J (eds) (1994) *An Enterprising Curriculum: Teaching innovations in higher education*, HMSO, Belfast

Webb, G (1996a) Theories of staff development: development and understanding, *International Journal for Academic Development*, **1** (1), pp 63–69

Webb, G (1996b) *Understanding Staff Development*, SRHE and Open University Press, Buckingham

Zuber-Skerritt, O (1992) *Action Research in Higher Education: Examples and reflections*, Kogan Page, London

Part One:
Supporting change within subjects and departments

2

Developing work based educators: professional and organizational issues

Maggie Challis

INTRODUCTION

Over recent years, higher education has increasingly sought to build closer relationships with professionals and to encourage the development of opportunities for work based learning. Implicit within this trend is an assumption that those who teach within the workplace understand their role as educators, and are able to undertake appropriate teaching and assessment activities within that context. However, as more emphasis is placed upon initial and continuing professional development for professionals within their own future work settings, it is important to consider how supervising staff can be developed to provide an appropriately supported and rigorous learning environment for their learners.

This chapter focuses on work done within the context of postgraduate medical education. However, it raises issues which are applicable across all areas where higher education and employers, in particular the NHS, and indeed the employer's clients (that is, patients and their families), have a legitimate interest in ensuring that the quality of training and assessment carried out in the workplace is of an acceptably high standard. It looks at work carried out to explore means of quality assuring the teaching of doctors in training during their first year of postgraduate work. It also explores means of identifying the learning needs of doctors who have the responsibility to teach and assess juniors who are in their first year of postgraduate work, but who are still officially under the auspices of the medical school from which they graduated. It is the duty of the university's representatives to certificate the achievement of these junior doctors in order for them to be entered on the General Medical Council's register of doctors. From this specific contextual example, some general principles emerge about the training needs of work based teachers, and how these might be addressed.

Background: the development of quality frameworks

After their five years of study in medical school, UK medical graduates undertake a year of work based practice as pre-registration house officers (PRHOs). This year, known as 'internship' in the United States and parts of Europe, enables them to gain experience in a range of clinical settings, and to begin to make choices about which specialty they are likely to follow as their training progresses. Traditionally the year is divided broadly into equal placements in surgery and medicine, but latterly it has become possible for three placements to be undertaken: medicine and surgery plus one of either paediatrics, anaesthetics, psychiatry or general practice. The teaching and supervision which takes place during this year is done by practising consultants within the hospitals in which the PRHOs are working. At the end of the year, PRHOs receive a Certificate of Satisfactory Service, issued by the university from which they graduated. This spread of location and expertise means that issues of quality assurance are complex, and it is at times unclear where responsibility lies: with the university; with the trusts in which consultants and PRHOs are working; with the postgraduate dean who ensures training posts are available and pays the salary of the PRHOs.

Such matters are set against a background of policy changes within both the NHS and higher education, all of which are aimed at improving the quality of education and training through the establishment of quality assurance mechanisms (which, in the case of the NHS, also have the intention of improving the quality of patient care). The governmental white papers *The New NHS: Modern, dependable* (Department of Health, 1997) and *A First Class Service* (NHSE, 1998) introduced the concept of clinical governance within the context of lifelong and multi-professional learning. Clinical governance introduces a framework through which the quality assurance required in health care can be monitored and delivered. It is intended to ensure that all components of the system – hospital organizations, primary care groups/trusts and health authorities and all the individuals working within them – can be accountable for their performance and the systems which support the provision of patient care (Heard, 1998).

Clinical governance is only one element of the 'new approach' that was signalled by *A First Class Service*. National quality standards are to be set through National Service Frameworks and together the National Institute for Clinical Effectiveness, the Commission for Health Improvement and the National Performance Framework will establish 'effective systems' for monitoring the delivery of these quality standards. The National Service Frameworks, together with other national and local protocols, give guidance on the use of best clinical practice, and clinicians will be expected to conform to their guidance. Improved arrangements for the education and training of health care professionals are an additional key element in the clinical governance process, including the introduction of appraisal and periodic revalidation of doctors in both training and career grades (GMC, 2000). The latter will bring medical staff in line with performance review procedures applied to other clinical and non-clinical staff across the NHS.

Formal quality assurance systems were well established in the polytechnics and by those colleges that offered programmes leading to the awards of the Council for National Academic Awards (CNAA). From the early 1990s the Higher Education Quality Council (HEQC) encouraged all higher education institutions to develop formal systems for assuring the quality of their provision, without prescribing the form that these systems should take. Institutions were also directly accountable to the funding councils (through the process of teaching quality assessment) for the quality of the taught programmes that they funded. The sector-wide quality assurance responsibilities of the funding councils and the HEQC were, in 1996, transferred to the newly-established Quality Assurance Agency for Higher Education (QAA). The quality of courses is currently assessed on the basis of their 'fitness for purpose', and institutions are responsible for defining the purposes (or aims and objectives) against which their provision should be evaluated.

The relatively permissive climate of the 1990s is, however, changing. The QAA has begun to publish the constituent elements of its *Code of Practice for the Assurance of Academic Quality and Standards in Higher Education* and, through the process of Continuation Audit and (from January 2002) institutional review, universities and colleges will be expected to demonstrate their compliance with the precepts of the code. The purpose of the code is to provide 'an authoritative reference point for institutions as they consciously, actively and systematically assure the academic quality and standards of the programmes, awards and qualifications'. In addition, under the Agency's new methodology for academic review, taught programmes will be assessed against national benchmark standards, the purpose of which is to ensure the comparability of academic awards offered by British higher education institutions.

There are important similarities (and an apparent convergence) between the developing quality assurance frameworks for higher education and the NHS. There is a common movement to external accountability, with the performance of organizations in both sectors being evaluated against national standards, and with central agencies tending towards prescribing the quality assurance systems and procedures that should be implemented by providers. There is also, for both sectors, an avowed commitment to reconciling professional and organizational self-determination with public accountability. *A First Class Service* stated that the government 'rejects the grey uniformity of central control as irreconcilable, both with clinical judgement and with individual patient needs' (para 1.12), and the *Report of the National Committee of Inquiry into Higher Education* (NCIHE, 1997) argued that:

Uniformity of programmes and national curricula, one possible approach to the development of national standards, would deny higher education the vitality, excitement and challenge that comes from institutions consciously pursuing distinctive purposes. . . The task facing higher education is to reconcile that desirable diversity with achievement of reasonable consistency in standard of awards.

(para 10.3)

The differences emerge when we examine the area of common concern: the education and training of medical, and indeed non-medical, staff. While organizations within both the NHS and higher education have legitimate interests in the quality assurance of post 'graduate' medical and non-medical education, the criteria against which this provision is evaluated are different. This difference is not adequately described by the principle of 'fitness for purpose' since this begs the question of whose and which purposes are being served. Where universities are involved in the provision of education and training, their ultimate and primary concern is with its 'fitness for award', and this is judged against the academic standards of the institution and sector; to the extent that NHS organizations (including the purchasing consortia) are involved, their primary concern is with 'fitness for practice', which might be ultimately judged against national standards of clinical effectiveness. The introduction of Workforce Confederations, signalled in *A Health Service of All the Talents: Developing the NHS workforce* (Department of Health, 2000), will take place from April 2001, and will bring into a single organization workforce planning across medical and non-medical staff, with merged budgets for training. Thus the notion of 'fitness for practice' has the potential to become more clearly located within a multi-professional context.

The distinction between fitness for award and fitness for practice, however, over-simplifies the situation. The purposes served by the higher education vocational programmes will include fitness for practice, and NHS trusts may have an interest in the academic value (and thus fitness for award) of the training programmes that they offer, in addition to organizational purposes that are not adequately described by the fitness for practice/award distinction. The distinction is also simplistic in that higher education institutions and employers are not the only stakeholders in the provision of medical and non-medical training: the others include not only the ultimate beneficiaries, the patients, but also the professional and statutory bodies, each with their own objectives and interests. While the professional and statutory bodies are concerned with fitness for practice, their interpretation of the meaning of this principle will not necessarily accord with that of employers; the interests of doctors in training and newly qualified non-medical staff (and thus the criteria against which they evaluate the quality of training) may include career advancement, personal satisfaction and cost; while the purchasing consortia have a proper concern with value for money, their definition of 'value' may differ from those of the other stakeholders.

BACKGROUND: MEDICAL EDUCATION

For generations medical education has been based largely on an apprentice-ship model, often characterized by the phrase 'see one, do one, teach one'. This has arisen from the fact that junior doctors have a heavy service commitment (seeing patients and playing a part in the organization of the trust) as well as learning from both formal and informal educational activity. There has been an assumption that a programme of lectures, plus watching and imitating those more experienced doctors with whom they work, will enable them to become competent in their own practice, and pass on their skills and knowledge to others. It is only relatively recently that the various Royal Colleges that oversee higher specialty training, and the General Medical Council (GMC), which maintains the register of doctors approved to practise, have developed curricula for doctors in training and a framework for revalidation.

In the case of the PRHOs, the minimum standards have been laid down by the GMC in its publication *The New Doctor* (1997). This document sets out the skills, knowledge and attitudes which should be developed and demonstrated by PRHOs during their first year in practice. It also indicates the roles and responsibilities of those with a duty to assure the quality of the training and assessment carried out in the name of the postgraduate dean, who represents the university in this context.

A complicating factor is that all those clinicians who are tasked with teaching and assessing the PRHOs are themselves practising doctors, with a full and increasing case load of patients and heavy management responsib-ilities. It cannot be assumed that they have had any training in teaching, learning and assessment processes, or even that they would normally spend enough time with the PRHOs to be able to make a valid judgement on their progress. Many of the older consultants spent their junior years in a climate where there was no maximum number of hours which could legally be worked. This meant that there was more chance of seeing many examples of routine cases and the probability of rarer ones. With the new restrictions on the number of years doctors may remain in post (NHSE, 1994; Depart-ment of Health, 1998) doctors in training now spend less time physically in the hospitals with patients. This, coupled with the fact that patients now tend to spend less time in hospital than in previous times, means that doctors in training actually have less patient contact on which to focus their learning. This combination of circumstances enhances the need for greater awareness on the part of more senior doctors about how to use the time for experiential learning more positively within the prevailing context.

The New Doctor (GMC, 1997) describes the responsibility for general clinical training as falling between four major parties: the GMC, universities with medical schools, the health departments and the PRHO him/herself. The role of the universities within general clinical training is clearly stated:

'The universities are. . . responsible to their PRHOs for ensuring that they are placed only in posts which will give good experience, supervision and training.'

The particular duties of the universities include:

a. regularly inspecting and approving hospitals and health centres and recognizing posts within them as suitable for the training of PRHOs

b. identifying educational supervisors and training them in teaching, appraisal and assessment techniques

c. ensuring that in every post PRHOs receive regular constructive feedback on their performance

d. taking early remedial action if major problems with the trainee or the training are identified

e. ensuring that each PRHO obtains the required balance of general experience in medicine and surgery

f. ensuring that PRHOs receive induction training and formal educational opportunities

g. certifying to the GMC that each PRHO has made the educational and clinical progress expected of a doctor at the end of basic medical education, and is fit to be fully registered.

These duties are usually delegated to the postgraduate dean or in some cases the dean, but they remain the responsibility of each university.

It is clear from this that there is an expectation on the part of the GMC that the postgraduate dean, on behalf of the universities, should have in place quality assurance systems whereby he or she is aware of the needs, skills and capabilities of both PRHOs and those charged with undertaking their training and evaluating their progress. If this is indeed the case, it should be possible to track the evidence used in order to make a judgement about each trainee and each training placement.

TRAINING THE EDUCATORS IN MEDICAL EDUCATION

Shortly after the publication of *The New Doctor*, the Chief Medical Officer established a working group to explore the assessment of PRHOs during their placement. This group developed a range of assessment instruments which might be considered appropriate in order to ensure that all aspects of the PRHO's development were monitored and assessed at a time and place appropriate to their training, and by staff appropriately placed to make a judgement on the individual's progress. These included criteria for acceptable performance against the syllabus set out in *The New Doctor*, a framework for reflecting and reporting on critical incidents, outlines for case presentations, and the use of 'learning scripts'. The instruments were distributed to deaneries, who were then at liberty to choose those which they felt were resource effective and would give a picture of the PRHO which would enable a judgement to be made about their suitability for the certificate of experience. The documentation used as a result of this process within the deaneries involved in this project was a key piece of evidence of the quality assurance processes in place within the region.

The attempt by the GMC to sharpen up the infrastructure supporting the education and training of PRHOs and other junior doctors is pre-dated by changes in the medical curriculum for undergraduates following the publication of *Tomorrow's Doctors* (GMC, 1993). This document highlights the need for medical education to move away from a heavily knowledge-dependent process to one which enables the development of skills and attitudes which will be appropriate for the medical world of the future. Towle (1998) summarizes the responses which medical education must make in order to respond to the context in which it operates:

- Teach scientific behaviour as well as scientific facts.

- Promote the use of information technology.

- Adapt to the changing doctor–patient relationship.

- Help future doctors to shape and adapt to change.

- Promote multi-professional teamworking and care.

- Help future doctors handle broader responsibilities.

- Reflect the changing pattern of disease and healthcare delivery.

- Involve health service employers and users.

The agenda for making doctors aware of, and able to meet, the requirements laid upon them as teachers is therefore large, and made more problematic by having to make any training offered to them accessible within their other commitments.

RESEARCHING MEDICAL EDUCATION

Within the Mid Trent Deanery, centred on Nottingham University, an in-depth exploration was carried out in order to ascertain how clinicians wanted to undertake their training as teachers and supervisors of PRHOs (Challis, Williams and Batstone, 1998; Challis and Batstone, 2000). This research revealed that three major aspects were seen as important needs: teaching, assessing and giving feedback.

In order to create a basis on which to build, we consulted clinicians with a defined educational role within trusts, to seek their views on their own training requirements in order to meet the demands of *The New Doctor*.

Through a series of focus groups and interviews with these clinicians, it was clear that respondents perceived that the current level of skill and knowledge was often insufficient to carry out the role of educational supervisor. While there was evidence of much good practice in supporting PRHOs, this had been developed on an individual rather than a coordinated basis. There were emerging models of good practice, such as the identification of lead clinicians in each specialty, interviewing of each PRHO by the director of postgraduate education, briefing booklets and documentation to monitor educational progress. However, these had been developed within individual trusts, without coordination between trusts or specialties. Clinicians have largely been responsible for following up their own perceived needs in relation to their educational supervision role, and acquiring the necessary skills and knowledge through whatever means were available, without any strategic or managed approach. While creditable in its own way, this has led to a diversity in practice that leads to inconsistency in approach.

We found that participants in our research believed that educational supervisors should have the following qualities:

- Enthusiastic commitment to the principles of educational development for PRHOs.

- Sensitivity to the needs of a range of learners, including both the 'high fliers' and those in need of additional support.

- An ability to give regular and supportive feedback on progress, both good and bad.

- Administrative and time management skills in order to coordinate and build on feedback from others with a role in supporting PRHOs.

- A knowledge of the structures within which PRHOs are working, and the key staff involved.

- An understanding of the generic skills of clinical practice as highlighted in *The New Doctor*.

Although acknowledging the need for a more structured process for their own learning, consultants taking part in this research were reluctant to undertake activities that would take substantial amounts of time, necessitate their being away from work on a regular basis, or require them to engage in self-directed learning. They declared themselves in general to be not particularly interested in gaining further qualifications, but felt that a course carrying continuing medical education credit might be a 'carrot' for some clinicians.

The role of the trust was deemed to be crucial in facilitating baseline training, demonstrating support for educational supervisors in attending briefing sessions and maximizing potential by attracting good doctors and reducing risk. Cooperation between the trust and the university was seen to be essential, with the university taking responsibility for providing the training, assessment and accreditation of the educational supervisors. It was stressed that education needs to be part of the core business plan of every trust and that the health authorities should be encouraged to take an active role in supporting educational activity within trusts.

RESPONDING TO THE RESEARCH

In response to our findings, we developed a course consisting of three modules, covering the basic skills of teaching; assessment; and giving feedback and guidance. These modules were all offered in each of the major trusts within our deanery. In accordance with our respondents' request, each module was designed to last one full day, with a follow-up half day two weeks later in order to review changes in practice. Participants were free to attend in their own trust or in another, depending on work timetable and convenience.

As this package had been developed in direct response to the consultation exercise, we were hopeful that attendance and commitment would be high. However, the workshops were very poorly attended, despite an initial apparent commitment from those whom we recruited. On further discussion with clinicians, we were able to attribute this to a range of reasons:

- The significance of the educational supervisor role as outlined in *The New Doctor* had not been fully understood as the document was still relatively new.

- Educational supervisors had not been formally recruited, and so there was a lack of clarity over who should be taking on the role.

- Modules taking place within the consultants' own trusts offered a 'temptation' to try to fit work and training into the same day, with the natural consequence that some potential participants found themselves called away.

- Trusts seemed unwilling or unable to give due weight to the role of educational supervision through the provision of administrative support or protected time.

Following the relative lack of success of the initial training programme, we then offered a two-day residential course, covering much the same ground, but in rather less depth, at a local hotel. By this time, there was greater familiarity with the contents of *The New Doctor*, and documentation prepared by the Chief Medical Officer's Steering Group on the PRHO year had been circulated for piloting. Most trusts were able to provide lists of educational supervisors who were willing to take on the role and who were aware, in outline, of what their duties would be. The result was a course that was full, and which we now offer on a regular basis.

We have, however, supplemented the enhancement of teaching skills through attendance at courses with a process whereby clinicians may seek individual support and feedback through being observed in their daily practice by an experienced educator. This process consists of one day's observation of teaching *in situ*, followed by an extended and detailed feedback session of one to two hours, and a further session observing practice to explore how far the feedback has been used to change or reinforce practice. The service appears relatively cost intensive but is proving highly effective in bringing about modifications to the culture of medical teaching where it is being afforded an appropriate high profile in the work of many clinicians.

LESSONS TO BE LEARNT

It is clear that the task of assuring the quality of work based learning and assessment for doctors is fraught with difficulty, and the tension between education and service delivery permeates all educational provision for health care workers. While there is no intention to imply that the current standard of teaching and supervision should be seen as inadequate for its purpose, it is, under present circumstances, quite difficult to be sure that quality systems are in place which will assure high standards in training the doctors of the future and meet the desired outcome of 'fitness for practice'. Each of the health care professions has its own systems for undertaking the training of its work based staff, and requires different forms of evidence that all knowledge and skills are kept up to date, including those of teaching, supervision and assessment. These are continually being modified in the light of drives from government and professional bodies, perhaps most notably through clinical governance.

However, issuing the directives and expecting compliance is only one part of enhancing the quality of education and training. Ensuring that the directives are disseminated and understood is clearly a key factor in their implementation, and it appears that not all relevant staff are aware of what they should be doing in order to comply, and fewer still felt that their views had been sought or represented in the development of new frameworks for practice. This becomes an increasingly large issue as the relevant staff are at some distance from the originating body, whether this be a higher education institute, a professional body, or a government organization.

In the case of doctors, the role of educator is not clearly identified within their work roles. It is therefore difficult to know how far teaching through 'goodwill' can be expected to continue amongst all the other pressures of the job, and how much pressure it is appropriate to exert to ensure that clinicians are trained to undertake their teaching responsibilities. Clearly doctors have a view about what they need to know and many appreciate where their greatest needs lie. Yet having the time to access appropriate provision is problematic, given that they are employed first and foremost as clinicians.

At the same time it is clearly imperative that universities can ensure that learners being educated under their auspices are receiving appropriate teaching and learning support. As employers, trusts should feel obliged to ensure that education and training provision by and for their staff meets their requirements in terms of clinical governance, and that clinical care is of an appropriately high standard.

The issue of quality assuring education and training within the workplace is therefore highly complex and involves the terms and conditions of employment of those undertaking the teaching role; establishing their training needs; meeting those needs using appropriate methods and timescales; agreeing whose responsibility it is to undertake and evaluate programmes to enhance teaching and learning skills; establishing a source of funding to enable needs to be met. The role of universities in working with trusts and other stakeholder groups also needs to be further explored in order to ensure that the quality frameworks across all sectors can be confidently expected to meet not only 'fitness for award' but also 'fitness for purpose'. A commitment to 'training the trainers' must be a key feature of such a partnership.

Clearly it is not in anyone's interests to ignore these matters, which are particularly highlighted in the case of junior doctor training. However, the issues appear to be pertinent across the NHS in its role as an educational organization, and probably into other public and private sectors where initial and continuing professional development is being undertaken in collaboration with or on behalf of higher education. The risks of ignoring the issue – complex though it is – are, however, profound.

REFERENCES

Challis, M and Batstone, G (2000) Educational supervision for PRHOs: getting it right?, *Hospital Medicine*, **61** (5), pp 352–54

Challis, M, Williams J and Batstone, G (1998) Supporting pre-registration house officers: the needs of educational supervisors of the first phase of postgraduate medical education, *Medical Education*, **32**, pp 177–80

Department of Health (1997) *The New NHS: Modern, dependable*, HMSO, London

Department of Health (1998) *Reducing Junior Doctors' Hours*, HSC1998/240, HMSO, London

Department of Health (2000) *A Health Service of All the Talents: Developing the NHS workforce*, DoH, London

General Medical Council (1993) *Tomorrow's Doctors: Recommendations on under-graduate medical education*, GMC, London

General Medical Council (1997) *The New Doctor*, GMC, London

General Medical Council (2000) *Revalidating Doctors: Ensuring standards, securing the future*, GMC, London

Heard, S (1998) Educating towards clinical governance, *Hospital Medicine*, **59** (9), pp 728–29

National Committee of Inquiry into Higher Education (NCIHE) (1997), *Higher Education in the Learning Society: Report of the National Committee of Inquiry into Higher Education*, (the Dearing Report), HMSO, London

NHSE (1994) *The New Deal: A plan for action, report on the working group on specialist medical training*, NHSE, Leeds

NHSE (1998) *A First Class Service: Quality in the new NHS*, HSC 1998/113, NHSE, Leeds

Towle, A (1998) Changes in health care and continuing medical education for the 21st century, *British Medical Journal*, **316**, pp 301–04

3

Evaluation as a tool for curriculum development: a case study of multimedia development in the teaching of creative writing

Peter Hartley, John Turner and Felicity Skelton

INTRODUCTION

This chapter examines the role of evaluation in the development of multimedia software to support the teaching of creative writing to undergraduate level 1 students. Although we only employed fairly simple and established methods of evaluation, we were able to generate results which supported the underpinning curriculum model, which provided the impetus to further enhance the materials, and which generated further important questions for research.

We stress the importance of an evaluation strategy which can be sustained and which has a developmental role, that is, it does not just focus on the specific, possible narrow, aims of the software and deliberately explores the broader context. As a result, our experience should be of value to tutors in many subject areas who are exploring the role of evaluation as a means to both developing the curriculum and generating educational inquiry, particularly when implementing new computer-based methods.

BACKGROUND

The development of the multimedia software we discuss in this paper was originally supported by Curriculum Initiatives funding in the School of Cultural Studies at Sheffield Hallam University. It was then completed and evaluated as part of the Fund for Development of Teaching and Learning (FDTL) project 175/96 – 'Extending the Professional Writer'. The main phase of this project ran from January 1997 till December 1999 and was then extended till June 2000 to support further dissemination and embedding.

National Teaching Fellowship funding supported a further round of evaluation in the first semester of the 2000/01 academic year.

The software is now fully embedded in the undergraduate curriculum at Sheffield Hallam and is also used in various ways at other institutions. This paper will concentrate on the experience at Hallam but will also comment in passing on lessons learnt from trying to help colleagues in other institutions incorporate the software in their curriculum.

More detailed descriptions of the background to and development of the FDTL project have already been published (Turner, Broderick and Hartley, 1998 and 1999; Hartley, P, Turner, J and Broderick, D, 1999) so here we shall simply summarize the main characteristics. The project aimed to elaborate and disseminate the curriculum and assessment model used at Sheffield Hallam to teach creative writing, and to further develop and complete computer based materials to support creative writing teaching at undergraduate level 1. The project funding came at a very appropriate time: we needed new approaches to meet the demands resulting from the expansion of HE in the early to mid-1990s. We had to redesign the curriculum to cope with pressures such as increasing student numbers, reduction of class contact time, increasing variety of students and so on. The challenge was clear-cut: how could we maintain our approach to teaching and learning under these increasing pressures?

DEVELOPING THE CURRICULUM APPROACH AND EVALUATION

Our response to the challenge outlined above can be summarized in three major steps, although it is fair to say that the actual development of our thinking was less ordered than this summary implies.

Step 1: identify the main curriculum ingredients (not starting with technology!)

Although we had already made some progress in developing software materials to support seminar teaching, we were aware of the dangers of assuming that technology could provide 'magic answers'. This caution is also expressed by authors at the cutting edge of ICT developments. For example, Dertouzos (1997) argues that 'Education is much more than the transfer of knowledge from teachers to learners' and that information technology cannot adequately substitute for essential features such as 'building student–teacher bonds' (1997: 187).

It was important to establish what we wanted to achieve in the curriculum before deciding on the appropriate methods. Here we were following guidelines on good practice which are emphasized elsewhere in this volume, for example in the chapter by Oliver and Conole. So we attempted to define the key features of the approach to creative writing at SHU and decided upon the following:

- Emphasis on the acquisition of technical skills as the basic building block to develop creativity. This reflects our views both on the nature of creativity and on the most appropriate teaching and learning methods for this area. We see creativity as a combination of 'craft' plus 'inspiration': producing creative work involves an integration of convergent and divergent thinking. This is in contrast to some educational approaches to creative writing where the free expression of ideas is regarded as primary.

- Making students thoroughly familiar with the best writing in the particular genres being discussed.

- Emphasizing the importance of 'delivery to audience'. In other words, we continually emphasize that any and every piece of writing is directed at some external reader who is likely to approach the text with certain preconceptions, expectations and assumptions.

- Providing a wide range of feedback on work in progress, both from the peer group and from the tutor.

- Emphasizing the processes of redrafting and revising. This notion of writing as a process of continuous development is supported by both professional experience and research (e.g. Sharples, 1999).

Step 2: work out ways to preserve the main ingredients (and specify appropriate use of technology if possible)

With weekly contact time decreasing by about 40 per cent due to pressure on resources, and with seminar groups getting larger, we had to work out a way of making the most effective use of the seminar time with students. There were two aspects to this: deciding what were the essential features of the seminar, and deciding which aspects of the current seminar experience could be dropped or replaced. Tutors readily agreed on the most essential feature: developing dialogue about (and the critique of) established texts and the students' own developing work. They also agreed on the least helpful or distracting components: the explanation of technical concepts, such as the metrical form of the sonnet which some students almost inevitably knew already because of prior educational experience or preparation before the seminar. The solution seemed obvious: giving students the basic technical material and concepts outside the seminar. We found reassurance that this was an appropriate path in the developing educational literature of the time, which showed how different methods could be combined to create an appropriate educational environment (as in Laurillard, 1993).

So we decided to use the computer to 'protect' the seminar experience by:

- Providing computer based materials to deliver 'the craft' of creative writing, introducing and explaining the basic technical concepts and showing how they work in various contexts.

- Using the seminar to focus on critical feedback and analysis.

- Integrating the two methods so that students were expected to master specific technical concepts through the software before they were discussed in seminars. This required more careful advance planning of the seminar programme and tighter coordination between the range of tutors who were involved in the class teaching.

We also felt that the computer could offer additional advantages over other possible strategies such as printed workbooks. Perhaps the most important advantage, especially for the work on poetry, was the ability to offer the spoken word as well as the written text. In many cases, we were able to provide a reading of a poem by its author so that students could experience the text as interpreted by its creator. The computer also offers students the opportunity to learn and review at their own pace (which you can obviously also do with printed material), as well as the chance to develop interactive exercises which could not easily be replicated in print. By providing context-sensitive feedback and further explanation, the computer could also act as non-judgemental support/friend. It is easy for experienced tutors to underestimate the anxiety experienced by first year students in seminars when they lose track of or fail to understand what is being discussed.

We were unsure how far this computer based approach would be success-ful with groups of students who were not especially IT literate and who had little if any prior experience of computer based learning. We now have evidence that our students' use of IT has developed dramatically, through annual surveys and through the demand for copies of the software to 'take home'. This demand has moved from virtually nil to around 25 per cent of the student group within three years. However, increased use of ICT does not necessarily mean increased acceptance of its value or more positive attitudes towards it, as has been shown by workplace and educational studies (Brosnan, 1998; Weil and Rosen, 1997). So we needed evaluation tools that could test the application of these new methods.

We were also careful to decide upon the type of software we wished to develop as we were not convinced by some educational materials with high production values (very slick production and almost extravagant use of advanced multimedia features) which seemed to lose the educational point. So it is important to emphasize the type of materials which we have developed. The software:

- provides a linear and cumulative sequence (it is not hypertext);

- adopts a very simple design in terms of screen layout and interface;

- makes extensive use of sound (especially important for verse) and some use of video (primarily showing interviews with writers discussing their experience);

- runs on stand-alone CD ROM or over the Web;

- is designed to run in parallel with the seminar activity but can be used as stand-alone.

The materials we developed were:

VerseWriter
This aims to cover all the technical aspects of metric and free verse which we need in the level 1 curriculum. This was piloted informally with a sample of students during 1997/98 and was first used as a compulsory component of the course in 1998/99. So we now have three years' evaluation results for this software.

StoryWriter
This aims to cover all the technical aspects of short story writing which we need in the level 1 curriculum. This was piloted informally with our students during 1998/99 and was first used as a compulsory component of the course in 1999/00. So we now have two years' evaluation results for this software.

This paper concentrates on the evaluation results from VerseWriter and highlights a few interesting parallels in the StoryWriter results.

All the students were given introductory sessions on the software in our newly developed multimedia classroom and then asked to work through the programme at their own pace. Because of the large number of students involved (around 200 each year), several different members of staff teach this unit. So we also had the experience in 1998/99 of supporting colleagues who had literally never seen the software before being told they had to use it in their teaching, and we comment on some of the staff development issues later. The software has also been used at other higher education institutions and has received generally positive feedback, but we shall concentrate in this paper on our own experience.

Step 3: design and implement the most appropriate evaluation strategy and methods

From a theoretical point of view, we would endorse current thinking which suggests 'that when evaluating the effectiveness of learning applications. . . an integrative approach should be taken'(Cairncross and Mannion, 2001: 162) For example, Draper (1997) argues that it is not sensible to test software applications using a simple summative evaluation as there are so many confounding variables, ranging from the actions of specific tutors to halo and Hawthorne effects. He suggests that all computer assisted learning is 'one rather small factor in a complex situation' (p 35).

As well as avoiding the potential trap of theoretical over-simplification, our evaluation strategy had to satisfy a number of practical criteria. The strategy had to be:

- *Achievable within the project budget*. At the time of our FDTL project submission, evaluation was not such a strong component of FDTL philosophy. In hindsight, we did not give it the attention it deserved within the initial project budget. Given the opportunity to start again, we probably would not have acted very differently in the evaluation with our own students (perhaps carried out more individual interviews with students). We probably would have developed more systematic measures for collaboration with other institutions and given this more attention in the early stages of the project.

- *Sustainable*. Having developed materials which were designed to be a lasting contribution to our undergraduate curriculum, we also wanted an evaluation strategy which could be similarly long-lasting. We did not want an evaluation strategy which only lasted as long as the funding, as this would not give us the feedback to sustain long-term development. We were aware that many educational technology projects have struggled because of a lack of a continuation strategy, and wanted to ensure that we could still maintain an appropriate level of evaluation in the long term.

- *Fit for the purpose*. The evaluation had to answer basic questions to satisfy us that the project was achieving its stated aims, for example, was the software helping students? Were they using it? Did the software achieve what it was supposed to?

- *Developmental*. As well as checking that it was satisfying its basic aims, we wanted to explore the impact of the software in more general terms. As a result, we did not restrict the questions for users to the specific aims of the software. For example, we asked users to compare the use of the software with conventional methods of teaching, and deliberately investigated learning outcomes which the software was never designed to achieve.

These criteria can conflict with each other. For example, an evaluation strategy which is very detailed and time-consuming may be eminently fit for purpose but not sustainable. Our choice of methods was designed to achieve an appropriate compromise and included:

- Observation of students using the software (and discussing with them any subsequent issues of implementation) and overall monitoring of the assessment results and outcomes.

- Exploratory and follow-up interviews with student users at all stages of the project to examine their experience with the software and their more general expectations of the learning experience. Detailed interviews were analysed in the early stages of the project to develop appropriate questions for the main questionnaire, and later in the project to check against the questionnaire results. As a result of this cross-checking we are now confident that our questionnaire identifies the most important outcomes for students. In the long term we are unlikely to have the resources to carry out many such interviews in future years. but we will aim to encourage students to provide informal feedback.

- A questionnaire. This was administered to all students taking the course, and sent to all users in other institutions. It is designed so that the main results can be scanned and automatically analysed. We shall be able to maintain this procedure in future years, although we are unlikely to achieve the return rate we managed this year when staff were able to devote time to extensive follow-ups.

- Exploratory and follow-up interviews with all the staff tutors involved in the course at Sheffield Hallam and with some external tutors. In the long term we are unlikely to have the resources to carry out such detailed interviews in future years, but we have no doubt that our teaching colleagues will continue to provide extensive feedback.

- Presentation of evaluation data and progress reports to the project steering group (which contained independent external members who were subject experts). This ensured that our results and progress could stand up to independent scrutiny.

EVALUATION RESULTS AND DISCUSSION

VerseWriter has been used at Sheffield Hallam by 180 students in 98/99 (115 questionnaire returns), by 160 students in 99/00 (108 questionnaire returns), and by well over 200 students in 00/01 (203 questionnaire returns). The results in the following tables give percentage figures based on these returns. We currently believe that VerseWriter is also used to some extent in around 25 other universities and colleges. This last statistic is approximate because of the difficulties of embedding software in other institutions where many staff have been less fortunate than ourselves in terms of the support they have received from their IT infrastructure (Hartley and Turner, 2000). Our own experience has not been problem-free and has reinforced the need to have coordinated organizational systems (Hartley, 2000).

In terms of pedagogic value, the general evaluation results have been very positive:

- Most students found VerseWriter interesting and useful.

- Most students worked through the whole programme, which again suggests that they found it valuable.

- Although we had expected VerseWriter to provide the greatest benefit to students who had the least background in English studies, students from the English Studies Course also received it very enthusiastically.

- Some tutors felt that the students had grasped the mechanics of verse writing more quickly than students had in previous years when the software was not used.

- Some tutors felt that using the software had, indeed, enabled greater depth and breadth in seminars by eliminating the need to go over technical issues in great detail.

- This pattern of results was repeated in the responses to StoryWriter, suggesting that the overall approach works for both software applications. Some tutors even felt that the introduction of StoryWriter had actually improved students' creativity and risk-taking.

EVALUATION AS DEVELOPMENT

The summary above suggests that the results generally support the curriculum model we have adopted. To show how the evaluation has contributed both to curriculum development and to the development of a research agenda, we can look at specific elements of the evaluation.

Questionnaire data

We can show how the evaluation results have been used to generate new ideas (and demonstrate the value of extended evaluation over several cohorts) by looking at answers to specific questions. For example, we asked students whether they found the software useful and the results are presented in Table 3.1.

Table 3.1   *Questionnaire results: did students find VerseWriter useful?*

Statement	Percentage of students in agreement		
	98/99	*99/00*	*00/01*
VerseWriter is effective/useful	67	64	88
VerseWriter is attractive to use	81	77	77
VerseWriter is easy to follow	98	100	99

The significant student agreement with these statements suggests that the software has made a valuable contribution to the learning experience. The increased numbers agreeing to its effectiveness in 2000/01 may be just an artifact caused by a slight rewording of the statement. This will be checked with next year's cohort.

Table 3.2 indicates how students used the software. Of course these results are based on self-report and may be inflated as a result. The drop in reported usage this last year could be explained in various ways: it might be a reflection of more honest reporting, or this year's cohort could have been under more time pressures, and so on.

Table 3.2   *Questionnaire results: how far students used VerseWriter*

Amount completed	Percentage of students		
	98/99	*99/00*	*00/01*
All	20	18	13
Most	47	51	39
About half	15	16	24
Some	16	14	21
None	2	1	3

Our review of these results (and our slight cynicism over the level of self-report) has led us to look for further technological support. As a result, we have developed ways of electronically monitoring individual use of the software. This will also allow us to see which sections of the programme are used (including when and how often) and provide additional information on which aspects of the course students need most help with.

The comparison between the following two questions on how students compare different methods of teaching illustrates how the use of 'developmental' questioning can generate significant questions for future development. (See Tables 3.3 and 3.4.)

Table 3.3   *Questionnaire result: is VerseWriter or conventional teaching better at helping you to understand scansion?*

Statement	Percentage of students in agreement		
	98/99	*99/00*	*00/01*
VerseWriter is better	30	24	23
Both are equally good	40	42	45
Conventional is better	25	34	32

Table 3.3 focuses upon a specific aim of the software. The consistent finding that around 65–70 per cent of the students feel that VerseWriter is at least as good at if not better than conventional teaching re scansion is very important. It supports our approach by affirming that most students are not disadvantaged by moving part of the teaching from contact to computers.

Table 3.4 covers an example of a question which tests the software beyond its limits. VerseWriter was not designed to help users 'write' poetry, yet up to 50 per cent of students feel it is as good as, if not better than, conventional teaching. This does not appear to be an indictment of our standard teaching as this receives excellent feedback from other surveys and feedback. What we have potentially uncovered here is an interesting educational question which we cannot answer at present. Perhaps it is related to an issue we look at next.

Table 3.4   *Questionnaire result: is VerseWriter or conventional teaching better at helping you to write poetry?*

Statement	Percentage of students in agreement		
	98/99	*99/00*	*00/01*
VerseWriter is better	2	7	8
Both are equally good	38	44	41
Conventional is better	56	49	52

The results in Table 3.5 again suggest some interesting conclusions:

Table 3.5   *Questionnaire results: what does the software help students to achieve?*

Factor	Opinion	*98/99*	*99/00*	*00/01*
Use of rhythm	Yes it did help	80	51	50
	Gave some help	12	41	40
	Did not help	8	8	10
Use of imagery	Yes it did help	16	14	21
	Gave some help	16	32	68
	Did not help	60	44	11
Self-confidence in writing poetry	Yes it did help	23	36	33
	Gave some help/not sure	17	42	43
	Did not help	40	22	23

- VerseWriter is helping students with use of rhythm (which it was intended to do). The drop in response from 80 per cent to around 50 per cent may reflect a range of difficulties with the technology which some groups experienced.

- VerseWriter is helping students with use of imagery (which it was not intended to do). We have no explanation for the year-on-year rise in positive response.

- VerseWriter is helping students with their self-confidence (which it was not intended to do). At first sight this looks quite a remarkable result, especially given the consistent pattern over the last two years. The drop in response may reflect difficulties with the technology which some groups experienced.

What we have unearthed here is an important relationship between the use of the software and broader emotional factors. Can it be that use of the software is building technical competence and hence self-confidence that then 'spills over' into other reactions to the software content? So we are developing a hypothesis (which is effectively a research question) which has been generated by sensible use of a broad evaluation strategy.

Comments from students

Comments by students generally supported the questionnaire data: 'more forgiving than tutor'; 'doesn't scowl at you for being late'; 'helps clarify things'. The comments did also show that some students were reacting to the software in terms of their interpretation of staff motives: 'You know as well as I do that it's a cheap substitution for a teacher because you can't afford to pay for the extra time.' Once again this shows the importance of recognizing the contextual influences on evaluation.

In terms of the broader context of the FDTL project, we interviewed a small sample of former students to ascertain whether their experience of creative writing at university had any long-term impact. They reported significant impact and this highlights the importance and the value of long-term evaluation, which is so often neglected for resource reasons (Jenkins, Jones and Ward, 2001).

Comments by staff

Because of the large number of students involved (around 200), several different members of staff teach this first year course. As a result, we had a staff group whose initial relationship to the software ranged from the totally committed ('I developed and wrote the thing') to the suspicious ('Will this software pose a threat to my autonomy in the classroom and undermine my position as tutor?'). One of the issues which we hope to explore in more detail in future evaluation is the precise relationship between the tutors' attitudes towards the software and the way in which their students approach it. At the moment we only have data on the changes in staff perceptions over time.

Most of the tutors with no initial experience of VerseWriter were 'converted' to the software and are looking forward to using it again, and have been similarly impressed by StoryWriter. Others are still not totally convinced that it is worth the time and effort needed, although no one has argued that it detracts from the student experience.

GENERAL IMPLICATIONS AND CONCLUSIONS

The feedback from this evaluation suggests that we have developed a valid and productive approach which can improve both the staff and the student experience.

In terms of general implications, we can highlight the way in which evaluation that adopts a broad contextual perspective (as we have tried to do) and that does not focus on simple summative measures can provide both important data to monitor and improve the application and can generate important developmental questions and issues.

REFERENCES

Brosnan, M (1998) *Technophobia: The psychological impact of information technology*, Routledge, London

Cairncross, S and Mannion, M (2001) Interactive multimedia and learning: realizing the benefits, *Innovations in Education and Teaching International*, **38** (2), pp 156–64

Dertouzos, M (1997) *What Will Be*, Piatkus, London

Draper, S W (1997) Prospects for summative evaluation of CAL in higher education, *Association for Learning Technology Journal*, **5** (1), pp 33–39

Hartley, P (2000) '*Of Course Your Software Won't Work This Term. We've Changed the Student Interface': Moving from institutional rhetoric to the effective implementation of new learning technologies*, Paper to SRHE Annual Conference, HE Futures: Policy Prospects and Institutional Change at the University of Leicester

Hartley, P and Turner, J (2000) *Can Best Practice in IT-Based Learning be Transported Successfully Across Institutional Boundaries?*, paper to Association for Learning Technology Annual Conference, Alt-C2000, UMIST, Manchester

Hartley, P, Turner, J, and Broderick, D (1999) *Liberating the Seminar Through the Use of CBL*, paper to Association for Learning Technology Annual Conference, Alt-C99, University of Bristol

Jenkins, A, Jones, L and Ward, A (2001) The long-term effect of a degree on graduate lives, *Studies in Higher Education*, **26** (2), 147–61

Laurillard, D (1993) *Rethinking University Teaching*, Routledge, London

Sharples, M (1999) *How We Write: Writing as creative design*, Routledge, London

Turner, J, Broderick, D and Hartley, P (1998) Using IT to liberate the seminar: the case study of creative writing, in *Humanities and Arts Higher Education Network (HAN) Conference on Information Technology in the Arts and Humanities Conference Proceedings*, Open University

Turner, J, Broderick, D and Hartley, P (1999) Using multimedia to support the teaching of creative writing, in *Innovations in English and Textual Studies*, ed C Bryan and G Wisker, SEDA, London

Weil, M M and Rosen, L D (1997) *TechnoStress: Coping with technology@work@home@play*, Wiley, New York

4

Researching teaching effectiveness as an experiential learning cycle: insights into practice

Shona Little and Gina Hefferan

INTRODUCTION

When research into teaching effectiveness is instigated by practitioners and addresses questions that are of immediate relevance and significance to them, it has the capacity to impact on practice in important and sometimes unexpected ways. It can not only inform and enhance the reflective processes that teachers are engaged with, but it can also provide a range of insights into the improvement of practice. In addition, it has the potential to provide a rationale for change as well as indicating possible directions for achieving any increased effectiveness. Research data about how to improve teaching effectiveness will generally have implications for staff professional development, because such data tends to identify what practitioners may need to do differently and consequently indicate their learning needs as individuals or as a group.

The qualities of immediacy and relevance in practitioner based research can be key motivators in engaging teachers' interest in and commitment to improving their effectiveness as educators. Research questions need to be framed so that they directly address the kinds of questions important to practitioners, and research outcomes need to be seen to be applied wherever appropriate.

The research study which is the focus of this chapter addressed the question, 'What do students perceive as the most important contributing factors to their development or otherwise of legal reasoning skills?' The ways in which the outcomes of the study have impacted on the teachers working on the programme are discussed, especially in relation to the induction of new staff. The sequence of events is analysed and parallels are drawn with the experiential learning process.

CONTEXTUAL BACKGROUND

The problem based module which is the focus of this study is a law discipline component embedded in an integrated third semester of a Bachelor of Business Studies (BBus) degree. The degree aims to prepare students for practice by developing appropriate skills and capabilities as well as holistic understandings of the professional areas for which they are being prepared. At the Auckland University of Technology (AUT), programmes are structured around a graduate profile which articulates not only the graduate outcomes but also the professional and academic capabilities that the programme is designed to produce. (AUT defines 'capability' as the personal and inter-personal qualities that enable people to take effective professional action.) Graduate outcomes for the BBus include the ability to adapt and apply the process of learning to any situation, a broad understanding of business and the relationship between different disciplines, and the development of capabilities related to the application of knowledge, conceptual thinking, teamwork, problem solving, technical competence, communication, the use of technology and research.

One valuable method of developing student capabilities is to use a problem based approach to learning. Such an approach is, according to Boud and Feletti (1997), the most fully articulated and trialled means of addressing some of the formerly intractable challenges of professional education. The Bachelor of Business Studies with its capabilities focus is a particularly appropriate context in which to implement problem based learning, and it can be a relatively straightforward process to persuade students of the relevance and value of acquiring process skills such as legal reasoning skills.

The content of the module is based on a series of case studies that closely approximate real life situations. These case studies are of increasing legal complexity, and students engage with them in ways that demand increasing finesse in legal reasoning. It is intended that the outcome of this engagement will be the integration of discipline knowledge with a developing under-standing of and skill with the legal problem solving process.

BACKGROUND TO THE RESEARCH PROJECT

As with many other modern universities, AUT students tend to be highly diverse in terms of academic ability, cultural background, English language skills, motivation and educational goals. In recent years this increasing cultural and social diversity has presented a considerable challenge to academic staff. Questions arise such as, 'How can we achieve what Biggs (1999) terms "high level engagement" when student groups are so diverse? And how can we structure learning experiences in ways that help such students to develop the confidence, skills and knowledge necessary to solve professional problems and become independent thinkers and learners?' (Little and Hefferan, 2000).

Evidence from both formal and informal feedback on the module suggested that the problem based approach to the course increased student motivation and interest, and contributed to the development of students' legal problem solving skills. However, such feedback, although providing useful data, did not indicate what aspects of the module might be contributing to its effectiveness, nor how that might be happening. The researchers wanted to obtain specific, in-depth and rich data comprising student generated concepts that identified students' beliefs about any specific aspects of their learning experiences that contributed to the success or otherwise of the course. Educators need concrete evidence, not only as a focus for reflection, but also as a sound basis for action.

METHODOLOGY

Collaborative research which engages the researchers in critical reflection on practice can inform both the theoretical and experiential knowledge of those involved. In this study a staff developer was the principal researcher and a discipline lecturer the co-researcher.

The researchers looked very carefully at the various research methodologies available to them. They considered ways of measuring student reasoning ability and generating quantitative data on this, but in the end they rejected such an approach. Such methods were unable to provide the depth of data required. The researchers wanted to get close to the heart of what was a very personal and individual experience for each student. In order to obtain student views, framed and articulated using their own concepts, a case study methodology was used (Merriam, 1998). This belongs within the interpretive naturalistic paradigm (Guba and Lincoln, 1994).

The most important reason for selecting a case study design was its particular suitability to situations in which it is impossible to separate the phenomena or variables in the study from their context (Yin, 1994). In addition to this, a case study design tends to emphasize insight, discovery, and interpretation in context, and it allowed an holistic approach to be taken to the exploration and analysis of a particular educational situation (Merriam, 1998: 29). Case studies also have an heuristic quality, and the potential to provide new meanings, identify new relationships, or highlight new insights into the situation being studied, thereby increasing their potential applicability to a wider audience (Merriam, 1998: 30–31). Although the findings of case study research are not normally generalizable, it is often possible for others to draw parallels with their own contexts.

The design for this study included the use of a brief questionnaire to obtain data, student focus groups to explore and clarify that data, and a modified grounded theory approach to the analysis of data (Merriam, 1998).

The important issues of student confidentiality and personal risk were addressed by having the principal researcher administer and collate data from the questionnaires, facilitate the focus groups and organize the transcription of that material. The co-researcher had access only to the collated and transcribed data.

The research group consisted of 18 student volunteers (10 female and 8 male with a range of ages and backgrounds) who provided thoughtful and constructive data.

Questionnaire

The student questionnaire was modified from Brookfield's (1995) 'Critical Incident Questionnaire'. That approach elicits students' recollections of specific classroom events that were significant in helping them gain insight into their learning experiences. Brookfield uses information from a very brief questionnaire (completed at the end of each week of classes), as the basis for direct dialogue with students about ways of improving their learning.

Persuading students to participate in research projects can be problematic. In this study it was felt that students were most likely to respond constructively to requests for questionnaire data when only a few minutes of classroom time was required and they were not being asked to give up their own time. Students completed the questionnaire in the final few minutes of class for eight consecutive sessions. The purpose of the open questions was to identify, firstly what new insights and understandings (if any) students believed they had gained in a session, and secondly their perceptions of particular learning experiences that they believed contributed to any new insights or understandings. Dialogue with students about this data occurred in the focus groups.

Focus groups

There is now a considerable body of literature on focus groups (for example Morgan and Krueger, 1998; Morgan, 1997). In this study, two focus group interviews were conducted, one in the middle of the course, and one near the end of the course. The purpose of the focus group interviews was to explore in depth the key themes and issues derived from the questionnaire data. The focus groups also provided an opportunity for the participants to ask questions and to clarify ideas and concepts. The opportunity to articulate ideas and reflect on experience during these group interviews helped learners recapture, focus on, and reevaluate experience, thus drawing meaning from that experience, and possibly extending or modifying meanings previously ascribed to it (Boud, Cohen and Walker, 1993).

The focus group interviews were audiotaped and transcribed verbatim. Note taking during these types of interviews can be off-putting and intrusive. The audiotaping process is an objective and useful means of obtaining data, and it is frequently important in case study research that the exact nature of relationships or the implications within data are fully recorded. Audio-taping helps ensure that as accurate as possible a record is acquired.

The structure of the focus groups was derived from the questionnaire data as is consistent with a grounded theory approach (Merriam, 1998). Emerging themes and issues as well as key concepts and ideas, were identified and used to develop the overall framework as well as the actual questions for the focus group interviews (Denzin and Lincoln, 1994).

IMPACT OF THE RESEARCH PROCESS AND ITS OUTCOMES

Integrating theory and practice

The experience of participating as researchers in a research project such as this informs both the theoretical and practical knowledge of the participants (Little and Hefferan, 2000). This is especially true when researchers move beyond the actual research process towards producing published material, as the analysis of the data in relation to relevant theory results in an integrative process that provides understandings and insights at a level new for those involved. For the staff developer in this study, a deeper understanding of practice explicated theory; for the discipline specialist, a deeper understanding of theory informed practice.

Current teaching practice

Most educators who are committed to the ongoing improvement of their practice engage in a cycle of critical reflection on that practice. An outcome of this research project was to feed valuable insights from students into this cycle for the discipline specialist. She was not surprised at the importance students assigned to small group work and the quality of the lecturer's questioning and discussion skills. However, it was a revelation to realize the extent to which students gained from 'legitimate peripheral participation' (Brown, Collins and Duguid, 1989: 40) in a whole class situation when they were intellectually engaged at the higher cognitive levels (Little and Hefferan, 2000). Brown, Collins and Duguid cite research which shows that 'important discourse in learning' does not have to be 'direct and declarative'. Students can learn a great deal from being active observers, especially of specific professional behaviours such as legal reasoning.

It was also interesting to reflect on the tremendous importance of skilled facilitation and the power of skilled modelling of professional behaviours to influence students' levels of motivation, interest, and perceptions of the effectiveness of their learning. These factors highlight the need for integrity and congruence between what is said and what is done by teachers.

Induction of new staff

All these insights had a powerful influence on the approach taken to the induction of new staff on the module. They also led to greater clarity and confidence in the approach taken by the module coordinator, who took pains to emphasize the factors that were critical to the effectiveness of students' learning experiences. However, this emphasis was not sufficient to help the staff develop the skills and strategies necessary to enable them to be effective in the classroom. It was one thing to hear about important teaching behaviours and principles, another to understand them, and yet another to implement them when faced with the various exigencies of practice. The need for further training in facilitation was obvious.

This led to a programme of ongoing staff development. The new staff met weekly to experience the process of working with a wrong answer. They practised on and with each other. Such peer feedback and interaction, together with the demonstration of skilled teaching by an experienced practitioner, can be invaluable in subtly modelling the values as well as the behaviours of effective facilitation while overtly addressing the process of teaching professional capabilities (in this case, legal reasoning skills).

The new staff valued the opportunity to observe a skilled, experienced facilitator in action. When staff witness (as teachers) as well as participate (as students) in developing professional reasoning skills, they gain a sense of how expertise is made 'manifest' in that discipline (Brown, Collins and Duguid, 1989: 40). This group of new staff proposed that in the future all induction for that module should include a similar experiential learning component, and attempts will be made to implement this in future.

Programme development

The insights gained from the research outcomes have guided the continuing process of programme development. Faced with the unending call to produce more with less, as well as with ongoing programme development, the module coordinator felt better equipped to distil and retain the essence of the module as a result of insights gained from this research study.

Staff development

The results of this study indicate clear directions for ongoing staff development, especially for courses where the primary goal is to develop professional and academic capabilities. There is no doubt that a lecturer's facilitative skills are of primary importance, as is an awareness of the power of modelling to affect student learning behaviours. Highly developed questioning and discussion skills are also very important, especially when it is vital to produce dialogue and engage students in contributing to it, particularly if they risk being wrong. It is imperative that teaching staff are equipped to work constructively with wrong answers.

A MODEL OF THE PROCESSES BY WHICH RESEARCH CAN IMPACT ON TEACHING AND LEARNING

In this study, the experience of the impact of research into teaching effectiveness was that it closely parallels the experiential learning cycle (Kolb, 1984). The experiential learning cycle provides a model of the interplay between the real worlds of professional practice and of learning (in which teachers and students engage with learning activities and applied processes), and the abstract world of concepts and theories (refer to Figure 4.1). The stages of this cycle as identified by Kolb (1984) are concrete experience, reflective observation, abstract conceptualization, and active experimentation. The researchers were aware of the parallels between the experiential learning cycle and the action research process (Zuber-Skerritt, 1991), but the focus here is on the learning process for the teacher rather than on the research process itself. In simple terms teachers engage with their practice, find ways of learning more about that practice (for example, engage in research), and use that learning to develop new theories of practice.

The primary cognitive and metacognitive processes experienced by the researchers before, during and following the study can be represented by the model in Figure 4.1.

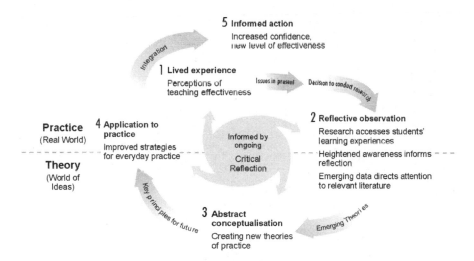

Figure 4.1   *Primary cognitive and metacognitive processes*

The term 'lived experience' is an appropriate one to describe the first stage of a process that inevitably includes ongoing reflection and analysis of educational experience. All teachers bring with them the values and theories of practice that are the sum of their earlier experiences, and these, together with current experiences, shape their everyday practice and decision making.

However, the teacher's experience of teaching is only one part of a more complex reality. The students' experience is the other key element, and this may be quite different from the teacher's perceptions of it (Zuber-Skerritt, 1991). It is therefore important for the teacher to carry out research and access information that will provide a more accurate picture of what is happening.

Because the cognitive and metacognitive processes experienced by researchers during and following the research process have some close parallels with the second part of the experiential learning cycle, Kolb's term 'reflective observation' is also an appropriate one for this stage of our model. The research data included students' self-observations and reflections on their learning experiences, observations and reflections that were explored in depth in focus groups. The emerging data further heightened the teacher's awareness and became a focus for reflection and analysis. This reflection and analysis informed the development of questions for the focus groups. The data resulting from this process directed attention to relevant literature on the subject. Critical reflection on the relationship between key themes from the research, together with relevant theory, led to the emergence of hypotheses about possible new theory.

The third stage of the experiential learning cycle is 'abstract conceptualization', an apt term to describe the third stage of our model. This stage is one in which the research outcomes are explored in depth in relation to existing educational theory. This process tends to lead to a range of insights and new meanings which in turn lead to the development of new theories of practice. The researchers were able to use some of the themes and concepts which emerged from the study to help identify literature likely to be relevant, that is, they were able to be relatively focused in their search of the literature because the research outcomes indicated clearly which aspects of theory were immediately relevant. In this particular study the literature on cognitive apprenticeship (Ryan and Quinn, 1994), facilitation (Boud, 1987; Heron, 1989), and good teaching (Ramsden, 1992), proved very useful.

The fourth stage is 'application to practice'. During that stage the researchers were able to use their new understandings of theory to inform their handling of the everyday exigencies of practice, especially in relation to the classroom experience, the induction of new staff and curriculum development.

Various writers have described the way in which the experiential learning cycle develops further cycles as inevitable outcomes of new learning (for example Kolb, 1984; Zuber-Skerritt, 1991). The fifth part of the cycle, 'informed action', is one in which the lecturer lives out future experience at a new level of effectiveness. This new level results from the profound shift that has taken place in awareness, knowledge and confidence. The outcome of this is a demonstrable increase in the clarity with which both everyday and problematic issues of practice are addressed. There is also a greatly increased confidence regarding the factors which are critical to student success, for example establishing trust, the ability to work constructively with wrong answers and the importance of engaging students at the cognitive and metacognitive levels in analysing and making decisions about their learning behaviours.

LESSONS LEARNT

The evaluation of a project such as this one happens on several levels. We were surprised at the richness and depth of the data we were able to obtain, and believe that we selected an extremely effective methodology for our purposes. We would therefore use a similar methodology again.

Our experience bears out Ramsden's (1992) assertion that it is important to engage in a committed (and we would add 'grounded') exploration of practice to improve effectively the quality of student learning. Routine evaluation is simply not enough.

At any point in a teaching situation, a lecturer is responding to, analysing, and interpreting the myriad signals and behaviours that indicate the extent to which factors such as motivation, interest and understanding are evident. If a lecturer can bring to this analysis a greater knowledge of strategic behaviours to improve learning at any given moment, then both the lecturer and the students benefit.

There is now a deeper understanding that new staff require educational experiences that enable them to move from their general beliefs and conceptions of teaching to theories of practice informed by experiential learning and critical reflection.

Learning from experience requires attention to the dynamics of learning, the processing of experience through critical reflection, and applications of learning to practice. Teaching, research and staff development are all about learning, but learning in all these areas needs to be embedded in a cycle of reflection and action based on appropriate evidence and integrated into ongoing experience.

POLICY IMPLICATIONS

The processes outlined in this chapter demonstrate a cycle of quality improvement of teaching effectiveness which needs to be undergirded in a variety of ways. In an environment where departments, faculties and individual universities have to compete for research funding it is important that policy makers overtly value research into teaching and learning and support this by setting aside funding for that purpose. As well as rewarding teaching excellence (as many universities now do), it is important to acknowledge and reward excellence in research into teaching. This will help to ensure continuing quality improvement at a time of ongoing change within a diverse and complex educational environment, both nationally and internationally. There are also policy implications for the ways in which the outcomes of educational research are promulgated in order to achieve the maximum benefit.

Perhaps it is inevitable that the research focus in higher education will continue to be discipline based. However, universities almost invariably claim a professional commitment to the very highest levels of education, and unless they actively support research into teaching and learning, and implement the findings of such research, they risk providing educational experiences that are of less than optimum quality.

One of the benefits of the developing professionalism in the management of universities is an increased awareness of the value of relevant training and staff development, and the importance of this is reflected in the policies of many successful universities. Research into teaching effectiveness can inform staff development and training, and help address the problems of practice that exist in all educational contexts.

REFERENCES

Biggs, J (1999) *Teaching for Quality Learning at University,* Society for Research into Higher Education (SRHE)/ Open University Press, Buckingham

Boud, D (1987) A facilitator's view of adult learning, in *Appreciating Adults Learning,* ed D Boud and V Griffin, Kogan Page, London

Boud, D and Feletti, G (1997) *The Challenge of Problem-Based Learning,* 2nd edn, Kogan Page, London

Boud, D, Cohen, R and Walker, D (1993) Understanding learning from experience, in *Using Experience For Learning,* ed D Boud, R Cohen and D Walker, SRHE/ Open University Press, Buckingham

Brookfield, S (1995) *Becoming a Critically Reflective Teacher,* Kogan Page, London

Brown, J, Collins, A and Duguid, P (1989) Situated cognition and the culture of learning, *Educational Researcher,* **18** (1), pp 32–42

Denzin, N and Lincoln, Y (1994) Entering the field of qualitative research, in *Handbook of Qualitative Research,* ed N Denzin and Y Lincoln, Sage, Thousand Oaks, CA

Guba, E and Lincoln, Y (1994) Competing paradigms in qualitative research, in *Handbook of Qualitative Research,* ed N Denzin and Y Lincoln, Sage, Thousand Oaks, CA

Heron, J (1989) *The Facilitators' Handbook,* Kogan Page, London

Kolb, D (1984) *Experiential Learning: Experience as the source of learning and development,* Prentice-Hall, Englewood Cliffs, NJ

Little, S and Hefferan, G (2000) Developing students' legal problem-solving skills: an integrated model, in *Problem-Based Learning: Educational innovation across disciplines,* ed Tan O Seng *et al,* pp 105–13, Temasek Centre for Problem-Based Learning, Singapore

Merriam, S (1998) *Qualitative Research and Case Study Applications in Education,* Jossey-Bass, San Francisco, CA

Morgan, D (1997) *Focus Groups as Qualitative Research,* 2nd edn, Sage, Thousand Oaks, CA

Morgan, D and Krueger, R (1998) *The Focus Group Kit,* Sage, Thousand Oaks, CA

Ramsden, P (1992) *Learning to Teach in Higher Education,* Routledge, London

Ryan, G and Quinn, C (1994) Cognitive apprenticeship and problem-based learning, in *Reflections on Problem Based Learning,* ed S Chen, R Cowdroy, A Kingsland and M Ostwald, Australian PBL Network, Sydney

Yin, R (1994) *Case Study Research: Design and methods,* Sage, Thousand Oaks, CA

Zuber-Skerritt, O (1991) *Professional Development In Higher Education,* AEBIS, Brisbane

5

Improving teaching and learning in chemistry: the national Improve project

Richard Moyes

INTRODUCTION

This chapter recounts the progress of a project looking at problems in chemistry, but it is typical of most of the practical sciences. The cost of laboratory work and the high staff–student ratios considered necessary to teach these subjects led to extensive reorganization at the end of the 1980s. Universities found there was a need to evaluate their chemistry teaching and research in relation to national trends. The report of the enquiry *University Chemistry: The way forward* (Stone, 1988) suggested redeployment of resources to fund 30 large departments each with 30 or more academic staff. At that time probably some 120 institutions offered degrees in chemistry, so the report caused some gloom, but there was expansion in some universities to produce very large chemistry departments. These tended to attract the majority of well qualified applicants. Many small departments have closed as a result, and others are likely to follow this lead.

Chemistry degrees are often looked upon as purely vocational, although the annual graduate output exceeds the needs of the chemical industry. The employment situation for chemistry graduates was reviewed recently (Mason, 1998). This report observed that in the period 1986–95, while universities underwent an expansion of 115 per cent, chemistry only grew by 37 per cent. Royal Society of Chemistry (RSC) statistics (RSC Web page a) show that in recent years the output of graduates in chemistry rose from 3,000 in 1989 to 3,900 and then declined to 3,500 (approximate figures) in 1997. A level statistics for chemistry (RSC Web page b) show the number of entries declining gently from the 40,000 mark. Applications for chemistry degrees were less than 10 per cent each year of the A level entries from 1991 to 1997, with a small variation in any year. Applications since then have declined annually by a few per cent (RSC Web page c).

Since the recruitment situation for chemistry degrees is declining, chemistry departments nationally have evolved methods for increasing applications. The first of these is the use of the modular system to produce degrees with attractive minor subjects, based on a strong chemistry core. A comment on the competition for applicants comes from the fact that the RSC accredits (RSC Web page d) more than 500 named courses for professional membership (Graduate Member of the RSC), that is, each course on average must have less than eight students annually! The second method of boosting applications, and hopefully their quality, has been the almost universal development of four-year undergraduate master's degrees termed MChem.

THE IMPROVE PROJECT

The HEFCE Fund for the Development of Teaching and Learning (FDTL) offered moneys to projects following the Quality Assurance Agency's (QAA) early assessments of the quality of learning. This offer was limited to departments attaining an 'excellent' rating, some 13 departments in England in the case of chemistry. The Improve project aimed to identify and promote the wider use of examples of good teaching and learning activities which could be drawn from the QAA's *Chemistry Subject Overview* report and the individual departmental reports. To do this, it needed to secure the widest possible involvement of institutions for the extensive dissemination and transfer of new, as well as tried and tested, teaching ideas, activities and materials which stimulate learning. The project also wanted to help chemistry students to develop the intellectual, scientific and professional skills needed to make the most effective use of their knowledge of chemistry.

A number of organizations already existed with similar aims for chemistry. Primarily, the Royal Society of Chemistry had a very active education department with an interest across the whole range of education, and with concentrated effort on the secondary area. Higher education was advised by the independent Higher Education Chemistry Committee (HECC), a six-monthly meeting for heads of departments which was serviced by the RSC. There was an active Chemistry Computers in Teaching Initiative (CTI) centre based on the University of Liverpool effectively run by Dr R Gladwin. The Network for Chemistry Teaching (the Network), led by Dr John Garratt (University of York), was already in place doing similar work, but, like the CTI, limited by funding. The project aimed to build a cadre of involved teachers by extending and consolidating these networks across the country, as all these activities could be improved by an injection of cash.

The operation of the Improve project

The Improve project used publications, meetings and electronic communication to support the development of the network of lecturers. It ran staff development workshops to explore, on a national basis, specific problems and developments in teaching the subject as well as 'open road' workshops. It published 'case studies' reviewing particular teaching areas. It published and circulated a series of regular newsletters and developed e-mail communication through the pre-existing network. On top of this, it initiated and supported a Web page to give a method of rapid publication and ready access to the project publications.

Another important aspect of its work was liaison and cooperation with existing bodies in the chemistry world. Particularly important were the three annual meetings of directors of study to bring together those with direct responsibility for teaching in chemistry departments. One of the most significant innovations of the Improve project was the secondment of staff to develop their ideas in the real situation and seeking ways to make them generally applicable.

Workshops and conferences

The staff development workshops were a major factor in the dissemination of the outcomes of the project. They grew in popularity and attracted, apart from a 'core' of regular participants, a number of people from a variety of other scientific disciplines, for example those concerned with students' mathematical difficulties. Workshops were of two kinds, small invited 'think tanks' to discuss a problem in detail, such as the shape of undergraduate courses, and open meetings without restriction on participants which offered a range of practical solutions, for example approaches to difficult branches of the subject. By using facilities at other universities where appropriate, the cost of some of the workshops was lower than anticipated, which enabled more workshops to take place. Thirty-six workshops were held. Some were repeats of popular subjects at alternative venues and some, like the chemistry projects and think tank meetings, were the second of their type.

At the suggestion of, and in cooperation with, the Liverpool Chemistry CTI, 16 'open road days' were organized at centres across the country. The project contributed to the funding of these events by awarding one and a half secondments principally to cover travel costs. Apart from the main purpose which was to enable busy colleagues to 'drop in' to discuss and evaluate the latest software, the events provided a showcase for liaison with other chemistry projects, such as the RSC's Cutter Bequest projects, the Teaching and Learning Technology Project (TLTP), Chemistry Video Consortium, Elaborate (a project based on York University), the FDTL project 'Personal and Professional Development for Scientists' (PPDS), and the DfEE Network for Chemistry Teaching.

In addition, the project contributed sessions to the Variety in Chemistry annual Conference each September and made presentations at the European Conferences on Chemical Education and to the Department for Education and Employment Physics Network in Leeds. Papers relating to the presentations have been published in relevant journals. Reports of meetings and workshops can be found on the project's Web page, now subsumed into the LTSN Physical Sciences centre Web page.

Case studies

Eight studies were produced; they were case studies only in the sense that they reviewed chemistry related approaches to the problems reported. Case studies as printed versions were disseminated to everyone on the mailing list and also published electronically on the project's Web page (Race, 1997; Johnstone, 1997; Bland and Rolls, 1997; Bennett, 1997; Rest & Brattan, 1998). They proved to be highly popular and some reprinting had to be ordered. One study, *Good Practice in Industrial Work Placements* (Murray and Wallace, 1998) was produced at the suggestion of the HECC. Two are the results of weekend 'think-tanks' on quality matters (Moyes and Overton, 1997, 1998) and were intended to disseminate the discussions to a wider audience.

E-mail and WWW discussions, Web page

The e-mail Chem-Education mailbase was set up by the Network in advance of the Improve project. Participants in the Improve events were invited to subscribe to the Chem-Education mailbase, and most did. E-mail was used to advertise project events and disseminate news and opinions. This contact with colleagues, maintained by the extensive and popular use of e-mail, improved the efficiency and speed of communication. This ready availability of participants for rapid communication was of enormous value to the project. Post was also used, but was costly and sometimes slow. The Web page contained all the latest information about project events and developments as well as publications.

Newsletters

Newsletters were published at six-monthly intervals throughout the project. Their content reflects the activities of the project with accounts of secondment projects, workshop reports and other items of interest. The mailing list for all project publications rose to 850, including about 30 institutions overseas.

Cooperation with other bodies

Cooperation with the Royal Society of Chemistry (the professional body) took place through the arrangements for joint meetings such as workshops, and through service on Society committees (its Education Division Council and Educational Qualifications Board). These arrangements were examined annually at an Improve Chemistry Projects Meeting, which also involved the

CTI and the PPDS project. Cooperation with the HE Chemistry Conference (HECC) took place through attendance at and contributions to their meetings and the production of the case study (Murray and Wallace, 1998) at the Conference's request.

Cooperation with the Network for Chemistry Teaching in HE took place through the invitation of the coordinator to sit on the management committee and through agreement on a joint timetable of events (at the Chemistry Projects Meeting). Improve also provided support and presentations at the annual Variety in Chemistry Teaching conference.

Meeting of directors of study

Four annual meeting of directors of study were held at the Royal Society early in the academic year. The meetings were concerned with project reports from seconded staff, reports of the activities from collaborating chemistry projects, discussion of recent developments from the Quality Assurance Agency and other progress reports, for example on the production of benchmarking standards for chemistry. The full attendance and the delegates reported satisfaction with the meetings confirmed the value of these annual events.

Secondments of staff to develop good ideas

Minor funding was awarded to lecturers for partial secondment to the project. Sums were calculated on a notional one day per week basis at 20 per cent of point 6 of the lecturer scale (£4,200). Funds were paid to the relevant department, not to individuals. These secondments were intended to develop and disseminate good, innovative teaching materials that were readily transportable and to support the project. Nineteen full secondments (on referees' recommendations) were agreed to, each for a notional 12-month period. One of those was awarded a further half secondment for continuation purposes. The funding for secondments was very popular, and for the projects to complete within the lifetime of the project, had to be operating by the end of the second year. The outcomes, mostly in the form of written reports, materials or publications, were available for free dissemination to all institutions. Secondees have also presented their work through workshops and events organized by Improve and at conferences. Referees reported satisfaction with the amount and quality of the work achieved. These relatively small sums initiated a great deal of activity perhaps not otherwise possible, and their success must be considered a useful pointer for future development. Reports of these projects were made available through the continuing project (until October 2000) and thereafter through the LTSN Physical Science Centre (Physical Science Centre Web page).

THE SUCCESSES OF THE IMPROVE PROJECT

Major meetings allowed the presentation of the work of the project as a whole and of contributors to it. Presentation was by short talks or the exhibition of posters. This latter was much the most flexible method, as the constituent parts could be adjusted to fit the expected audience.

The Directors of Study meeting identified the staff in departments with responsibilities for teaching management and curriculum development, in many cases for the first time. It has clearly provided a useful platform for developments and is to become a permanency under the umbrella of the Royal Society of Chemistry. No charge was made for registration or catering, and the travelling expenses of each participant were met. This made the meetings expensive, but ensured a good attendance. A new group of influential teachers was initiated and the final meeting was used, in part, to plan future developments.

The programme of workshops by discussing important problems meant that chemists now recognize in each other those with an interest in developing teaching skills and new approaches, and can take up more readily the experience of others. We found that chemists in general prefer discipline related meetings, and the workshops set a pattern for future continuing professional development. The venue for meetings was important as a move from the university ambience could be very helpful, so that many workshops were held in hotels. Making no charge for registration or catering helped attendance, but each participant met his or her own travelling expenses.

The WWW page was a useful publication of project papers and attracted some overseas interest. It came as a surprise to learn how effective e-mail could be in keeping in touch with busy colleagues, and the use of the Network's original mailbase idea has been a major contribution to success. The publications have been well received, if demands for copies are a measure of success. This measure is difficult to quantify, as there was free circulation to all on the mailing list.

The open road days with the CTI offered an opportunity to stimulate interest in individual departments (and to encourage enthusiasts). It was noticeable that the participants were different from those attending the workshops, so some different penetration was seen here. This feature is worth considerable further development as travel costs are limited to the team providing the open road day, and it is intended to develop these days into teaching days with some degree of interdisciplinarity.

Secondment provided a relatively inexpensive route to innovation and the opportunity to encourage enthusiasts. The sums involved were only notional, and provided a lever for the staff concerned to obtain the necessary time for the development. It was an excellent use of funds which should be supported in the future. It was important to ensure that outcomes were available, in a variety of ways, to those who wished to make use of them.

LESSONS LEARNT

We have learnt about the power of networking and the value of building a cadre of involved chemistry teachers in HE through the project's activities. The connections with the Royal Society of Chemistry and the Physical Science Subject Centre provide channels through which some permanence can be achieved. In a desire to spend available funds on activities, we perhaps underrated the cost of effective managers, and would spend more on management in future developments. We would stress the need for active involvement of practising teachers rather than staff development managers *per se*, so that where part-time secondment is possible, it should be the preferred choice. There is no substitute for real personal experience.

Chemistry and physical science teaching in general face a number of crises, and there are two important matters to resolve. The first of these is making courses more interesting and attractive to students through careful consideration of content. Workshops relating to the schools/university interface and the 'Chemistry Courses for the Millennium' and 'Inspirational Chemistry' suggested routes forward. Second, there is the need to develop student autonomy through increased use of independent learning. Three workshops addressed this directly, while the TLTP workshops set out to customize existing material for local use as an answer to the 'not invented here' syndrome, and this added to the development of independent learning approaches. Only when these matters have been given due emphasis and priority are the current problems likely to be alleviated.

A related but different problem is the balance between the professional training of chemists and the general requirements of a comprehensive higher education. Career opportunities for trained chemists are declining and there is a need for the wider view. The adoption of the four-year undergraduate Master's degree raises new difficulties which need to be faced and dealt with through curriculum development, and substantial discussion of this arose at the project workshops.

EVALUATION

From the outset, the FDTL management required an approach to evaluation. In our case we chose to approach it at a series of levels. Evaluation at the activity level, where the major activity was in the form of meetings and workshops, was by use of a feedback form given to participants, the results of which were analysed and acted upon. This led to useful information about the venue and management of these central activities. The 36 workshops attracted in all 810 participants, averaging 23 from, on average, 17 institutions at each workshop. An analysis of 20 workshops where the participants and their institutions were known showed that, of 485 attendances, there were 293 separate individuals from 63 universities and 28 other institutions.

This can be construed as reasonable penetration of the target group of university teachers which then probably numbered about 1,200. It also reflects the size of the teaching network that developed during the project. A further activity was 'secondment' to produce a piece of work. Each application was sent to referees and their reports transmitted to the applicants, often resulting in helpful alterations. Of the sums involved, half was allocated at the beginning and half on completion and receipt of a report.

At the general level we circulated the usual questionnaire to all on the mailing list seeking opinions on the various activities. Disappointingly, only 40 replies were received (from 850!), so that the analysis is of limited value as most responses were from committed enthusiasts. We had hoped to repeat the exercise at the final directors' meeting, but were frustrated by a postal failure. A general response also came from preparing a bid for the Physical Science Centre when we solicited support and a number of congratulatory letters were received.

At the administrative level we tried to measure participation and penetration in terms of numbers of individuals involved. The circulation list contained 850 names. We estimate the national size of the community at about 1,500. The (independent) management committee met regularly to receive reports on progress and provided evaluative advice. The preparation of these reports (at approximately six-monthly intervals) forced a pause to reflect on the activities and their relative success.

At a consultancy level, bearing in mind the HEFCE and therefore English funding, three external consultants were appointed. Two were Scottish academics, one a professor with an education background, and one a professor of chemistry. The third was a biochemistry professor based in Wales who had taken part in the HEFCE quality assessments. All were chosen for their extensive subject experience and lively interest in educational development. They reported annually on progress with evaluative comments and suggestions for improvement. They were also invited to observe the activities. This they did with helpful comment as feedback. The executive summary of their final report represents evaluation from outside the project and therefore is probably the most valuable.

This is a quotation from the external evaluators' report (Executive Summary):

> Project Improve aimed to identify, promote, and provide mechanisms for the dissemination of high quality teaching and learning activities. . . The project delivered substantially more than was originally outlined, holding twice as many workshops as planned, in addition to the open road days that had not been in the proposal, and in all other areas the original deliverables were essentially achieved. It is clear that participation in Project Improve was extensive across universities in the UK, with new and older universities being well represented. Most Chemistry Departments had at least three or four members of staff

who were, in one way or another, involved in some aspect of Project Improve.

It is hard to assess the real impact of the project on chemistry teaching in the UK, but it is our impression that it has had a substantial effect by raising the profile of teaching at HE level, by encouraging individuals who wished to develop new activities, and by providing a springboard for the development of new material over the next five to ten years.

CONCLUSIONS

Workshop and meeting evaluations were valuable, particularly for content relevance, venue suitability and highlights. Results were generally approving, but criticisms did appear and were taken seriously. The refereeing of secondment activities has been useful, but not so useful as withholding half the cash until a report is received! The organizational evaluations were also valuable, but the committee tended to leave administration to the directors, probably because the project was considered successful. The consultants' reports have been very useful, full of considered opinion on the activities and feedback analyses. Reporting at annual intervals seems appropriate, except if there is a crisis.

The final overall evaluation drew together all the sections above and their relation to the expected outcomes for chemistry teaching at this level. The final paragraph reads:

Lessons to be learnt: Perhaps the greatest lesson to be learnt from Project Improve is that such programmes need to be well managed, and to have strong dialogue with the community, if they are to succeed. Project Improve had both of these.

REFERENCES

Bennett, S (1997) *Designing Independent Learning Material* [online], Improve project Web site: http://science.ntu.ac.uk/chph/improve/improve.html
Bland, W and Rolls, D (1997) *Design of Objective Questions for Assessment* [online], Improve project Web site: http://science.ntu.ac.uk/chph/improve/improve.html
Improve Project Web site: http://science.ntu.ac.uk/chph/improve/improve.html
Johnstone, A (1997) *Evaluation of Innovation* [online], Improve project Web site
Mason, G (1998) *Change and Diversity: The challenges facing chemistry higher education,* Royal Society of Chemistry
Moyes, R and Overton, T (1997) *University Chemistry Teaching: Challenges and opportunities* [online], Improve project Web site: http://science.ntu.ac.uk/chph/improve/improve.html

Moyes, R and Overton, T (1998) *Exploring the Opportunities Offered by the Benchmarks*, [online], Improve project Web site: http://science.ntu.ac.uk/chph/improve/improve.html

Murray, R and Wallace, R (1998) *Good Practice in Industrial Work Placements* [online] Improve project Web site: http://science.ntu.ac.uk/chph/improve/improve.html

Physical Science Centre Web page: http://www.physsci.ltsn.ac.uk

Race, P (1997) *Changing Assessment to Improve Chemistry Learning* [online] Improve project Web site: http://science.ntu.ac.uk/chph/improve/improve.html

Rest, Λ and Brattan, D (1998) *Customising Multimedia Packages for Chemistry Teaching* [Online], Improve project Web site: http://science.ntu.ac.uk/chph/improve/improve.html

RSC Web Page a: http:// www.Chemsoc.org/pdf/LearnNet/rsc/stats/UK-qual.pdf

RSC Web Page b: http://www.Chemsoc.org/pdf/LearnNet/rsc/stats/2.pdf

RSC Web Page c: http://www.Chemsoc.org/pdf/LearnNet/rsc/stats/3pop.pdf

RSC Web Page d: http://www.RSC.org/members/accred.htm

Stone, F G A (1998) *University Chemistry: The way forward,* University Grants Committee

6

Planning and understanding change: toolkits for course design and evaluation

Martin Oliver and Grainne Conole

INTRODUCTION

Changing educational practice involves a leap of faith, particularly when unfamiliar techniques (such as teaching with new technologies) are involved. In any such example of change, some of the wide range of issues – technical, pedagogical and cultural – are likely to fall outside academics' areas of expertise. Consequently, ways of providing guidance and support have become particularly important. Processes of planning and reflection can be adopted to ensure that these changes are based on an understanding of their role and context, rather than on blind faith or fashion, particularly if these processes are underpinned by expert knowledge, theory and examples.

Although these processes are useful, they remain problematic. One particular issue is that current practice is often poorly understood, meaning that the first stage in any debate about educational change must be to discuss existing approaches. Furthermore, as a result of a strong tradition of disciplinary cultures in higher education (Becher, 1989), educational developers frequently find themselves challenged with, 'It's different in my discipline.' However, finding out precisely how it is different – let alone why – can be difficult, since many disciplinary practices and values are tacit, and remain hidden. As with the need to discuss current practice, recognition of and engagement with these cultural differences is essential to educational change.

The focus for this chapter will be the role of a particular type of resource – a 'toolkit' – in planning and understanding changes in educational practice. By defining and illustrating what a toolkit is, and providing a case study of the use of a toolkit, the role of these resources in supporting change will be investigated. In addition, issues of difference in practice – between individuals and between disciplines – will be considered.

BACKGROUND

The current climate of globalization, combined with the introduction of new technology into the mainstream of higher education, has had a significant impact on academic practice and roles. Several strategies for coping with these changes have been proposed, including, for example, programmes of academic development that focus on reflective practice as a way of guiding change (Smith and Oliver, 2000).

A complementary approach involves the development of resources that can guide the process of integrating technology with existing practice. Such resources are not intended as a substitute for reflective practice or expert advice; however, they can – if carefully designed – promote reflection and discussion by representing practice and making intentions explicit, and thus open to critique. This process of planning and representing changes to educational practice provides a bridge between the superficial adoption of off-the-shelf 'solutions' and informed, critical engagement (Conole and Oliver, submitted). This goal is helped by the format of the toolkits, which make expert information available to practitioners, help them choose approaches that best suit their context through a process of elicitation and simple inference, and thus attempt to embed theory in practice.

Toolkits are particularly useful where a range of approaches could be used, and where there is no single right answer to a problem. Although they need not be implemented as software tools, doing so can support the processes of modelling and information management that they involve; it also provides an easy mechanism for revisiting and revising output from the toolkits over time. This allows toolkits to identify implications or recommend suitable approaches, based on the information and assumptions elicited from the user. Rather than the toolkit deciding on the best approach on behalf of the user, the practitioner uses these inferences to make informed, professional decisions about whether certain changes would be appropriate. In this way, toolkits can provide the paper required by processes such as quality enhancement without forcing practitioners to adopt pre-defined, 'generic' solutions (Oliver and Conole, 2000).

Two examples of toolkits are discussed in this chapter: the pedagogic and the evaluation toolkits, which cover the processes of (re-)developing and of evaluating courses. The metaphor of a 'toolkit' is used to refer to a specific kind of resource: one that is structured around either a theory or an expert model of a design process, where each decision is supported by an activity that guides users towards appropriate options. In addition to supporting the process as a whole, this metaphor requires the individual components of toolkits (the activities and tools) to be useful in isolation to tackle particular problems or decisions as they arise.

Early evaluations of these toolkits confirmed the usefulness of the approach as a way of guiding change, but also challenged the notion that the toolkits might be developed to a point where they could be used in a stand-alone, unsupported format. Instead, these studies highlighted the value of group based activities involving the toolkits (Kewell, Oliver and Conole, 1999). When they were incorporated into an educational development workshop, it became clear that the structure of the knowledge base within the toolkits acted as a simple language that allowed academics to describe their own practice. This provided a valuable starting point for reflection and for cross-disciplinary discussions of pedagogy and practice.

In retrospect, this should have come as no surprise; it simply reflects the diversity of values, beliefs and methods held by disciplines (Becher, 1989; Shabajee, 1999), and the fact that this diversity extends even to the way in which terms such as 'tutorial' are used (Condron, 1999). As has been observed, discussion of such disciplinary differences provides a rich ground for reflection on academic values, roles and processes (Rowland, 2000). Recognition of this adds a valuable critical dimension to the use of toolkits: not only can they be used to support judgements about the appropriateness of change, but they can also contribute to a deeper understanding of current practice and the potential impact of changes through a process of group enquiry into assumptions, meanings and values.

The pedagogic toolkit

The pedagogic toolkit was developed as a way of helping academics to select appropriate teaching techniques when redesigning their courses (Conole and Oliver, 1998). Recognizing that any interpretation of 'appropriate' must depend upon context and personal practice, the toolkit focuses on eliciting actual practice and drawing inferences which can be used to support professional judgement, rather than on prescribing 'correct' solutions. It involves five steps:

1. A review of the current course structure, identifying the teaching techniques used and opportunities for learning.

2. An analysis of the current course structure to identify areas of learning that could be supported more effectively.

3. The comparison of alternative teaching techniques in order to identify those that might usefully be added to or substituted for current methods. Importantly, the descriptions provided are required to reflect the user's actual or intended practice, rather than representing some 'generic' caricature of a 'typical' session.

4. A comparison between different possible course formats, with decisions as to the final format taking into account:

    i.   the development/preparatory work required;

    ii. the breadth of educational experience supported, expressed in terms of Laurillard's (1993) conversational framework;

iii. how flexible the course is, in terms of constraints on the time and location of participation.

5. Specification of the final course format.

Elements of the pedagogic toolkit were subsequently implemented as a software tool called Media Adviser. This concentrated on the process of describing, modelling and comparing teaching techniques. Two elements of this are particularly relevant here: the 'media rater', which is equivalent to step 1 in the above process, and 'course modeller', which is used to support steps 2 and 4 (ii). These components are illustrated in Figures 6.1 and 6.2.

Although the modeller relies on quantitative descriptions of techniques ('ratings'), users are encouraged to use this information qualitatively, as the basis for professional judgement. Weightings are indicative rather than absolute, and are based solely on users' characterization of their teaching practice and their intentions for and beliefs about changes to practice. It is this feature that allowed Media Adviser to act as the basis for cross-disciplinary discussions of education, as described above, since it highlights differences in approach from user to user in a visual, easily understood way. Once such differences have been identified, it is then a simple matter to steer group discussion towards an exploration of the reasons why approaches differ.

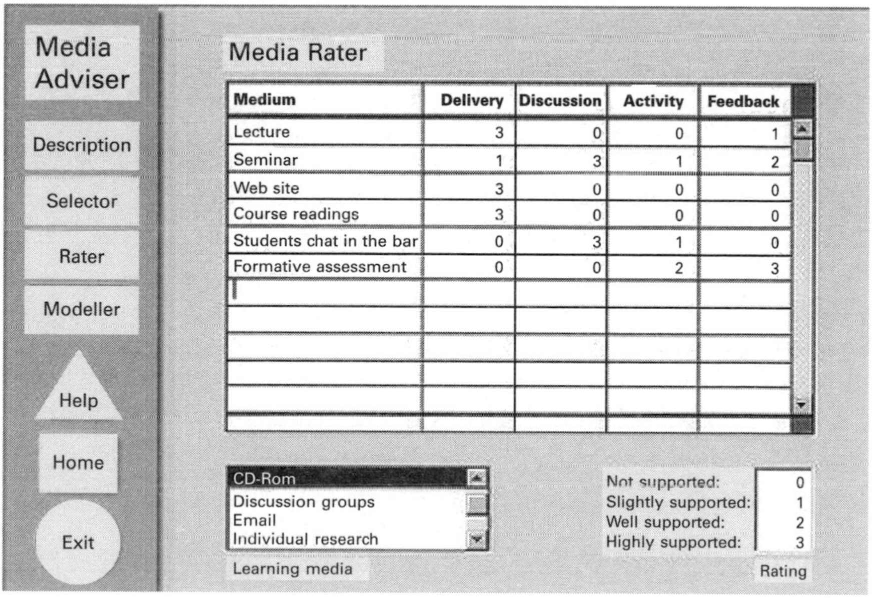

Figure 6.1   *Media Adviser's 'media rater'*

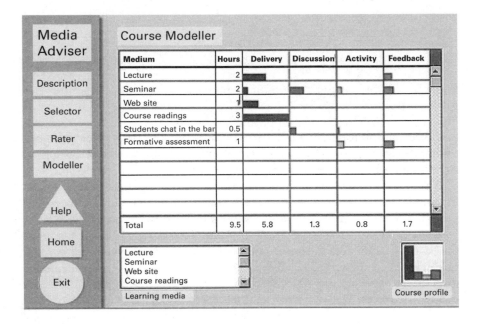

Figure 6.2   *Media Adviser's 'course modeller'*

The evaluation toolkit

As with curriculum design, evaluation is a process that is heavily influenced by context and for which there is no universally applicable approach. The evaluation toolkit was developed to help academics design and plan evaluations of their teaching practice (Oliver and Conole, 1998). This was subsequently implemented as an online resource (Conole *et al*, 2001), a detailed evaluation of which is reported elsewhere (Oliver *et al*, in press).

The model of evaluation planning incorporated in the online toolkit incorporates the following steps:

1. Scoping the evaluation.

   i. Identifying the focus of the study, reasons for undertaking it and important contextual features.

   ii. Identifying stakeholders and their concerns.

   iii. Devising appropriate questions to address.

2. Planning the evaluation.

   i. Selecting appropriate data capture methods.

   ii. Selecting appropriate data analysis methods.

3. Presenting the evaluation.

    i.   Assessing the validity of the study.

    ii. Planning action to be taken as a result of the study.

    iii. Selection of appropriate presentation techniques for each stakeholder group.

The evaluation toolkit forms a useful complement to the pedagogic toolkit, supporting academics in the process of understanding and communicating the impact of changes in practice. Whereas the pedagogic toolkit concentrates on plans and intentions, the evaluation toolkit focuses on outcomes. The evidence of success and accounts of change that evaluation provides can then make an important contribution to the process of understanding change.

METHODOLOGY

This section will outline the methodological approach to developing and using 'toolkits', a central tenet of which is that the development of a toolkit is an iterative process, involving a series of evaluative steps.

The first step involves identifying theories and taxonomies that can be used as a framework for the area under discussion. The pedagogic toolkit, for example, involved developing a framework for course design, within which various models were used (for example, models of costing resources, of the learning process and of different ways in which courses could be made more 'flexible') to differentiate between teaching techniques (Conole and Oliver, 1998). This framework was evaluated by asking an academic to work through it as part of the redevelopment of one of her courses, with the developers on hand to troubleshoot the process. While working through it, the academic followed a 'talk aloud protocol', so that her reasons, doubts, problems and insights were available to guide subsequent refinements. The process was recorded on video, transcribed and analysed. This approach was selected because it provided significant amounts of rich data. This was used to highlight the shortcomings of the resource and to provide an understanding of the way in which the academic related to and interpreted the framework.

After refining the framework, the next step involves redeveloping it as a paper-based toolkit by devising activities that allow users to interpret their practice by interrogating the framework. This is also piloted using a talk aloud protocol, allowing improvements to be made in terms of both clarity and conceptual structure. With the evaluation toolkit, for example, users had problems framing the scope of the evaluation they wanted to carry out; this prevented them from engaging with the toolkit until substantial intervention and support was provided by the developers. This incident led to a whole new section being added to the beginning of the toolkit to help users to think about the audience and context for the study.

Once such refinements have been made, the toolkit is used in a workshop setting. This part of the evaluation process tests whether the initial refinements have been effective, and whether other users engage with the resource in the same way. The workshop incorporates feedback sessions after each part of the toolkit, each of which is run in the style of a focus group. This allows the thoughts and reflections of users to be elicited in a similar way to the talk aloud protocol used in the individual studies, providing a far richer source of data than end of workshop feedback sheets or just copies of the plans produced by participants.

The participants in these evaluation workshops were carefully selected to represent a range of disciplines and levels of expertise (from complete novices through to experienced researchers). It was difficult to predict who might use the toolkit or how they might use it, all of which would have had a bearing on its effectiveness. This complexity meant that it would have been unreasonable to generalize about any generic impact these resources might have had. Rather than attempt to do so, for example by using randomized control trials, these qualitatively rich evaluation methods allowed the development of deeper understanding of issues and of the use of the toolkits, with the sampling of participants providing some insight into the way in which these experiences varied.

Once this workshop evaluation has confirmed the suitability of the structure of the toolkit, the next stage involves identifying the most time-consuming elements of the process – particularly those that involve routine activity rather than active reflection – so that these can be facilitated by implementing the toolkit as a piece of software. As before, this resource was subjected to trials with individual users for the purposes of refinement, followed by evaluation in a workshop setting. Again, participants were carefully selected to ensure that a wide sample of potential users was represented. Moreover, since this represented the final developmental step for the toolkit (barring refinements for usability or the potential need for redesign in the light of feedback from the workshop), the workshops were organized so as to allow sustained engagement and discussion over the course of a complete day. In addition to the normal feedback on usability and relevance, particular attention was paid in these sessions to the way in which the toolkit supported reflection and discussion.

It is this last point that will be taken up in the following case study.

A CASE STUDY

Central to all the discussion above has been the idea that the value of toolkits arises from the way in which they require assumptions and approaches to be made explicit (and thus open to critique), and their ability to suggest options or illustrate consequences that users might not otherwise have considered, prompting reflection and debate. The advantages of this in planning and understanding change are clear; however, toolkits also have a role to play in laying the groundwork for change by helping academics to develop a better understanding of their current practice, and providing a mechanism for them to articulate their future needs more precisely.

In this section, a study is described that focuses on the workshop format outlined above to investigate the issue of differences in teaching practice. The workshop was kept small in order to allow deep discussion within a half-day session; there were three participants, two drawn from one course team and one drawn from a different faculty. Each had experience of teaching on a number of courses, but had chosen one course that they felt needed changing. The jointly taught course was a first-year unit in a medical programme, taken by around 120 students, roughly three-quarters of whom were taking the course as part of a subsidiary subject. The other course was also a first year course, but was about economics, and involved a mix of historical review and case studies. It is taken by around 20 students, half from within the economics department, and half from the faculty of social sciences. This mix allowed differences in practice both within and between faculties to be illustrated. The workshop was run by one facilitator, with an additional observer taking notes and helping out when required.

The format of the workshop was simple: participants introduced themselves and outlined the course they were thinking of redeveloping. The facilitator then introduced Media Adviser. Participants worked at computers to characterize their current teaching practice using the rating tool, and then shared their descriptions with the other participants, leading to a discussion about differences in approach. After this, they modelled their courses, based on their descriptions of practices, and then these models were shared and discussed. These discussions were then used to formulate plans for course development. The session ended with open questions and answers. Participants were encouraged to challenge the format and assumptions of the tools they were using at any point during the workshop.

Even from the first activity – which simply involved listing the teaching methods used during the course – participants started to reflect on fundamental issues of course design, such as the difference between a teacher centred and a student centred description of the course.

Are these teaching or learning media?

Similarly, there was reflection on the fact that 'different groups of students might have different experiences of our lectures'. They also distinguished between their intentions and the reality of what might actually happen, showing sensitivity to the limitations of a modelling exercise such as this:

Not so easy to determine – was there any discussion? – but can't force this from students; [it] may happen or may not (ie no guarantee that will get discussion or how much).

The process also prompted critical reflection on related issues, such as the way in which quality is measured:

There is a tendency to equate weighting [ie emphasis] with time, which is not accurate.

This led the lecturers to challenge their current course design, which they felt reflected tradition rather than need. This discussion drew on the earlier consideration of student centred rather than teacher centred models of course design, emphasizing the values that they felt were central to their practice.

It makes you reflect on what. . . are possible for the student. Often one feels the number of lectures, tutorials etc is given and immutable. It's useful to see how the course breakdown looks.

The second activity, which involved using the rating tool to describe their teaching, led to further questioning of the role of different educational techniques. On discovering that he had characterized lectures and handouts in an identical way, one participant asked,

Why not replace lectures with handouts?

This led to a rich discussion of student expectations and institutional policies, raising participants' awareness of the marketing and political aspects of course design. It also highlighted the way in which familiar formats can appear to be engaging without actually involving the student in anything more than a passive, receptive role.

Students seem to want to feel that they have participated, and some-how, by sitting through a lecture, they think they have done.

The descriptive process also highlighted differences in teaching style. For example, one participant characterized his lectures as involving a high degree of activity and discussion for students; this contrasted with the two lecturers who both taught as part of one course team, for whom lectures were primarily a means of disseminating information to students. Similarly, all three had differing views about what constituted a tutorial. Importantly, there were differences between the two members of the course team that had not previously been recognized. This led to a discussion of how the participants ran their tutorials, and an exchange of suggestions about how they could be made more interactive and engaging. As one participant noted, such discussions provided obvious opportunities to extend lecturers' repertoires of techniques by learning about 'the different ways in which people use handouts, tutorials, lectures, etc'. The result of this was the early sharing of plans for change that were grounded in participants' own experiences.

As part of these discussions, the participants began to identify reasons why teaching techniques such as lectures differed. 'Disciplinary differences' were initially cited as one possible reason, but the existence of differences within the course team led to a more critical discussion of what this phrase might actually mean. Eventually, a number of influences were identified, each of which contributed to the process of determining the format of teaching, including:

- Whether the teacher has a teacher centred or student centred view of learning.

- Current trends in learning and teaching. ('If we'd done these ten years ago, the differences between us might have been much narrower.')

- The status of knowledge and the type of discourse within a discipline. ('In arts, if a department came out where delivery [of information] was high there would be something very wrong'; 'In science, there is a mass of basic information you need to have, whereas in history, it is different – it doesn't matter if you know nothing about the 19th century.')

- The content covered in the course.

- The level of students being taught. ('For first years, the emphasis is on the delivery of information. Further on, they are expected to discuss rather than receive, so most lectures will change.')

- The size of group being taught.

- Student expectations and requirements. (For example, are they intrinsically or extrinsically motivated by the course?)

- What other teaching techniques are used in the course.

In recognition of these influences, the participants recognized that there would never be agreement as to the 'right' way to describe a lecture, tutorial, etc. However, descriptions of techniques would 'start off differently, but might converge' as users of the toolkit debated their understanding of the descriptive language and reached consensus over the meanings of terms.

In a similar vein, the participants discussed whether or not to introduce less familiar techniques, such as Web based teaching, computer mediated communication, and so on. Importantly, there was valuable discussion about what these terms meant to the participants, and what role they might have in teaching and learning. One participant, for example, decided that what he meant by 'Web pages' conflated at least two distinct activities: the use of the Web to deliver lecture notes, and the use of online bulletin boards to supplement class discussions. This clarification enabled him to plan changes to his course in greater detail, concentrating on pedagogic requirements rather than the technical systems available to him.

One interesting point that was noted was that, at present, the introduction of techniques such as Web based teaching was seen as an add-on to the 'real' course.

At the moment, anything that is done online takes place by the students' volition.

Technology has been added to courses, but has never replaced traditional teaching methods.

This led to an exploration of the tension between the rhetoric of independent learning, often associated with the use of technology enabled learning, and the reality within the participants' departments. Use of the modelling tool within Media Adviser showed that what happened in practice was that the introduction of technology extended the formal elements of teaching, eating into the undefined notional learning hours that students were expected to spend on the course. This had the effect of reducing students' scope for independent study and activity, often replacing it with the delivery of supplementary reading materials in an electronic format. The discussion allowed participants to develop a deeper understanding of unanticipated potential consequences of change; it also led all three participants to reconsider the balance of teaching methods they wished to use on their courses.

One final area of discussion introduced by the workshop facilitators addressed the way in which the descriptions and models produced by working with Media Adviser could be used as the basis for discussion between different interest groups. Based on their experiences in the workshop, the group suggested a range of settings in which the tool could contribute to the understanding of practice and the potential impact of change.

Interestingly, given that background literature and the earlier discussion concentrated on interdisciplinary differences, the first proposed role for Media Adviser was to support course teams' discussion of teaching and learning. This was suggested by one of the pair of lecturers, and reflected his experiences in the session, where he had learnt a wide variety of things about his colleague's practices that had not been apparent in the previous two terms' worth of shared course delivery. This included discussion of 'private' information, such as practice within tutorials and lectures, which does not normally come to light unless programmes of peer observation are in place. One important proposed outcome of such discussions would be to define a sense of identity for the course team, in which personal styles of teaching were framed in relationship to a shared view of how teaching on the course 'ought' to be done.

Another related proposal was that this would be useful for departments. Participants suggested that it could provide a catalyst for thinking about teaching and learning issues in departments where these concepts were treated unproblematically. Starting points for discussion might arise, for example, out of apparent discrepancies between individuals' approaches.

> There might be value if these charts were added to unit descriptions. We would then be able to discuss why similar units 'looked' different.

Again, it was felt that such debate might lead to the emergence of a sense of identity, of agreement over what an appropriate educational emphasis for a particular subject or course was.

> For an individual or department, getting a sense of the balance between the four different categories [delivery, discussion, activity and feedback] would be very useful.

Finally, it was suggested that there would also be value in using these models to discuss and debate lecturers' intentions for different elements of the course with their students.

> The other area – and perhaps the more useful one – is to display it to students. . . Giving them this information will enable them to make judgements about what you as a lecturer are doing.

Interestingly, participants were cautious about the value of interdisciplinary discussion involving the toolkit. One participant, for example, only felt that 'it would be useful where departments are similar'. Given the rich discussion that took place in this simple interdisciplinary workshop, such comments seem somewhat ironic. However, such feelings are understandable given that the primary concern in all the uses outlined above is to achieve convergence – at least as an ideal to which all concerned can subscribe. The format of the workshop, however, relied on divergence, in that it used difference as the starting point for an investigation of personal styles, preferences and beliefs. For this reason, it is less surprising that the participants felt slightly less confident about the value of such an approach.

CONCLUSIONS

Changing educational practice is a risky business, full of uncertainty. These problems are often compounded by the fact that both the proposed changes and the current situation are poorly conceptualized. Resources that support decision making processes, such as toolkits, can help address these problems. Most obviously, they can do this by providing a systematic structure to guide planning; between them, the pedagogic and evaluation toolkits provide a way of planning an entire cycle of educational change, from conception through to summative judgement. Equally importantly, however, they can help by allowing academics to describe and debate their practice.

In the case study above, it is this latter role that has been most closely explored. Here, Media Adviser allowed users to explore practice by describing apparently shared terminology using a simple rating scale. In effect, this acted as a shared 'meta-language', allowing participants to move beyond the scope of their normal disciplinary discourse and to provide a 'window' on their culture and its practices. In doing so, differences and similarities were identified and then debated, allowing a deeper understanding of individual approaches to develop. What is particularly important about the case study is that these debates prompted participants to reconsider both their traditionally determined current course format and their initial ideas for introducing new techniques such as Web based teaching and learning. Instead of grand but poorly understood changes to the course, much of the discussion concentrated on small but important changes arising from differences in practice.

Importantly, the participants felt that discussions such as this would be of benefit in a wide range of settings, including:

- within course teams, for example, to understand how students' experiences of the course will vary with different teachers and tutors;

- within departments, as the basis for discussion about shared approaches and values;

- across disciplines, in order to develop an understanding of different approaches to teaching and learning, as illustrated in the example above;

- between staff and students, so that expectations about the purpose of particular learning and teaching opportunities are shared.

In a context where change has become the norm, it is perhaps more important than ever to ensure that developments are not merely planned, but also understood. Toolkits such as those described above offer one approach that can support both of these requirements.

ACKNOWLEDGEMENTS

The toolkits described in this chapter were developed with funding from BP, the Joint Information Systems Committee and the European Social Fund.

REFERENCES

Becher, T (1989) *Academic Tribes and Territories: Intellectual enquiry and the culture of the disciplines*, Open University Press, Buckingham

Condron, F (1999) Measuring the effectiveness of electronic resources in small-group teaching: the ASTER project, *Proceedings of the 1999 Humanities and Arts Higher Education Network Conference*, Open University

Conole, G and Oliver, M (1998) A pedagogical framework for embedding C&IT into the curriculum, *ALT-J*, **6** (2), pp 4–16

Conole, G and Oliver, M (submitted) Using toolkits to embed theory into practice, *Journal of Interactive Media in Education*

Conole, G, Crewe, E, Oliver, M and Harvey, J (2001) A toolkit for supporting evaluation, *ALT-J*, **9** (1), 38–49

Kewell, B, Oliver, M and Conole, G (1999) *Assessing the Organisational Capabilities of Embedding Learning Technologies into the Undergraduate Curriculum. The Learning Technology Studio Programme: a case study*, ELT report no 10, University of North London

Laurillard, D (1993) *Rethinking University Teaching*, Routledge, London

Oliver, M and Conole, G (1998) Evaluating communication and information technologies: a toolkit for practitioners, *Active Learning*, **8**, pp 3–8

Oliver, M and Conole, G (2000) Assessing and enhancing quality using toolkits, *Quality Assurance in Education*, **8** (1), pp 32–37

Oliver, M, MacBean, J, Conole, G and Harvey, J (in press) Using a toolkit to support the evaluation of learning, *Journal of Computer Assisted Learning* special issue on evaluation

Rowland, S (2000) *The Enquiring University Teacher*, Open University Press, Buckingham

Shabajee, P (1999) Making values and beliefs explicit as a tool for the effective development of educational multimedia software: a prototype, *British Journal of Educational Technology*, **30** (1), pp 101–13

Smith, J and Oliver, M (2000) Academic development: a framework for embedding learning technology, *International Journal of Academic Development*, **5** (2), pp 129–37

7

Enhancing transferable skills elements within a subject discipline: an example of how project initiatives can be implemented across a diverse subject discipline in the higher education sector

Ruth Pilkington

INTRODUCTION

The Fund for the Development of Teaching and Learning funded project on transferable skills development for non-specialist language learning, TransLang, ran from September 1997 to July 2001. It received continuation funding from FDTL up to July 2002 to transfer outcomes into specialist languages, other subject disciplines and staff development.

Background to the project

The TransLang project was devised by the heads of department from the University of Central Lancashire and Anglia Polytechnic University for submission as a proposal under FDTL Phase Two. Both heads had a history of active involvement in the development of institution-wide language programmes, and the success and development of their own programmes reflected the pattern of history and trends outlined by Fay and Ferney (2000). They were both convinced of the particular role and benefits associated with the study and provision of non-specialist language programmes at higher education level. They felt that the nature of teaching and learning on these programmes, under the heading of 'applied language study', contributed to specific pedagogic, skills and learning-related innovation and experiences, which were worthy of dissemination and further development.

The aims of the TransLang project were therefore to improve practice in teaching, learning and assessment in modern languages in higher education institutions by enhancing the role which is played by transferable skills in programmes of languages study, particularly for non-specialists.

TransLang developed strategies for focusing on:

- the transferable skills elements of students' language learning;

- ways and means of supporting the acquisition process of these skills.

The aims of the project reflected the applied nature of its context. The means by which TransLang achieved its goals also evidence a reflexive and thoroughly researched approach. It is an example of action research in practice. It is characteristic of the approach of the 'reflective practitioner' (Schön, 1983), which is the hallmark of those involved in project work, and certainly of many of those encouraged through the FDTL initiative.

Activity and structure of the project

The project team comprised a group of more than 20 colleagues from language departments at nine institutions of higher education (HEIs) who worked collaboratively over two and a half years from October 1997 to March 2000 in the development of teaching, learning and support materials, resources and approaches for enhancing transferable skills within non-specialist language programmes.

The HEIs involved were:

- five consortium members: University of Central Lancashire, Anglia Polytechnic University, Liverpool John Moores University, Newcastle University and Staffordshire University;

- four co-opted HEIs: Chester College of HE, University of Luton, Oxford Brookes University and Southampton Institute.

A steering group meeting four times a year oversaw and contributed to the strategy for the project. It comprised heads of department or their representatives from the five consortium members, the project manager and project officer, a representative from the National Languages Training Organization (NLTO), and student representatives. It played an active role in editing documents produced by the project. There was also an external evaluator whose role was critical in devising the strategy for evaluating the impact of the project's activities.

Staff were organized into three task groups for the first stage of the project, each with a particular focus regarded by the team as being critical:

- *Task Group 1*: curriculum design and module development, working on the process of identifying skills in learning, teaching and assessment tasks and how to emphasize those skills elements.

- *Task Group 2*: learner autonomy: autonomous language learning and providing students with independent learning skills. This area underpins the applied language learning experience.

- *Task Group 3*: assessment of transferable skills elements within language learning.

The three elements were each regarded as essential elements, which inter-linked and supported the overall curriculum design process. Staff members working in the groups were released on a pro rata basis to work on the project and were all practising lecturers from eight of the participating HEIs, between them covering a range of languages, including English as a foreign language. They brought with them particular interests and areas of expertise in fields such as assessment, module design, skills training, learner autonomy and computer aided language learning (CALL). Two of the co-opted HEIs had institutional approaches to skills profiling, and TransLang benefited from the insight and experience of these colleagues.

The continuation activity of TransLang reflected the changing nature of project work: a core team of original contributors have replaced the project manager role, and they were supplemented by a number of new members who took up and adapted TransLang products. The approaches and method-ology were now sufficiently well established and clear that project activities could continue, guided by a clear set of goals, structures and plan.

Output from the project

TransLang offered a series of products including training workshops, simulation activities and dissemination of practice and materials for achiev-ing these aims. There were in all 50 workshops and consultancy visits, and 48 contributions to conferences and other events during the first stage of the project. There were also a number of published resources from the project, which can be obtained by application through the project Web site: http://www.uclan.ac.uk/facs/class/languages/translang/tlweb.htm

The survey of non-specialist language provision in institutions of higher education in the UK
The investigation into non-specialist language provision across the UK in November 1997 produced a wealth of information on the nature of provision. This survey (Pilkington, 1998) contributed considerably to understanding of this particular area and to research by others in this field. It came at a particularly critical point in the development of provision, after a period of consolidation and rationalization of programmes. Hitherto there had been little large-scale investigation into what the survey clearly identified as a growing and important area of language provision. It provided an important baseline from which to measure change within languages over the intervening period.

The guide to transferable skills in language learning

This (Pilkington, 2000) was a key output to the work of the project and provides a basis for colleagues to redesign learning outcomes and modules, train students and staff, and adapt and use tools and materials for enhancing the transferable skills elements of language learning. The guide uses a model as its core for identifying transferable skills elements within the teaching, learning and assessment activities of a subject. Around this, the three task groups developed materials and approaches to support the design of skills into the curriculum, the assessment of transferable skills elements within a subject, and the development of autonomous learning skills. The guide contains photocopiable resources for practitioners, discussion of key issues, and a series of case studies giving examples of the application of the TransLang materials and resources. Materials for students are primarily in English, although certain key materials have been provided in the three main foreign languages studied: French, German and Spanish. The guide has been designed to be a flexible and user-friendly resource for use by practitioners who are teaching under considerable time and resource pressures.

Finally, there are two other publications arising from the continuation activities of TransLang: a set of case studies illustrating how TransLang approaches and materials can be transferred into other subject contexts, and a work-based language simulation, the TransLang Flytours Language Game, which has also formed the basis for a new module on Employability Skills for Language Learners. The latter product has become a focus for extensive further development of project outcomes. It links language learning and skills acquisition with issues relating to graduateness, employability of graduates, work experience, as well as experiential and problem based learning. Clearly project work is fraught with potential!

THE ROLE OF THE TRANSLANG PROJECT IN CONTRIBUTING TO RESEARCH AND EDUCATION DEVELOPMENT

Context

The simple description of the project and its outcomes given above indicates how wide reaching it was. The project was not based within an institution but operated across a sector, which included *old* and *new* universities with differing cultures and systems. The members were involved with non-specialist language provision at a range of levels, from different languages, and different experiences. Some were very much part of institution-wide language programmes, some were staff members working in language subject specialisms, but with non-specialist teaching responsibilities. They presented a microcosm of what was non-specialist language provision across the UK, a perception confirmed by the results of the survey (Pilkington, 2000).

The project ran in a period in which non-specialist language provision and specialist language provision were experiencing a crisis in terms of funding, role and management. Non-specialist language provision had been undergoing a period of tremendous growth and was at the time attempting to consolidate its position and purpose. The area was also affected by the general crisis in language teaching across the UK, which had resulted in disastrously falling rolls at undergraduate specialist level in the late 1990s. At the same time the project was operating in a time of huge opportunity because the key skills and graduate skills debate was reaching its height.

Profiling skills, benchmarking requirements for subjects, employability of graduates, the issue of learning and teaching quality, the creation of Subject Centres, the inauguration of the Institute of Learning and Teaching and the development of Institutional Learning and Teaching Strategies had all entered the stage since TransLang took up the issue of enhancing the skills element within the learning and teaching of languages. This meant that the project was able to highlight these drivers in its dissemination, but the restructuring of languages across institutions has led recently to loss of programmes and potentially a loss of impetus for the project. This experience for TransLang indicates the susceptibility of projects in an environment of developing trends, and sectoral and institutional change.

The context for the project raises a number of issues relating to research, staff development and evaluation. The applied language nature of non-specialist language provision means there was limited or no research culture (in the Research Assessment Exercise sense), but there was a very high level of expertise in pedagogy, and an interest in learning and teaching innovations and methodology among participants. Lecturers within this area tend to have high class contact workloads, high levels of administration, and low status in terms of research for RAE purposes. They are often part-time or hourly paid staff and therefore very much under time pressure (Pilkington, 2000). This meant products had to be flexible, practical and user-friendly. It also meant that workshops were complicated to arrange and the take up of TransLang output was hard to measure. Often participants at workshops would move on or might find it difficult to implement long-term embedding strategies.

That the project ran during a period of immense change was advantageous. On the one hand it was discussing and feeding into issues of the moment and was providing highly relevant tools. On the other hand it was unclear whether materials and resources from the project were being adopted for their own sake, or because of institutional and national drivers. The biennial institution-wide language provision conference did provide a forum for discussion of such topics, and also for tracking ongoing trends and measuring the impact of projects such as TransLang. The case studies arising from the continuation phase of funding likewise provided an indication of the wider applicability and adoption of the project's work. Finally, all the languages projects cooperated together under an umbrella organization, the Languages Committee, which met regularly at the Centre for Information on Language Teaching and Research in London to discuss issues affecting projects and to coordinate joint activity. As a result of this coordinated approach, the impact of the languages projects was extensive. The full extent of this impact was evident in the way they fed into the newly established Subject Centre and subject benchmarking. The TransLang survey certainly contributed to the latter.

The TransLang project was not really subject specific. It related to a specific 'type' of language provision within the HE sector, and therefore its impact can be seen across individual programmes, such as in the adoption of portfolio based learning and assessment grids. Where the project worked on a national and sectoral level the extent of impact was hard to trace. It also covered a wide range of themes: skills development, assessment, curriculum design, learner autonomy, use of portfolio, language acquisition. This meant it was able to feed into a number of other projects operating nationally and in individual institutions, as well as into staff development, non-specialist and subject specific initiatives.

The TransLang Language Challenge is a good example of this potential. It began life as a three-day, work-based language simulation to demonstrate how skills developed by language learning relate to the work environment. Its development led to the creation of a completely new module in 'Employability Skills for Language Learners'. This was aimed at specialist language learners and greatly extended the skills aspects of TransLang's work. The Language Challenge provided a means of certificating skills, and became a starting point for many other developments. It was then developed into an independent resource, the Language Game. In this guise it could be used as a tool for motivating language learners, measuring and structuring language or skills learning, for linking the work environment and work related skills to language learning. It has been used for specialist language students in HE, non-specialist linguists, and with sixth form A level language students, and year 10 secondary school pupils. It has also fed into the development of a work experience project and into research on experiential learning and game design.

Staff participation

Project work is an excellent way for participants to gain a foothold in the area of research and to benefit personally and professionally. Participating staff came from a range of backgrounds but they all gained positively from working on the TransLang project. Many did not have a research profile to start with, but have acquired one through writing articles (for example those by James (2000) and Fay and Ferney (2000) listed under References), giving conferences and running workshops. A useful starting point came through writing case studies and through the task groups themselves. They were a means of developing materials, but also of discussion, developing ideas and obtaining feedback. The work of the project was largely developmental, and project members have been able to develop research interests in a number of fields: curriculum design and skills sequencing; convergence of non-specialist and specialist languages; metacognitive skills; simulations and games; portfolios; learner autonomy; linguistics; cultural awareness.

Working on the project also created opportunities for gaining new skills and management experience, which fed into individual staff members' professional development. This was achieved through applying TransLang experience in a number of ways: devising materials; writing up activities they had developed for the project; managing a team or task group; planning and designing activities; presenting at workshops or conferences; managing time and resources for project work; editing; and contributing in their own institutions to working parties, committees, course development and so on.

Project work can be lonely, but on the other hand can prove extremely productive. Participants in projects assume the role of 'champions' within their institutions or departments, for example. At one institution in particular, participating on the project led to involvement in the development of the University Learning and Teaching Strategy and a new module for students, and it fed into very important collaborative activity with three other projects. These were funded by other means but were running concurrently. The project leaders collaborated because they perceived clear linkages in content: key skills; employability and career management; and learning from work. Collaboration took the form of exchange of ideas and mutual support through a form of action learning sets, and became a basis for work on papers and contributions to the Staff and Educational Development Association.

TransLang activities and structure

The activity and *modus operandi* for the project were designed from the outset to be managed collaboratively and to mirror the expertise, interests and individuality of the institutions and departments involved. The project consortium was extended from five at the outset in order to ensure a balance of new and old institutions, northern and southern representation, and to gain the benefit of experience from institutions already well advanced in terms of mapping and profiling skills elements. The survey was an important tool in getting the debate started across the sector by taking dissemination and information gathering into institutions across the UK.

Contributors to the guide worked intensively within their task groups on their particular area of investigation and development of materials. Task groups met regularly once or twice a semester to discuss issues and progress and to support each other through exchange and feedback. Each task group fed into the annotated bibliography for the TransLang guide. This mode of operation encouraged reflection and debate, and a critical approach to gaining and giving feedback.

There was a very strong task focus to the project, partly because of its structure and management, but also as a result of the clear goals and objectives inherent in the initial bid. This is an important aspect of project management where there is a short time limit, and measurement is largely output driven. It is both a necessity for project work and a disadvantage, especially where, as with so many short projects and government initiatives, the real aim is to implement change to practice. The developmental nature both of the project's work and the national context provided a useful balance, in that it ensured reflection, a long term approach and (in the creation of the guide) a tool both sensitive to its audience's needs in that it could be implemented quickly, and also one which emphasized the importance of a staged, evaluative approach to that implementation.

Overall the project undertook activities in three clearly defined stages: development and trial, evaluation and feedback, and finally revision and rewriting for publication. The focus of creating materials, piloting them in classroom or learning situations, and writing them up in case studies promoted a reflective approach. This was further encouraged through workshops and the pressure of dissemination to peer groups through events. This whole process was underpinned by strong formal and informal means of recording and feeding back on this discussion, as well as by debate through the internal communication channels of the project (electronic and personal in the task groups), and through regular task group leader meetings.

Debates were lively and constructive. Exchange between task groups was encouraged through joint meetings and whole project workshops. Wherever possible workshops were also used as a forum for feedback and discussion of issues on implementation and on the materials themselves. The resulting reworking of ideas and issues led to a sense of clarity about the TransLang model and its rationale, and a sense of ownership. At the same time it led to an awareness of the difficulty in translating that message into reality at other institutions and in other contexts. It is easy to fall into a proselytizing mode with project work, but the process of discussion made project members strongly cognizant of the contextual difficulties and issues around adopting and embedding the TransLang approach. At institutional level it is extremely difficult to enact 'culture change'. It is even more difficult to do so at a national level, where the levers are out of the control of individual project participants, and in a sense one has to rely on the value of the 'message' or 'product' itself.

Evaluation of progress and impact was complicated to track across the sector, although there were a number of tools designed and put in place, namely questionnaires, feedback and debriefings from visits and workshops. Student and other stakeholder views were regularly solicited and they fed into design and development processes. This collaborative process was part of the ethos of the project, and played an extremely valuable role in ensuring receptiveness to TransLang approaches. It worked best through feedback at workshops and face to face through meetings and through consultancy visits. Questionnaires issued by mail elicited the expected poor response. Employer views were sought early on, too, in order to confirm the relevance and links perceived as existing between languages and work. This process acquired focus through the TransLang Language Challenge initiative. This approach was vital to achieving acceptance by the sector of the validity of TransLang work.

The steering group played a very active and proactive role in evaluating progress and impacts across the sector. Members participated in regular quarterly meetings and contributed directly to achievement of several objectives. Members were heads of department and active stakeholders in non-specialist language provision. They had a strong expertise and understanding of the project's work and its value. Because of their involvement in project work, they were critical in contributing to the debate at middle management and strategic level.

A second role, which was of considerable importance in evaluating the work of Translang, was that of the external evaluator. The project was fortunate in being able to engage a person who was experienced in such activity, was able to keep at a sufficient distance, but who also possessed a keen understanding of the issues and the context. He was therefore well placed to see the potential impact, but he also encouraged us to adopt tools and methods that encouraged reflection and an evaluative approach in achieving project objectives. Early on he met the task groups, and spent time with them in order to understand their work. He then required each task group to reflect on the issue of evaluation and to identify its own means of measuring impact and progress: a form of negotiated contract. It worked extremely well and is transferable to other contexts. It involved participants at all levels of the project in the discussion of what we were doing, how, why, and to what end. It ensured all participants had ownership of key objectives within TransLang work.

LESSONS LEARNT: OUTCOMES AND POLICY IMPLICATIONS OF THE EXPERIENCE OF THE TRANSLANG PROJECT

Certain of these lessons relate directly to project work and are applicable to the individual and to those embarking on project management in future:

- Project work has a clear and important role in the personal and professional development of staff, and should be promoted with this in mind.

- Lecturing staff should be encouraged to see project work as a valuable 'leg up' on the research ladder and not as a devalued lesser brother of RAE-registered research.

- Project participants will become, and should be seen to be, champions for the project's work locally. They require support and skills to make the most of the opportunities in this role.

- Project work can be lonely and isolating within an institution if the project is operating nationally. Action Learning Sets can be used as a valuable support and learning tool (McGill and Beaty, 1999).

- Project work is a reflexive and evaluative activity and participants should be involved in identifying objectives for the evaluation of their work, and encouraged to participate in reflexive debate and feedback. This can be achieved through a 'negotiated contract' approach and transfers well to departmental activities.

- It is important for projects to ensure that output is matched and appropriate to the needs of the target audience. This requires investigation into and understanding of those needs at the outset. A collaborative approach to gaining feedback in the developmental period is therefore desirable.

- The short-term, objectives driven nature of project work is suited for a very task based focus to its management, which has implications for management style.

- Good communication is vital, to involve stakeholders and ensure acceptance of the project and its outcomes by the target audience.

- The lessons learned from TransLang can be adapted to the process of implementing departmental culture change.

Finally, in terms of the role of projects within government policy and initiatives, it is evident that higher education is very much at the mercy of the government with regard to its interpretation of what education is and what it should do. Projects are, however, an important means of ensuring that education providers can structure and shape such changes. Projects make a valuable contribution to change and implementing government goals, despite being short-lived. They can have a cumulative effect across a sector. That was certainly the case for the many languages projects in Phase Two of FDTL.

Projects also ensure that there is a degree of expertise, interest and preparedness for innovation. They are also an enjoyable activity in which to participate, rewarding personally and professionally, and their use as a tool for implementing change should be endorsed and continued. Projects highlight a need for government, or rather the establishment, to reconsider the RAE-driven agenda when so much project based research is that of a reflexive practitioner. The current emphasis on one over the other devalues a huge area of innovative research in curriculum design and learning.

REFERENCES

Fay, M and Ferney, D (2000) *Current Trends in Modern Languages Provision for Non-Specialist Linguists*, CILT, London

James, P A (2000) Blueprint for skills assessment in HE, in *Assessment and Evaluation in HE,* Oxford, Carfax **25** (4)

McGill, I and Beaty, L (1999) *Action Learning* 2nd edn, Kogan Page, London

Pilkington, R (1998) *Survey of Non-Specialist Provision in Further and Higher Education in the United Kingdom, November 1997*, TransLang, Preston

Pilkington, R (ed) (2000) *The TransLang Guide to Transferable Skills in Non-specialist Language Learning*, TransLang, Preston

Schön, D (1983) *The Reflective Practitioner*, Basic Books, New York

FURTHER READING

Blaxter, L, Hughes, C and Tight, M (1997) *How to Research*, Open University Press, Buckingham

Johnson, G and Scholes, K (1993) *Exploring Corporate Strategy*, Prentice Hall, Hemel Hempstead

Walford, G (ed) (1996) *Doing Educational Research*, Routledge, London

8

Translating research into disseminated good practice: the case of student residence abroad

James A Coleman

INTRODUCTION

For very many years, at local and national level, efforts have been made by both generic staff developers and disciplinary specialists to enhance the quality of the student learning experience in modern foreign languages. The series *Current Issues in University Language Teaching*, for instance, published jointly since 1992 by the Association for French Language Studies and Centre for Information of Language Teaching and Research, has been a major instrument for dissemination and discussion, recognizing that the primary loyalty of university staff is to their discipline, and thereby foreshadowing the recent adoption by the university funding councils of a discipline based approach to quality enhancement (in TLTP, FDTL and most recently LTSN). Yet the relative failure to persuade departments to innovate, to incorporate pedagogical research findings into their teaching, or to adopt the best available practices, has been quite frequently lamented, not least by the present author. The reports arising from HEFCE Quality Assessment (HEFCE, 1996), which for modern languages took place in 1995/96, fairly early (phase 2) in the cycle of subject assessments, confirmed that existing good practices were not necessarily widespread, and that a number of key quality issues remained unresolved.

This chapter discusses the particular challenges which the FDTL (Fund for the Development of Learning and Teaching) Residence Abroad Project, coordinated by the present author from Portsmouth University, faced in addressing one key feature of language degrees. It describes the strategies adopted and the relative success and failure of different approaches.

MODERN LANGUAGES IN THE CONTEMPORARY CONTEXT

All disciplines tend to see themselves as unique fields of specialism, where generic approaches have only limited application. Languages are no exception. Like many disciplines, modern languages incorporate both a corpus of knowledge and a spread of specific skills. But while other subjects may be acquired within one's own culture, and without major modification of one's own identity, a foreign language demands that learners step out of their own culture to explore another, and that they willingly abandon the security of their own personal and social identity. Otherwise, they will never acquire foreign language proficiency, which embraces not only grammatical competence (vocabulary, syntax, morphology, orthography, phonology, semantics and pragmatics), discourse competence (supra-sentence grammar, showing coherence and cohesion) and strategic competence (coping productively and receptively with messages which exceed the learner's current resources), but also sociolinguistic and sociocultural competences which demand direct engagement with the target language community and its culture.

Consequently, the learning process has very significant motivational and attitudinal components which teaching strategies must recognize. Additionally, languages are learned through use. The process of internalizing and automating language processing, of moving from conscious (declarative) to unconscious (procedural) manipulation of the target language system, depends on intensive, interactive use of the language, in which the focus is on meaning rather than on form. In other words, social learning is an essential part of mastering a foreign language.

Various other factors have been claimed to separate language study from other disciplines, not least the inclusion of 'learning to learn' in many language syllabuses. The acquisition of language learning strategies – which are different in nature from generic study skills and which have an extensive research literature of their own – is particularly important before students go abroad. There is also the fact that, unlike other university disciplines in the UK, many classes are not held in English. Naturally, all disciplines have a particular discourse which students must acquire along with the discipline itself, but in modern foreign languages two sets of learning objectives are addressed simultaneously: the content and the medium. Thus, for example, a class in French on French cinema poses distinctive challenges to the teacher, who must balance the cognitive content and its expression with the target language proficiency of the students.

The learning and teaching of foreign languages also draw on a huge body of research literature. Its extent can be gauged by logging on to any online university library catalogue, and conducting a search of *s + teaching* and of *s + learning*, where *s* is any subject or subject grouping. Typical results of such a search are shown in Table 8.1.

Perhaps because language learning draws not only on subject knowledge and pedagogy, but also on substantial research in social, personal and

Table 8.1   *Library catalogue search results, subject + teaching and subject + learning*

Subject	+ Teaching	+ Learning
Science	60	55
History	35	18
Economics	17	13
Engineering	10	7
Business	5	12
Language	331	269

developmental psychology, many language academics have a tradition of reflecting on the learning process, and were among the first to integrate, for example, learner autonomy (the research literature on autonomy in language learning goes back at least to the 1970s), information technology (both computers and video have particular applications to language learning, explored and evaluated since the early 1980s) and transferable skills (widely integrated into language syllabuses from the late 1980s: see for example Coleman and Parker, 1992). The principal target community for residence abroad insights may therefore be characterized as subject focused and research based like any other, but with above-average interest in teaching and learning issues.

However, most academics see themselves primarily as researchers, and the same is true of university linguists: 'In the eyes of the world (government, colleagues, their own students) they are language teachers, but, with a few exceptions, this is not at all obvious to themselves' (Evans, 1988: 102). Taking responsibility for student learning is not what motivated most to enter the profession, and the current climate does not encourage them. Research Assessment Exercises have become the dominant feature of most academics' lives, and a largely uncontroversial one. This *récupération* contrasts strongly with the fate of teaching quality initiatives, especially the first round of the Quality Assessment process. Stained by the inaccurate, dismissive and undetachable label TQA, it has been consistently rubbished over several years, and has been undermined, in the view of many, by cynical game-playing resulting in demonstrable grade inflation without any accompanying enhancement of the actual student learning experience. The Institute for Learning and Teaching in Higher Education has been threatened with boycott by the university teachers' principal professional association. The Quality Assurance Agency has met consistent, entrenched hostility, and effective opposition which in autumn 2001 saw the departure of its chief executive and a considerable watering down of its proposed methods of assessment.

Personal rewards in terms of prestige, promotion and salary too often go to effective researchers not teachers. An observant and self-interested young academic will soon learn that innovation in teaching requires team agreement, planning and substantial documentation. It is subject to student feedback and tied to the home institution. Pedagogical research is highly complex, requiring multi-disciplinary theoretical knowledge and complementary methodologies to encompass interacting factors. Although, for the first time, the Research Assessment Exercise of 2001 specifically acknowledged the validity of pedagogical research, its status remains below that of traditional academic research, and it may not help promotion or job moves. A teaching-focused career plan is politically uncertain, given the flak directed at TQA, the ILT and the QAA. External funding is small and hard to obtain. On the other hand, research is a good guide to promotion, professional mobility, status and respect. It depends little on others, and can help you travel to interesting places. External funding is more easily obtained, yet earns more credit. Any criticism is expressed politely and within a limited professional circle. In the political domain, it has plenty of heavyweight defenders who have shaped the RAE to meet their requirements in a way the teaching and learning community have signally failed to do.

Provided basic thresholds in teaching quality are reached, at institutional level investment in research is also rewarded much more generously. HEFCE allocates some £900 million annually on the basis of the Research Assessment Exercise, but only £30 million to the Teaching Quality Enhancement Fund, stretched across national, institutional and individual initiatives. RAE income rewards past performance and has few strings attached. TQEF funding is tied to detailed actions which are closely monitored and evaluated. Institutions know that RAE funding can easily be lost by substandard performance, while major shifts in teaching funding would be logistically and politically unacceptable. Consequently most institutions, whatever their public pronouncements, favour research over teaching, and ensure that their individual academics do too. Ours was not the only FDTL project to have come up against systemic problems: staff development events from which active researchers are absent, individuals discouraged or forbidden from active participation in teaching related activities in case it detracts from their research output, senior staff and decision makers away on extended sabbatical to ensure RAE-eligible publications.

Thus official policy reinforces the split between research and teaching in funding streams, in institutional priorities, in individual short-term and long-term career choices. Paradoxically, this led the Residence Abroad Project to reject the explicit, administratively convenient and artificial division between teaching and research, and to seek to involve the subject community by integrating research into the teaching and learning project. In common with other FDTL projects, to meet the funders' criteria we have had to label what is by any definition 'research' as 'evaluation' or 'feedback'. Our funding is ineligible for RAE entry, although the outcomes resulting from that funding constitute significant research findings.

If the institutionalized divide between research and teaching is one contextual hindrance to successfully enhancing the quality of learning in any discipline, the collapse of student recruitment in modern languages is another and more specific one. Since peaking in 1992, applications to specialist language degrees have first declined and then plummeted. Of 30 representative HEIs surveyed in summer 2001, all but two had lost staff in the previous two years, and more than three-quarters had cut courses or whole languages. Several hundred posts have been lost, often by compulsory redundancy, during the four years (1997–2001) of the Residence Abroad Project, and many universities have ceased to offer foreign language degrees once and for all. It has not been an easy climate in which to encourage staff to reflect on the quality of their residence abroad provision.

RESIDENCE ABROAD

Residence abroad has traditionally been a feature of UK language degrees, and has been extended over recent decades to other disciplines. UK students concerned with their graduate employability in international careers have increasingly opted for a period abroad within the degree programme. At the same time it has been enthusiastically taken up by the European Union's successive schemes (Joint Study Programmes 1976, ERASMUS 1987, SOCRATES 1995), from which over half a million students have already benefited. Worldwide, over a million students a year spend part of their degree programme in another country. It is therefore a significant area of study for educational research, particularly for applied linguists, since learning a foreign language is very often a principal reason for undertaking residence abroad.

Unsurprisingly, given that students are highly autonomous and away from their home institution, the learning process explored by residence abroad research is a highly complex one. A model of the variables involved in language learning through residence abroad (Coleman, 1998a), based on a thorough, 'state of the art' survey of the research literature (Coleman, 1997), separates 34 distinct variables into three time periods (before, during and after), and five categories (linguistic, biographical, cognitive, affective, personality). These factors naturally interact amongst themselves, as well as impacting on the dependent variable – foreign language proficiency – which itself is divided into BICS (basic interpersonal communication skills) and CALP (cognitive academic language proficiency: Cummins, 1979). Progress across the different language skills is typically uneven, with spoken skills (fluency, accent and intonation, vocabulary, sociolinguistic competence) improving more than grammar or written skills.

Complex as it is, this model encompasses only one of the possible learning objectives of residence abroad: there are always others. Indeed, even before the Quality Assurance Agency for Higher Education (QAA) had issued its draft guidance (December 2000) and its *Code of Practice for Placement Learning* (July 2001), the Residence Abroad project had identified a comprehensive, alphabetical taxonomy of learning outcomes – academic, cultural, inter-cultural, linguistic, personal and professional – and built around these a model for preparation, curriculum integration, support and monitoring, debriefing and follow-up, and assessment and accreditation (Coleman and Parker, 2001). It is to this project that we now turn, albeit to focus on data collection and dissemination, rather than the recommendations for good practice themselves.

LOCATING INFORMATION ON RESIDENCE ABROAD

In September 1997, contracts were awarded under the Fund for the Develop-ment of Teaching and Learning (FDTL) to 10 projects related to language learning, of which no fewer than three concerned residence abroad:

- the Residence Abroad Project, coordinated from Portsmouth, with its RAPPORT Web site;

- the Learning and Residence Abroad (LARA) project coordinated by Oxford Brookes;

- the Interculture Project at Lancaster.

The successful bids had incorporated experience of research, teaching, course management and delivery, and staff development. They built on the precedent of similar initiatives, and subsequently on advice from the FDTL National Coordination Team. Essentially, the task of such projects was firstly, to identify and evaluate good practices, and secondly, to disseminate and promote them effectively. This section reviews several potential sources of information on residence abroad within university programmes. The next section looks at the relative effectiveness of different dissemination routes.

The most immediate source of information was and remains public university documents such as prospectuses and Web sites: a survey of these reveals the vast majority to be purely descriptive (if not hyperbolic), inform-ing potential students of residence abroad arrangements, but not their rationale. Public statistics, notably those gathered by the Higher Education Statistical Agency (HESA) and the Universities and Colleges Admissions Service (UCAS), have been notoriously unhelpful as far as languages are concerned, largely because the category 'languages and related subjects', until 1999/2000, included also English and American studies, linguistics and comparative literature, but also because, for at least a decade, the majority of language students have been not specialists following single or combined honours but specialists in other disciplines pursuing language study through an institution-wide language programme (IWLP) or similar

(Thomas, 1993). It is possible to track the shift from single to combined honours and the subsequent decline of both in favour of language as a support discipline to other subject specialisms. It has been impossible to trace numbers where language study represents less than 25 per cent of the curriculum, although UCAS does provide, for each institution, the number of students on a placement or study period abroad (but excluding compulsory language course placements). The move towards recording individual module choices will help establish actual statistics of students going abroad. The Central Bureau, which oversees assistantships, has always published detailed data, but this form of residence abroad represents a minority option even among language students: the majority choose a university exchange or another form of work placement.

We know this thanks to the largest ever survey of UK language students, coordinated by the University of Portsmouth in 1993–95 and known as the European Language Proficiency Survey (Coleman, 1996). The study used a questionnaire and proficiency test to map several features of the population of advanced language learners. It estimated the number of UK students abroad at any given time at about 12,000, and identified typical patterns of residence abroad for language students, by previous foreign travel experience, length, type and target country. It also explored the link between residence abroad and proficiency, confidence, attitudes and motivation, finding support for the presumed impact on L2 proficiency and confidence, but also a small shift towards more integrative motivation, and identifying for the first time a worrying change in attitudes towards a more negative view of the target language community (Coleman, 1998b). Although the survey portrayed for the first time the overall picture of residence abroad within UK institutions, its scope did not extend to identifying good and bad practice.

However, the Quality Assessment of 1995/96 had raised a number of quality issues with regard to residence abroad (Coleman and Parker, 2001). Against examples of effective preparation, support and debriefing, were set shortcomings which made residence abroad the biggest problem of all in UK modern language courses. Preparation, integration, support, assessment and quality control were frequently inadequate.

In preparing a national response, account was taken of previous research into residence abroad and the principal books and articles devoted to it (Coleman, 1995, 1996, 1997; Freed, 1995, 1999; Parker and Rouxeville, 1995) including the longitudinal evaluation by questionnaire of the EU programmes (Teichler, 1997). A summary of research findings, and a searchable bibliography, were mounted on the project Web site which, following its transfer to the Subject Centre for Languages, Linguistic and Area Studies in September 2001, is now accessed at www.lang.ltsn.ac.uk.

Once the projects were established – and each represented a consortium, pooling considerable pre-existing expertise – they undertook data collection, both separately and jointly. LARA and the Residence Abroad Project undertook a national survey of current practice, but the time constraints imposed by HEFCE's three-year project format hampered its success. If year 3 is for feedback, analysis, evaluation, reporting and dissemination and in year 2 students are abroad, then year 1 has to include setting up the project, identifying good practice, turning it into a model *and* delivering the model – a very challenging timetable. The national survey was therefore compressed into the same five-month period as recruitment of staff and establishment of the projects themselves, with the unfortunate result that our questionnaire was imperfect and the survey findings consequently limited.

Although, thanks to the reminders and chasing which are the only way of increasing response rates, we ended up with a least one completed questionnaire from every UK higher education institution involved in language teaching, we did not achieve full, accurate coverage of all courses. Nonetheless, we confirmed that the number of UK students at foreign universities exceeds those in work placements, even including language assistants. We found that 92.5 per cent of students who go abroad do so in year 3 of their course, that two-thirds of work placements are arranged by the students themselves, that most students find their own accommodation, and that there is often a mismatch between institutional learning objectives and patterns of assessment. Other findings are on the Web site.

The three projects together adopted the banner RESIDENCE ABROAD MATTERS, and held a series of regional workshops in 1998, attended by a majority of relevant HEIs. The agenda for each workshop ensured that while attenders were made aware of the tasks to be accomplished by the FDTL projects, most time was devoted to discussion of issues and to finding out from attenders what different solutions were available. A similar dual function was performed by over 30 visits carried out by the Residence Abroad Project to individual institutions in 1999–2001.

These visits provided one opportunity for gathering student opinion through focus groups. The Residence Abroad Project also conducted individual interviews and used learner diaries in an effort to obtain qualitative data which would flesh out the quantitative data obtained from over 3,000 students representing what we christened the 'Seven Ages of Residence Abroad': pre-A level, end of university year 1, end of university year 2, during year abroad, start of university year 4, end of university year 4, and in later graduate employment. Although much of the survey was cross-sectional, there were some participants in longitudinal case studies whom we followed from pre-departure through residence abroad to return. Analysis of the findings is incomplete, but has shone new light on students' views of the objectives of residence abroad, on whether they are achieved, and on levels of support, as well as confirming or nuancing earlier findings on proficiency, confidence, attitudes and motivation. Graduate responses show clearly that residence abroad enhances employability; 96 per cent of them felt the time and expense had been a good investment.

The other projects also used student informants, the Interculture project developing a sophisticated, indexed database of student narratives of residence abroad, which allows exploitation for both research and teaching purposes.

EFFECTIVE DISSEMINATION

An analysis of the different strategies adopted by the 10 FDTL Language projects has already been carried out on behalf of the projects and presented at an international conference of linguists (Coleman, 2001). Uniquely in the history of such projects, they worked together. The sector might have overlooked a single project, but could not ignore the joint action of all 10. The Coordinating Group for Languages (FDTL-CGL), as well as overseeing national surveys to avoid overlap, contracted London's Centre for Information on Language Teaching and Research (CILT) to provide for all 10 projects a secretariat, a single enquiry point, a Web site, a common visual identity, biannual newsletters, leaflets and folders, and an annual conference. Projects did, however, develop their own visual identities, acronyms and logos, with the three residence abroad projects sharing the RESIDENCE ABROAD MATTERS slogan on leaflets, published reports and staff T-shirts.

Once the obvious has been stated – namely that dissemination comes not *after* development of a model, product or methodology but *simultaneously* and *co-terminously* with it, and that we need to distinguish between dissemination for awareness, understanding and action – my taxonomy of dissemination techniques would include four categories, in ascending order of effectiveness.

In the first (necessary but not sufficient) 'passive' category, end-users must take the initiative, and are rewarded with reading material: paper in the case of leaflets, reports, bookmarks, newsletters, packs and professional journals, electronic for e-mail lists, CD ROMs and Web sites. The latter offer the advantage of matching the pace of change and being up to date, provided resources are allocated to keeping them so. But nothing obliges end-users to engage with the process of professional development.

The same is true of the second 'reactive' category. Again initiative lies with the end-user, but he or she is offered more than reading matter. Interactivity can be assured through searchable databases, competitions or online forms – the Residence Abroad project's electronic postcard competition combined two of these – while presentations at professional conferences and workshops equally achieve the objective of helping the user to engage with the activity. Online discussion, however well managed, generally stutters to a halt.

The third 'semi-active' category sees project personnel taking the initiative to users' own territory, be it press coverage, a research conference or journal, or a subject association, although again user involvement is not guaranteed. The *Higher* is the professional journal of all UK academics, but most clearly skip the 'Teaching' section – my article in the 'How to. . .' series brought just two enquiries.

Only the 'active' category of dissemination, with project and users working together, assures engagement. In site visits and workshops, academic and administrative staff are directly involved in identification and discussion of real issues related to their own institution, and such events have often demonstrably served as a catalyst for changes in institutional practice. So too as has the 'Residence Abroad Matters Game', an engaging simulation devised by LARA's Linda Parker involving real-life scenarios and resource based decision making (Coleman and Parker, 2001). At the end of recent workshops, delegates have drawn up individual action plans, leaving a copy with the project for monthly follow-ups.

'Active' dissemination has also been achieved through accredited staff development. The Residence Abroad project's online Supporting Residence Abroad unit, delivered for the first time in 2000 and highly praised in feedback, demands commitment from the student/colleague's institution in registration fees, teaching relief and comment from line managers on completed assignments, which themselves have to describe, critique and propose modifications to the institution's own residence abroad arrangements. Completion of the course has contributed to successful applications for membership of the ILT (Institute for Learning and Teaching in Higher Education) and to several documented changes in institutional practice.

Concurrent project evaluation – a task for an external steering committee for most FDTL language projects – was in our case conducted by the experienced academics from consortium institutions who made up the management committee. Regular meetings (face to face or by audio/video conference) continuously monitored and reflected on progress and achievement of targets. Despite the comprehensive discussion which had shaped the initial bid, ongoing evaluation prompted modifications in three areas.

Firstly, technological improvements and the more widespread use of the Internet encouraged us to enhance the disseminatory role of the project Web site, and to undertake an evaluation of the 'virtual visit' – desktop video conferencing using cheap webcams and free networking software to maintain contact with students and partner institutions abroad.

Secondly, the recognition that helping students directly would also help staff led us to develop an extensive section of the Web site for student use, with content (mainly advice and links) discretely targeted. And thirdly, whereas the original bid had not envisaged institutional visits, our growing awareness of the differential impact of the various dissemination routes outlined above meant moving resources to achieve a higher level of interactive contact with end-users than had been foreseen in 1997.

CONCLUSION

A recent publication (Coleman, 2001), analysing the impact of the FDTL programme in languages, criticized HEFCE's selection on the basis of bid quality not coverage (which led to duplication and omission, and may have deepened the split between language teachers and 'content' researchers) and the three-year timetable (which created problems of scope and staff turnover with related loss of expertise): both of these have been addressed by the creation of the Learning and Teaching Support Network and the Subject Centre for Language, Linguistics and Area Studies. It remains only to review the approaches adopted by the Residence Abroad project.

To identify good practice, we have used university documents, HESA/UCAS statistics, consortium expertise, a survey of previous research, HEFCE QA reports, a national institutional questionnaire, student questionnaires, interviews, diaries, focus groups, dialogue with staff, pilot evaluations, conferences, regional workshops and institutional visits: all but the first two provided valuable data, and the incorporation of research methods and findings gave the Residence Abroad project greater authority, increased credibility and enhanced subject community interest. Continuous monitoring allowed the project to evolve more effective dissemination routes, and to incorporate new developments in support technologies.

To disseminate, we used a single multi-project contact point, newsletters, leaflets, posters, Web sites, searchable databases, an Internet discussion forum, e-mail discussion groups, CD ROMs, papers at research and teaching conferences, press coverage, and bookmarks. Formal project evaluation endorsed our multi-strategy approach, but could not include quantitative measures of actual impact. We can demonstrate 100 per cent awareness and even 100 per cent institutional involvement in Residence Abroad Matters events: those who wanted to understand have been helped to do so. Auditable change will always be hard to prove, but despite the context of the worst ever recruitment crisis in university modern languages, and other obstacles alluded to in this article, we have demonstrably developed new staff expertise and, in many institutions, helped introduce new practices, syllabus, materials and assessments to the support of student residence abroad.

REFERENCES

Coleman, J A (1995) The current state of knowledge concerning student residence abroad, in *The Year Abroad: Preparation, monitoring, evaluation, current research and development,* ed G Parker and A Rouxeville, pp 17–42, AFLS/CILT, London

Coleman, J A (1996) *Studying Languages: A survey of British and European students. The proficiency, background, attitudes and motivations of students of foreign languages in the United Kingdom and Europe,* CILT, London

Coleman, J A (1997) Residence abroad within language study, *Language Teaching,* **30** (1), pp 1–20

Coleman, J A (1998a) Student preparation for residence abroad: two stages in acquiring cross-cultural capability, in *Cross-Cultural Capability: The why, the ways, the means – new theories and methodologies in language education,* ed D Killick and M Parry, pp 32–44, Leeds Metropolitan University

Coleman, J A (1998b) Evolving intercultural perceptions among university language learners in Europe, in *Foreign Language Learning in Intercultural Perspective*, ed M Byram and M Fleming, pp 45–75, Cambridge University Press

Coleman, J A (2001) Lessons for the future: evaluating FDTL languages, in *Language Learning Futures: Issues and strategies for modern languages provision in higher education*, ed J A Coleman, D Ferney, D Head and R Rix, CILT, London

Coleman, J A and Parker, G (1992) *French and the Enterprise Path: Developing transferable and professional skills*, AFLS/CILT, London

Coleman, J A and Parker, L (2001) Preparing for residence abroad: staff development implications, in *Teaching Languages in Higher Education. Issues in training and continuing professional development*, ed J Klapper, CILT, London

Cummins, J (1979) Cognitive/academic language proficiency, linguistic inter-dependence, the optimum age question and some other matters, *Working Papers on Bilingualism*, **19**, pp 121–29

Evans, C (1988) *Language People*, Open University Press, Buckingham

Freed, B F (ed) (1995) *Second Language Acquisition in a Study Abroad Context*, John Benjamins, Amsterdam/Philadelphia

Freed, B F (1999) *Retrospective Views from the President's Commission on Foreign Language and International Studies and Prospects for the Future: Study abroad and language learning* [Online] http://language.stanford.edu/about/conferencepapers/freedpaper.html

HEFCE (1996) *Subject Overview Reports, Quality Assessment of French (2/96), German and related languages (3/96), Iberian languages and studies (4/96), Italian (5/96), Russian and Eastern European languages and studies (7/96)*, Higher Education Funding Council for England

Parker, G and Rouxeville, A (eds) (1995) *'The Year Abroad': Preparation, monitoring, evaluation*, CILT, London

Teichler, U (1997) *The ERASMUS Experience: Major findings of the ERASMUS evaluation research*, Office for Official Publications of the European Communities, Luxembourg

Thomas, G (1993) *Survey of European Languages in the United Kingdom*, CNAA, London

9

Incorporating change through reflection: community based learning

Irene Hall and David Hall

The idea that something I have produced will help such a worthwhile organization. . . is something that fills me with pride and satisfaction. I cannot believe I have achieved such a feat, no other assignment in my academic career has produced such a feeling of pride within me. This alone has made all the hard work and stress worthwhile as well as boosting my self confidence dramatically.

(CW, student reflective report, 1999)

I have developed useful skills in working with professionals, especially in learning that they are not perfect and do not have all the answers, but are human and prone to make mistakes like anyone else. I found it important to note also that in many real life situations, there are no 'ideal' answers to problems and that compromises have to be made.

(PJ, student reflective report, 1997)

INTRODUCTION

These quotations come from reflective reports written by students to discuss their experiences in conducting community based research for local voluntary organizations. Reflective reports, directed towards the academic audience of supervisors and examiners, allow students to comment on what they have discovered through practice about the 'messiness' of real life research, as well as the skills and personal development which they have experienced. These reports accompany client reports written for the organization with which the research has been negotiated. Together both reports form the equivalent of a dissertation, at the level of either a final year undergraduate programme or postgraduate degree.

The comments reveal a positive sense of experience in the face of challenges in conducting the research. They show evidence of learning but also point up some key issues, such as how the complexity of understanding revealed in the quotes can be incorporated into the curriculum and how community based and reflective learning can adequately be assessed.

But what is the long-term impact of such learning? Experiential and work based learning strategies imply that students will be changed in fundamental ways by the acquisition of skills and understanding, and that their subsequent careers will benefit. There may be changes, too, to the organizations involved, to the academic supervision, and to the departments involved. Evidence is presented below which explores some of these issues, along with information on strategies which are currently being developed to embed community based learning in the curriculum.

THE COBALT PROJECT

The dissemination of good practice was the major aim of the CoBaLT (community based learning teamwork) project. As a consortium between three partners, the project shared a variety of practice in community based learning. This ranged from viewing the community as a site for exploring theory to community based research with the aim of benefiting community groups and voluntary organizations.

The student projects reported here build on an established knowledge base of a research methods course, which has to be completed satisfactorily before students are accepted on to the community research course. Projects can be conducted individually or by teams and require two semesters for completion. Students are given considerable responsibility for the negotiation, design, progress and analysis of the research, under the overall guidance of the tutor, and are expected to spend one day a week on their projects. Assessment is by the completion of two reports, the client report (which can be a joint report) and a reflective report, which together comprise the equivalent of a dissertation.

Central to students' learning are the requirements:

- to keep a research diary for records of events, meetings and so on, together with the students' evaluation of their thoughts and feelings at the time;

- to draw up a research plan, in agreement with the community group or organization, on the understanding that this may need to be modified in the light of research problems encountered;

- to analyse and present the findings in clear and accessible language, appropriate to the audience.

These projects therefore demand the active engagement of the students in finding out about and responding to the client's needs, in thinking through the application of research methods and responding to the inevitable problems of carrying out the research plan, and in reporting the results in a way which is usable by the organization concerned. They provide an example of community based learning, developed over a decade of practice in sociology departments.

The CoBaLT dissemination strategy envisaged a two-way process: of learning from other (predominantly sociology) departments about their practices in this area through a series of 'guided conversations' and sharing this, along with the consortium's experiences, with a wider academic audience. Over the four years of the project, the dissemination strategy altered in focus in the light of feedback from the external evaluator and FDTL adviser and from participants at workshops and conferences. Responses from users of the earlier project materials (videos and workbooks) were crucial to their later development, moving them from being promotional to being more interactive and adapted for student learning.

Reflection is a key component in all the videos (for details of availability, see the endnote). Students, staff and community groups all reflect on the learning processes involved. While students and staff mainly reflect on the way students developed new knowledge and skills and increased in confidence, organizations reflect on their own learning experience and other benefits to the organization.

If community based projects are perceived as solely being of benefit to the students as a learning experience, then they may be seen negatively by the local groups, as exploitative or requiring the groups to provide training (which is properly the responsibility of the university). Negotiation and consultation are essential in ensuring benefit to both parties and result in groups recognizing the value of student projects.

> Having a student coming in and doing this kind of research is good for voluntary organizations, because it teaches them to manage a researcher; it's cheap; it saves a lot of time, and very often work that they would like to do but cannot see any way of getting done can be done. And they also feel they are helping the students.

> (Caroline Hayes, CoBaLT Video Two, 1999)

WHERE THE LEARNING IS IN COMMUNITY BASED LEARNING

The context

There is increasing emphasis upon learning in, from and with the community. Thus, in the UK, the Dearing Report (NCIHE, 1997) concluded that students need more than just books and lectures:

> they also need practical experiences that rehearse them in the professional or scholarly skills of their field, and the opportunity to develop

their own understanding and point of view in an environment that gives constructive feedback. (Section 8.3)

This may be achieved through work experience, involvement in student union activities, or work in community or voluntary settings. (Section 9.26)

By emphasizing the importance of students experiencing 'real life' situations and tackling the attendant problems, proponents of community based learning argue that some of the limitations of traditional forms of learning can be overcome. A variety of educational 'good practices' can be drawn upon to support the case for this kind of learning.

- It makes connections between abstract concepts learned in the classroom and real applications in the world outside.

- As a form of experiential learning (Kolb, 1984) it promotes learning through a cycle of action and reflection.

- Through the engagement of students and interaction with others, it fosters a deep rather than a surface approach to learning (Gibbs, 1992a, b).

- It develops general and transferable skills that are useful in other contexts, particularly the world of work.

- It encourages students to engage in work of 'social value', such as service to others, reciprocal learning and community involvement. (Stanton, Giles and Cruz, 1999).

Community based learning is however a broad and inclusive term, which can include a multiplicity of forms of learning, which have different goals and offer students different kinds of experiences. Buckingham-Hatfield's (2000) edited collection of examples, published by Community Service Volunteers (CSV), exemplifies the range of academically assessed community based learning in the UK across a range of disciplines. Case studies include opportunities for volunteering (within Community Enterprise modules), for independent study (as part of a Community Partnership Scheme), for critical engagement with local communities (for a Citizenship and Community Studies degree), and for community based research projects.

Further evidence for the variety of practice within the discipline of sociology is reported by the CoBaLT project, on the basis of a qualitative survey (through 'guided conversations') with colleagues in a number of British sociology departments. The resultant report is published at http://www.hope.ac.uk/cobalt/Guided.htm

Community based research is a form of collaborative applied research, in which, as Nyden notes: 'Community perspectives as well as academic perspectives are put on the table as the research is designed, data collected, and results analysed. . . Community leaders' interest in the research is also increased because they have a voice in the research' (Nyden *et al*, 1997: 8)

Tutors have felt that students respond well to the challenge and the experience: 'They gain a lot in confidence, they enjoy doing it, you actually see happy faces coming through your door' (CoBaLT Video One, 1998).

The model of learning

Community based learning fits into the broader pattern of experiential learning. Discussions on this subject tend to begin with the work of David Kolb, whose influential book, *Experiential Learning: Experience as the source of learning and development* was published in 1984. Using a structural model derived from research in psychology, philosophy and physiology, and based on the works of Dewey, Lewin and Piaget, Kolb defines learning as 'the process whereby knowledge is created through the transformation of experience' (Kolb, 1984: 39).

In his analysis, Kolb develops a four-stage cycle of concrete experience, observation and reflection, abstract conceptualization and generalization, and active experimentation, which can be represented as a circular process. Other learning theorists, such as Cowan (1998), have adapted the model, using slightly different terms for the four stages, but essentially agreeing on the order and process involved. Cowan uses the verbs:

- experience;
- reflect;
- generalize;
- test;

to indicate the four stages. He views the cycle as an iterative progress that can be repeated many times. Experience is reflected upon, generalized knowledge is acquired, and new actions are taken which form the basis for further reflection and analysis. Cowan also suggests that reflection can take a number of forms, and that each of the four stages is not necessarily of equivalent length in an individual's learning progress.

Cowan draws particularly on Schön (1983) to give more depth to the reflective process, which is seen as critical to the whole process of learning. He distinguishes between the retrospective reflections on recent experience of 'reflection-on-action' to the more prospective use of reflection as 'reflection-in-action'. The aim is to facilitate the 'reflective practitioner' who is able by generalizing from experience to think creatively about problem solutions.

Using reflection in student reports

Traditionally, research reports rarely paid attention to the learning process of the researchers. Instead they focused narrowly on aims, methods, and results, often in ways which replaced the 'messiness' of actual research processes with 'sanitized' accounts. This approach has been eroded through the work of researchers with commitments to ethnography, feminist methodology and participatory action research (amongst others) who emphasize the importance of the 'person' of the researcher in the creation of the research text or report of findings. Such reflection challenges the positivist notion of the researcher as objective or neutral and recognizes that the researcher is located within the research in terms of personal or political attributes, experience and feeling.

The need to provide such reflection lay behind the requirement for students to produce both a client report and a reflective report for their assessment, where they could draw upon their research diary to analyse, generalize and make suggestions about their research and the learning they derived from it: 'reflection-on-action' as compared with the 'reflection-in-action' of the tutorial process.

Research into community based learning

To find out if there was any long-term impact from the experience, in terms of skills and personal development, and in relation to subsequent career, it was necessary to conduct a follow up survey, to explore 'reflection-on-action' after the lapse of some years.

Qualitative evaluation of student experience was chosen, on the grounds that the aim was not simply to count responses, but rather to gain some insight into what the students themselves considered to be important. The questions were open-ended with minimal prompting being used. The interview team was keen to enable former students to give their spontaneous responses to the questions, rather than use a structured response approach, and to allow students to express feelings as well as opinions.

A sample was chosen of students who had completed projects between two and nine years previously. In order to cover possible sources of variation, the sample included those who had completed projects on their own and in teams, male and female students, younger and more mature students. The sample was in practice limited because of contact problems (many past students were difficult to trace), but did provide variety of experience.

Thirty former students were interviewed, and none of those approached refused to be interviewed. The interviews were mainly conducted by telephone (two respondents preferred to be interviewed face to face) and took about 35 to 40 minutes to complete. All were taped (with the informants' permission) and transcribed.

The questions related to the graduates' current evaluation of their community based learning experience:

- What were the highlights of the experience?

- What difficulties had they encountered, and how did they solve them?

- Did they acquire skills from their practice that proved to be transferable across to other jobs and activities?

- On reflection, what did they think they gained from the course, and from working with a local voluntary sector organization?

- Had the experience of working in the community affected their subsequent career direction?

- What would they have changed to improve the experience and their learning?

Findings from the graduate survey

Highlights
When asked to recall what were the 'highlights' of the research projects, former students emphasized their personal engagement with the projects. Twelve replied in terms of the people they had met, especially the service users. For some students, the people were remembered for their friendliness and helpfulness. Others mentioned the specific needs of those with whom they conducted research, and how this had opened their eyes to a hitherto unknown group in society.

> Just a fantastic experience, I absolutely loved it. I learned a lot about autistic youngsters (and that's what I do now).

> Meeting people with special needs, and appreciating they do have a place in society.

For some too, there was a sense of having the privilege of being able to participate in other people's lives.

> Building up relationships and interviews with people I didn't know.

> meeting those lovely ladies, sharing their experiences.

Interviewing
Some found survey research particularly enjoyable, but also challenging. Others used more in-depth qualitative research and found the quality of the experience deeply meaningful.

> Interviewing real people on the street, I was fascinated, I thought it was wonderful.

the interviewing itself, I felt I was on a journey of their lives, it was a privilege – not just shopping research, but I felt they owned it as well.

Three students used the term 'hands-on' to define the highlight, in contrast to their other university learning:

The interviews because that was hands-on stuff.

Conducting hands-on research.

Doing hands-on questionnaires and interviewing.

Worthwhile and useful
Seven people said the highlight was participating in a project to benefit others, and this had given both satisfaction and motivation to their work.

I felt I was doing something worthwhile, there was a point, they were appreciative.

I felt I was putting something back into the community.

For five people it was the practical use of the research that was seen as a highlight, though most people who mentioned usefulness qualified their responses, 'hoping' that it would be useful, rather than assuming it would be.

Real world and dissertations
Three students talked about 'getting out into the real world', being 'out and about' and 'going out into Liverpool, nice to go out into the community'. This positive view contrasted with those who saw the applied research as an escape from dissertations, so that the highlight for them was 'doing something more useful than a dissertation'.

Problems and problem solving
Only four people reported that they had had no difficulties, or 'none we didn't overcome'. The others listed 35 difficulties between them. The largest category (eight) concerned difficulties gaining access to people to interview. For many of those who mentioned major difficulties with access, the informants they wished to contact were outside the organization itself and access had to be gained either through other gatekeepers in the community and/or through using what the students themselves termed 'persistence' and 'perseverance'. A common outcome of such problems was for the research itself to change direction.

Although the research was negotiated with the organization concerned, as many as seven respondents felt that 'unhelpful staff' had posed major difficulties for them. However, there were only two situations where the problems required the supervisor to intervene (and only after discussion with the student concerned). Lack of interest by an organization 'made it harder' for a student, though motivation was sustained 'because obviously you had to get the project done because it was part of your dissertation'.

Time pressures
Time management was an issue for six people, both team members and those working on their own. Time problems were often compounded by transport difficulties and use of a car (which had to be negotiated with other users) was seen as essential for fieldwork outside the city centre. A common finding in this group was 'I got too involved'.

Career destinations
Two-thirds of the sample stated that their project had influenced their career direction, with 12 replying unequivocally that there had been an influence, while another six added a 'perhaps' and two felt there had been an indirect effect. Of the remaining 10, seven said there had been no influence on their careers, and the remaining three were unsure or did not respond.

For five students, the project encouraged them to enter careers working with people. Typical responses were:

> It helped concentrate my mind in that I wanted to get out more and do more in the community.

> It convinced me that I really wanted to work one to one with people.

For one student, the career direction directly linked with where the project had been conducted.

> It made me aware that the Health Service was an area that I felt I wanted to go back into.

Current use of project in work
Of lasting benefit seemed to be some of the skills that students had acquired through their research projects, plus their awareness of the context of social issues. One former student now a teacher saw the project as helping her to plan work 'rather than just dive straight in'. A voluntary sector worker found that the project experience 'helps you do things in a logical and methodical way'. Communication skills were also enhanced. For instance, teachers asking children questions knew how to rephrase them when answers were not forthcoming. An insurance worker felt better able 'to talk to people, negotiating, that kind of thing'.

Report writing skills were also in daily use. One teacher noted that such skills were essential, given the many reports teachers have to write. A voluntary sector worker also felt that report writing was particularly important in her work:

I have to do reports all the time for the board and for our funding.

Approaches to learning

The effects of community based learning can also be related to differences in learning styles, such as 'surface' and 'deep' approaches to learning. Here distinctions are made between reproductive learning, where facts are memorized and reproduced, and transformative learning, where the focus broadens from the immediate task itself to wider comparisons and an interest in the process of learning itself. Gibbs is one of the foremost proponents of a deep approach to learning, characterized as an attempt 'to make sense of what is to be learnt. . . this involves thinking, seeking integration between components and between tasks, and "playing" with ideas' (Gibbs, 1992b: 2).

Gibbs argues that the choice students make between surface and deep approaches to learning is not solely due to students' preferred learning styles, but is also affected by the characteristics and requirements of the courses they are studying. Hence, it becomes important for courses to be structured in ways which encourage deep learning. He argues that 'good teaching' includes the following key elements: motivation; active involvement; interaction with others; and a well-structured knowledge base (Gibbs, 1992a: 155–56).

Altogether 17 former students noted that they had been motivated by their involvement in work which was seen as worthwhile, 'putting something back into the community', or potentially usable by their organizations. In the Dearing Report, such motivation is seen as part of the emerging role of higher education 'to play a major role in shaping a democratic, civilised, inclusive society' (NCIHE, 1997: Section 23). This is already an emphasis in the United States, where service learning is widespread in the curriculum of higher education. Eyler and Giles (1999) found that service learning increases tolerance and aids personal development, promotes critical thinking and the development of new perspectives on social issues, and combines knowledge, skills and commitment which they argue underlies 'effective citizenship'. Community based learning may not share quite this agenda, but it does have the potential to provide a 'deep' learning experience where motivation is enhanced through partnering with the community, and students have the opportunity to produce quality research for academic assessment (unlike most service learning which emphasizes volunteer work).

Disseminating CoBaLT: can videos really make a difference?

The CoBaLT project existed to disseminate good practice in community based research. It did so through sharing videos and workbooks as ready-made teaching resources, and providing regional workshops to share the vision and the problems (and solutions where possible). It also held a joint national conference with Sociologists in Placements (SIP), a further sociology project on work based learning (for contact details, see endnote). The conference was evaluated very highly by participants. However, CoBaLT could not offer financial support to departments, nor help them resource the development of their own work in the community.

Video as a way of conveying information on community based learning has advantages and limitations. The advantages lie in being able to see examples of actual student projects and getting a feel for what is actually involved. The limitations are due to video being a poorer medium for conveying information than for atmosphere, hence the decision to include workbooks as supplements to the video.

The dissemination moved from the initial 'feel good' video through interactive videos for student learning to the fourth and final video aimed at survey methods teaching (albeit in a community context). Punch (1998) has used the term 'infiltration' to describe a strategy of 'access and acceptance' in qualitative fieldwork, and the term also fits this latest model of dissemination: using a common issue, the teaching of research methods, to implant the idea of community based practice.

CONCLUSION

The projects provided an opportunity for experiential learning which involved both action and reflection on action as an integral part of the activity. Students did not just accumulate skills as the outcome of their course, but through the process of active participation they learned how to face problems and develop strategies for resolving them. Arguably, it is this 'deep' learning which is providing long-term benefits.

Former students were capable of reflection-on-action in their ability to respond at length to the survey, but were they reflective practitioners in the crucial sense of being able to 'reflect-in-action'? Some responses do support this. For instance the teacher who saw the project as helping her to plan work 'rather than just dive straight in' and the social worker who reported the project helped her to 'do things in a logical and methodical way' were reflective practitioners. So was the teacher who had to think on her feet when children did not understand the question she was asking and who had to rethink and rephrase, applying the experience gained in interviewing.

It was noticeable that problems had inevitably arisen in the 'real world setting' of the research, and that some, though not all, were resolved. Time management was not always successful. Difficult staff in the organizations required intervention by academic tutors on two occasions, although in terms of problem solving, the students may have learnt that there are sometimes conflicts which need to be handled by someone higher in authority or detached from the situation. The major problem was a research issue – of access to informants to gain data – and for all the students a creative solution was found, to enable their reports to be completed. For some students, they felt this required personal development such as 'patience' and 'persistence'.

Over time, the tutors' learning has also developed, and the assessment of the modules has been altered in two significant ways. First, the students' individual reports have been changed from 'methodology reports' to 'reflective reports' as the emphasis on reflection has increased. Second, skills have been explicitly recognized and rewarded through appropriate assessment criteria, and additionally through accreditation programmes for key skills where these have been available in the institutions.

Community based research provides students with opportunities to participate in 'deep' learning through structured programmes. Because it works in partnership with the local voluntary sector, it is also in a position to deliver some of the ideals concerning the wider role of higher education as an agent in building civil society. The problems which face community based learning are not so much with devising forms of learning which can operationalize this idealism, as with requiring support from the institutions to make it practical. Such support includes placement provision and mentoring for students, otherwise the high ideals of Dearing, among others, will fail to materialize.

NOTES

Four videos were eventually produced by the CoBaLT project, for dissemination to higher education institutions. At the conclusion of the CoBaLT project in September 2001, the remaining stocks were transferred to two of the National Centres for Learning and Teaching, the Centre for Sociology, Anthropology and Politics (C-SAP) at the University of Birmingham and the Centre for Social Policy and Social Work (SWAP) at the University of Southampton. The videos are available on request from these centres. C-SAP may be contacted via its Web site www.c-sap.bham.ac.uk and SWAP is located at www.swap.ac.uk/

Sociologists in Placements (SIP) is a further project funded through HEFCE's Fund for the Development of Teaching and Learning, coordinated at the University of Newcastle. Its reports are accessible through the Web site www.unn.ac.uk/academic/ss/SIP/home.html

REFERENCES

Buckingham-Hatfield, S (ed) (2000) *Student Community Partnerships in Higher Education: Promoting skills for life and work*, Community Service Volunteers, London

CoBaLT (1998) *Learning in the Community: A real sense of achievement*, video and Workbook 1, CoBaLT Project, Liverpool

CoBaLT (1999) *Researching in the Community: A positive partnership*, video and Workbook 2, CoBaLT Project, Liverpool

Cowan, J (1998) *On Becoming an Innovative University Teacher: Reflection in action*, Society for Research into Higher Education (SRHE)/Open University Press, Buckingham

Eyler, J and Giles, D (1999) *Where's the Learning in Service-Learning?*, Jossey-Bass, San Francisco, CA

Gibbs, G (1992a) Improving the Quality of Student Learning through Course Design, in *Learning to Effect*, ed R Barnett, SRHE/Open University Press, Buckingham

Gibbs, G (1992b) *Improving the Quality of Student Learning*, Technical and Educational Services, Bristol

Kolb, D A (1984) *Experiential Learning: Experience as the source of learning and development*, Prentice-Hall, Englewood Cliffs, NJ

National Committee of Inquiry into Higher Education (NCIHE) (1997) *Higher Education in the Learning Society* (the Dearing Report), HMSO, London

Nyden, P, Figert, A, Shibley, M and Burrows, D (1997) *Building Community: Social science in action*, Pine Forge Press, Thousand Oaks, CA

Punch, M (1998) Politics and ethics in qualitative research, in *The Landscape of Qualitative Research*, ed N Denzin and Y Lincoln, Sage, Thousand Oaks, CA

Schön, D (1983) *The Reflective Practitioner: How professionals think in action*, Basic Books, New York

Stanton, T, Giles, D and Cruz, N (1999) *Service-Learning: A movement's pioneers reflect on its origins, practice and future*, Jossey-Bass, San Francisco, CA

10

Developing an evaluation design: a multi-dimensional case study

John Winter and Chris Foggin

INTRODUCTION

The Built Environment: Appropriate Technology for Learning (BEATL) project is a collaborative initiative which involves three universities, De Montfort, Westminster and the University of the West of England, Bristol (UWE). The main emphasis of the project is on promoting the use of new technologies embedded in the teaching and learning strategies employed in built environment higher education programmes.

This chapter provides a provisional assessment of the effectiveness of the evaluation framework used in the BEATL project. Initially the background to the project is given, followed by a description of its main operational elements. The chapter then outlines BEATL's evaluation framework, based on a case study approach, before reflecting on how effective that structure has proved to be in operation. A number of initial findings emerging from the first stages of evaluation are then given followed by conclusions on the general validity of the case study approach for such 'real world' research.

BACKGROUND TO THE BEATL PROJECT

BEATL is a three-year project funded by the Higher Education Funding Council for England (HEFCE), as part of the third phase of the Teaching and Learning Technology Programme (TLTP3), and is scheduled to be completed in August 2001. The emphasis in BEATL, as in TLTP3 as a whole, is on integration and embedding rather than development. This focus, coupled with BEATL's complex methodology, has together posed very interesting challenges for evaluation.

The general aims of the project are:

● to develop effective methods of integrating technology based learning materials into the delivery of modules within the undergraduate modular programmes at the Universities of the West of England, De Montfort and Westminster;

- to share with and promote to all higher education institutions, good practice in embedding technology-based learning materials.

The principal project outputs are:

- case studies for a range of built environment technology based innovations designed to share good practice with the higher education community for delivering the built environment curriculum;

- a Web based staff handbook on good practice for embedding appropriate new technology to promote the development of effective teaching and learning strategies;

- a communication strategy to ensure project clients and stakeholders are kept informed and engaged in the project throughout its development;

- a series of staff development workshops, at both individual university and national level.

How the BEATL project operates

Scale and project management

BEATL is a large-scale project. It involves more than 90 academic staff, working on 30 innovations in three universities. Each partner university has identified an experienced academic as university project manager, to lead project implementation there, and appointed an educational technology officer to provide technical support for module innovation. BEATL is coordinated on a day to day basis by a project director and research associate, both based at UWE. Monitoring and review of project progress is undertaken by a project management group which meets on a two-monthly cycle and at a more strategic level by a project steering group on a six-monthly basis. An important project link to the wider academic and professional communities is provided by the project consultation group which was initially convened twice per year.

Research questions

The principal aim of BEATL is to embed technology based learning materials into the built environment curriculum, but the project was also designed to examine the following research questions:

- How can module leaders most effectively embed technology based applications and learning materials into a range of built environment modules?

- What is the impact of these applications and materials on the quality of the student learning experience?

- What are high quality innovations and why?

- What are the resource implications of the project innovations and how does one identify cost effective solutions?

- In what ways can faculty/institutional take-up of educational technology be reinforced?

- What collaborative arrangements can be identified among the consortium universities, for testing transferability of good practice?

Partnership

BEATL involves partnership, or collaborative working, which operates at two different levels in the project. The first is at the more general level of three collaborating faculties/schools in the partner universities. The second is at the more operational level of the module innovation, which involves partnerships between two or three module leaders, normally at different universities.

Partnership at the operational level comes from the identification of modules in similar subject areas where there is a shared interest in embedding the same technology based materials. Each innovation is first embedded within a pilot module and evaluated at the pilot institution. After review the partner institution runs the module innovation and again the overall results are evaluated. The results are finally written up as a case study. These module partnerships are significant for evaluation in a number of ways, including the opportunities for insights into the transferability of such learning innovations from one module team to another.

There will be one further dimension to partnership within the BEATL project. It is intended to widen that partnership to include the wider higher education community when the outputs and findings of the BEATL project are disseminated.

Content and delivery

BEATL involves a wide range of subject disciplines. Built environment undergraduate modular programmes typically include programmes that range from architecture, town planning and housing to building surveying, estate management and construction management. These programmes offer a test bed of considerable variety for embedding technology based materials in teaching and learning programmes.

The range of learning technology materials being embedded through the project includes:

- tutorial Web sites containing interactive tutorials, reference material and self-assessment quizzes;

- customized spreadsheets used for analytical project work;
- CD ROM multimedia resources presenting a practice-related case study;
- Web authoring software used by students to present case studies;
- software designed to assist students to categorize objects through images;
- audio tapes to reinforce learning in relation to housing accounts.

This wide range of applications, coupled with the range of learning contexts in which they are being introduced, poses particular challenges for evaluation methodology.

PROJECT EVALUATION

Thorough evaluation of the impact of BEATL innovations is an integral part of the BEATL commitment, as indicated by the large number of project objectives that relate to evaluation. This emphasis arises out of the need for advice and guidance to academics on which of the multitude of ICT applications they might look to take up in their teaching, and to what purpose. The project team is mindful also that the potential audience for BEATL outputs, the 'early majority' and 'late majority', in Everett Rogers' terms (1995), will only be persuaded to take up innovations if there is clear evidence for educational benefits.

The first big question for the BEATL team was what type of evaluation methodology to use. Two contextual sources of influence had a strong impact on the team's choice: first the advice and requirements of the project funders, and second the recent academic debate in educational literature about alternative approaches to the evaluation of pedagogic research.

BEATL, in common with all TLTP 3 projects, has been set a range of requirements and expectations in relation to project management and evaluation by HEFCE's National Co-ordination Team. These requirements include:

- setting project objectives, preparing a list of project activities for each year, and having a variety of mechanisms in place for monitoring progress;
- identifying project stakeholders and keeping them informed throughout the work;
- ensuring the project team learn through project implementation, which may, in turn, lead to adjustment of project objectives.

The project team welcomed this direction and advice, recognizing that the unusual scale and complexity of the project required strong management and evaluation structures if it was to deliver its commitments. These directions had a significant impact on the evaluation framework for BEATL in terms of both principle and detailed design. Of most importance was the opportunity to learn from project implementation which required the evaluation approach to have the flexibility to accommodate change through the life of the project. In more specific terms, for example, one of the project team's responses to the early identification of stakeholders was to ensure their views were able to influence project development from the outset, by the adoption of front end evaluation. Though aimed at overall project level, HEFCE's directions also have implications in BEATL at the level of module innovation.

The second external source of influence on the choice of evaluation approach for BEATL was the background academic literature on pedagogic evaluation. Most significant for BEATL among recent academic debates has been the promotion of case study and action research approaches at the expense of traditional scientific methods of enquiry. Gunn (2000) catalogues the writings that have exposed the limitations of the scientific, experimental approach, from the difficulty in accommodating individual and contextual influences on results (Elton and Laurillard, 1979) to the problems associated with the indiscriminate choice of study populations (Draper *et al*, 1996). Out of this critique has come a return to more grounded approaches to enquiry, based in individual, real world teaching and learning situations. Yin's description of the case study method emphasizes its use for examining 'contemporary phenomena within some real-life context' (Yin, 1994: 1). Case study research is more than survey methodology. Yin compares the single source of information about individuals or settings produced by survey methodology, with that of the case study which uses multiple sources of information about a limited number of individuals or settings.

Zuber-Skerritt's (1992) action research approach is similarly grounded in the student learning experience as a whole, with all interested parties, including teachers, actively engaged; this approach is as much concerned with practical improvements to learning, through the action–reflection–modification cycle, as with understanding for its own sake. The principal limitation of such approaches is that there is little scope for generalization, with findings being applicable to one group of teachers and learners at a particular point in time. But Gunn concludes that this objective has proved very difficult to achieve in any form of educational research, and she holds out the hope for the long-term development of more grounded theory based on common findings from individual cases. It can be helpful to conceive these different approaches less as alternatives and more as at different points on a methodological continuum. Bhattacharya, for example, proposes an action research continuum with student feedback at one end and full scientific research at the other, with action research fitting in between (Battacharya, Cowan and Weedon, 2000).

The case study approach

These powerful trends in the academic debate in favour of more grounded, 'real world' research had a strong influence on the choice of evaluation approach for BEATL. Given the applied nature of research enquiry in the project, the BEATL team was clear that a 'real world' approach had to be adopted. It was decided, therefore, to take a case study approach using both qualitative and quantitative data collection methods. Yin supports the use of case study as an evaluation strategy for two reasons: 'first, the ability to incorporate an investigation of the context directly satisfies an evaluation's need to monitor and assess both the intervention and the implementation process. Second, the case study is not limited to either qualitative or quantitative data, but can incorporate both' (Yin, 1994: 59).

The BEATL team also considered that the case study approach fitted best the particular characteristics and challenges of this large scale, complex and dynamic project. The following advantages of the case study approach are seen as particularly significant to our choice:

- It is the most appropriate framework for the examination and description of contemporary events in the student learning process.

- It best enables us to focus on the impact of innovation on the quality of the student learning process.

- It recognizes that there are many more variables impacting on that learning experience than data points, and recognizes the significance of contextual conditions.

- It readily accommodates a variety of techniques and instruments felt to be central to our investigations, including direct observation and systematic interviewing.

- It enables learning to take place from project implementation, during the life of the project.

The project team recognizes that there are a number of limitations and dangers of the case study approach, which we have both sought to address in the design of the evaluation framework and kept in mind during project implementation. At a fundamental level care has to be taken in relation to generalization from project results; case studies are generalizable to theoretical propositions and not to populations or universes. In this sense, the case study does not represent a sample, and the investigators' goal is to expand and generalize theories (analytic generalization) and not to enumerate frequencies (statistical generalization). At the more operational level, as with all action research, there is a danger of bias through project researchers becoming personally involved in the innovations they are examining. The project team would maintain that these dangers are far outweighed by the flexibility and sensitivity offered by the case study approach.

The overall evaluation framework adopted for BEATL may be characterized as a multi-dimensional case study, mirroring the multi-faceted complexity
of the project itself, and providing for 'requisite variety' in the evaluation
function. This multi-dimensionality is expressed in a number of ways. First,
evaluation operates at a number of different levels in BEATL, from the level
of individual innovation and of module partnerships (formally written up
as case studies); through the level of the faculty and institution where
structures and policy may support or constrain innovation; finally to the
scale of the project overall, where the challenge is to pull together evidence
from the other levels of evaluation to address whether the project objectives
have been met. There are, therefore, case studies within an overall case study,
which provide a meta-evaluation. The project team has formally identified
three main levels at which evaluation operates in BEATL, in ascending order
of scale:

- the module and module partnership;
- the faculty and institution;
- the project.

BEATL's evaluation framework is multi-dimensional also in terms of the
range and types of techniques employed in the collection and analysis of
evidence. The team has sought to maximize the potential of the case study
approach for tailoring the methods to the individual task in hand. The
instruments used include:

- structured and semi-structured questionnaires;
- commentaries on questionnaire responses;
- semi-structured interviews, both face to face and telephone;
- classroom observation;
- module documentation;
- student assessment results;
- student profiles;
- university and faculty policy and other documents.

The selection of techniques has sought to strike an appropriate balance
between flexibility and appropriateness to the subject matter under assessment, on the one hand, and standard frameworks, providing a stronger basis
for generalization, on the other. Table 10.1 sets out the main surveys undertaken against the three principal levels of evaluation identified in the project.

A final way in which BEATL evaluation may be perceived as multi-
dimensional is the adoption of different appropriate techniques at each stage

Table 10.1   *BEATL evaluation framework*

Level	Evaluation aims		Evaluation methods
A *Module and partnership*	To investigate: • the extent to which the technology is embedded • impact on the quality of student learning • impact on the tutor's experience • cost effectiveness of the innovation • the extent to which innovations were transferred • the effectiveness of the partnership • the factors that affected the impact of the innovation • why initial innovation proposals not progressed	A i) ii) iii) iv) v) vi) vii) viii) ix)	module staff evaluation project associate's (PA's) structured interviews in standard format with module leaders student module evaluation educational technology officers' (ETOs') commentary on module leaders' (MLs') questionnaire responses module assessment results structured interviews with ETOs re general views on innovation module specific methods such as observation in action review of module documentation after first delivery monitor the second year of delivery through a brief standard questionnaire to module leaders
B *Faculty and institution*	To investigate: • the organisational context of each faculty and university relevant to BEATL innovation, and the differences among them • motivations of faculty/ university managements for participation in BEATL • contextual factors which supported and impeded project innovation • BEATL impact on uptake of IT in teaching and learning • organisational frameworks/ procedures	B i) ii) iii) iv) v) vi)	PA's interviews with BEATL managers, faculty/ department heads, and module leaders annual follow up of survey B i) to identify change faculty/institutional analysis of IT provision and organisational frameworks in each university, baseline and terminal staff questionnaire on IT usage structured interviews with University Project Managers (UPMs) and ETOs re the faculty/university factors which have affected BEATL innovation (including why innovations have not

Table 10.1   *BEATL evaluation framework (continued)*

Level	Evaluation aims		Evaluation methods
			progressed) possible survey/analysis through the Tavistock working group on institutional change
C *Project*	To investigate whether the project objectives have been met; the objectives relate to:	C i)	the evidence will in the main come from evaluation methods under A and B
		ii)	minutes of project management group (PMG) meetings and PMG papers
	i) embedding	iii)	structured interviews with ETOs, UPMs and project director in relation to overall delivery of the first 5 project objectives
	ii) impact on learning		
	iii) cost effectiveness		
	iv) institutional take up		
	v) transferability		
	vi) accessible courseware	iv)	feedback from the Tavistock on the draft project report
	vii) 8 or more case studies		
	viii) staff handbook	v)	pilot the BEATL access guidelines with 1 or more modules in 1999/2000 and 2000/01
	ix) 3 staff development workshops nationally		
	x) inform stakeholders		
		vi)	consumer feedback on case studies, staff handbook and workshops

of the project, to inform the work of the project team throughout the implementation process. Front end analysis was carried out at the beginning of the project with stakeholders; this was partly to establish a baseline for personal expectations from the project and partly to guide project planning and implementation. Second, formative evaluation is a key commitment throughout the project, including most importantly the use of module partnering methodology. The institution carrying out the pilot innovation undertakes an initial evaluation, which is used as a basis for discussion of how the pilot can be moved forward for second delivery and transferred to the module team in the partner institution.

This evaluation is based on our belief that a close systematic examination of particular innovations *in situ* will result in data revealing the extent to which the innovation has been effective, and where improvements may be made. Less scientifically, formative evaluation also takes place through quarter and annual progress reports, as required by HEFCE. Finally, summative evaluation is undertaken at the level of each module partnership through a case study analysis in standard format, and at the level of the project overall, through the final BEATL project report. This report will draw on all project evaluation sources including the set of module partnership reports, to address, at the meta-level, the outcomes of the project against the overall project objectives.

REFLECTIONS AND FINDINGS

This section discusses in turn, first, some modifications to the evaluation framework introduced during project implementation; second, some lessons about successful embedding; and third, initial views on how effective our evaluation methodology has been.

The quality and relevance of the data that the evaluation strategies have produced have enabled the team to begin to address the research questions posed at the outset of the project. Inevitably the most productive of the data sources has proved to be the 30 module innovations, each of which has been evaluated using a variety of instruments, providing rich qualitative and quantitative data. These evaluations have been written up as 14 case studies in a standard format, 12 of which are likely to be selected for inclusion in the BEATL electronic staff handbook, where they are scheduled to be accessible from January 2002 (http://uwe.ac.uk).

The flexibility of the case study approach proved invaluable in enabling the project team to adapt the evaluation framework in response to learning during project implementation. This adaptation did not happen haphazardly but was planned as a 'mini review' during the early part of the middle year of the project. The review confirmed the appropriateness of the case study approach and of the overall framework but suggested modifications in a number of areas. In the first instance a number of additional surveys were proposed to ensure more comprehensive and better quality data against all project objectives (Table 10.1). These additions included structured interviews to a common format with the members of the project team providing technical support, on their general views on module innovations they had supported.

There were also a questionnaire survey of academic and research staff in each faculty on their use of IT in their teaching, and structured interviews with each member of the project team in relation to a wide range of project issues, including institutional factors which have impacted on BEATL innovations. A second adaptation, confirmed through the 'mini review', was to move from a more general freedom for module leaders to choose evaluation techniques relevant to their innovation. This was an attempt to move towards greater standardization through the introduction of a structured survey questionnaire directed at the module leader. This important adaptation was to enable a greater degree of generalization from evaluation results across the set of module innovations.

A further modification was to reduce the relative importance given in the original evaluation design to the continuing canvassing of stakeholders' views. The number of meetings of the project consultation group was reduced from two to one per year, and the frequency of the original commitment to return to those surveyed in the front end analysis to identify whether perceptions had changed was also reduced by half. A final important modification was the decision to appoint a project evaluator from outside the BEATL team to both give formative advice during the final year of the work and contribute to the summative final report.

It is the team's view that the capacity of the case study approach to accommodate these adaptations significantly improved the value of the evaluation results. A number of these changes could be characterized as a move back from a more open case study approach in the direction of a more scientific methodology, along the methodological continuum discussed by writers such as Battacharya, Cowan and Weedon (2000).

The loudest early message to emerge from the choice of innovations made by module leaders has been the clear preference among most staff for small scale generic applications rather than large off the shelf, content specific software packages. Eleven out of 14 case study innovations chosen by module leaders were of the generic type, such as the use of Web pages or formative self-assessment quizzes. This was not at all what the project team had anticipated at the start of the project and appears to be due in particular to the increased accessibility of the latest technology and to its intrinsic flexibility to accommodate the individual academic's home-grown content. It was essential for overall project relevance that work structures were capable of adjustment to reflect this change of direction, and in turn equally important that the case study evaluation approach selected was able to accommodate such change.

The area of most extensive learning during project implementation has been in relation to the central principle of module partnering, normally involving a pilot innovation in one university and receiving partner in a second. Partnering enables the project to explore the process of product change and improvement, brings a comparative dimension to the educational context of embedding innovation packages, and most significantly introduces testing of transferability and the potential for wider dissemination. The human and technology dynamics to the partnering process have proved both challenging and frustrating, with each partner module leader tending to want adaptations to suit his/her particular context. Once again flexibility in project approach has proved indispensable, though inevitably at the expense of some uniformity in innovation content across module partnerships. This evidence underlines once more the attractiveness of customizable generic tools to module leaders, and the importance of flexibility in evaluation frameworks.

The overall aim of BEATL is to embed technology into undergraduate modules in ways which are appropriate to the student learning experience.

As a wide variety of technological applications and ways of embedding are being tried and evaluated, it will be possible to assess which types of application and embedding strategies are more effective. One key element in the BEATL approach to embedding has been to require that module leaders adopt a planned approach to the innovation, ensuring that it is fully integrated as a meaningful part of module learning. Module level evaluation in BEATL has already confirmed the crucial importance of such a planned approach in terms of effectiveness in delivery: it not only helps ensure educational relevance but also enables technical support issues, resource matters, academic training issues and others, to be identified early and overcome.

This experience is in contrast to many of the early experiments introducing IT into teaching. For example in the earlier phases of the Teaching and Learning Technology Programme, many projects were often technologically rather than educationally driven and as a consequence were rarely transferred beyond the authoring institution and tended to become obsolete quickly.

While it is too early to be clear, in general, of the extent to which gains to student learning have taken place through project innovations, two main areas appear to lead to learning enhancement:

- Formative, rapid feedback quizzes consistently receive positive responses from students, who appreciate the immediate access to explanatory materials and the ease of electronic communication with tutors. An important design issue to emerge, which can further promote learning enhancement, is to ensure such quizzes are open ended, inviting students to engage in further exploration of topics.

- The potential of technology to provide rich varied content in support of student project and coursework. Built environment disciplines lend themselves well to such multimedia resources, particularly for project work; as with formative self-assessment quizzes, such rich content helps to reinforce the student's position at the centre of the learning process, providing choice, and enhancing autonomy.

On the important matter of barriers to effective embedding, initial analysis of module leader questionnaires has indicated two main concerns: limitations on the time available to module teams to undertake the advance planning required, and limitations to the on-demand availability of technical support staff. Staffing resources rather than ICT infrastructure appeared to present the major frustrations for module leaders, even though BEATL funds provided a .6 post dedicated to technical support in each university, and made modest hours allocations to module leaders working in the project. Departmental managers need then to be alert to the danger of investment in ICT infrastructure, propelled by the 'ratchet effect', being out of balance with investment in time for academic planning and technical support.

Experience to date on the project has indicated that organizational and policy matters at institutional level may have an impact on technology innovation at module level. There is evidence of a general concern among teaching staff that ICT policy and development at university level were too often driven by administrative imperatives rather than by educational need. This might result, for example, in infrastructure which is not as accessible or consumer friendly for staff and students as it could be.

Another currently problematic area for institutional decision making is achieving an appropriate balance between *standardization* in respect of applications such as computer based quiz tools, computer aided design (CAD), geographic information system (GIS) packages, virtual learning environments, and the *discretion* for staff, locally, to set up and employ non-standard tools in their teaching. This is a particularly tricky area for universities to resolve, given the current speed of technological development, but it is of great significance for take up of the new technologies in teaching and learning, as it touches on the crucial areas of accessibility and of customization.

The project team also experienced difficulties in transferring a number of innovations to the partner due to infrastructure differences between the universities concerned. The degree of standardization of ICT systems in universities, nationally, can clearly have a major influence on the potential for dissemination of project products. A final point to emerge in relation to university organization is the need, as ICT infrastructure expands, for parallel investment in resources to ensure effective maintenance of operational systems. On a number of occasions during the project, progress in development of tools or the delivery of the innovation was hampered by system unavailability.

These initial project results have proved informative and should prove also to be robust, with the triangulation of data using quantitative and qualitative sources both within individual module evaluations and across the 30 innovations and other survey sources. There are, however, a number of ways in which BEATL's evaluation framework might have been improved further:

- A further shift towards standardization of evaluation surveys might have been introduced through a common student evaluation questionnaire, at least at a minimum level, still allowing the individual module leader to include additional elements through choice.

- A more comprehensive baseline survey of departmental and university policy and organizational structures relevant to teaching and learning innovations across the three partner universities.

- A resource note, the allocation of more staff time to help ensure all elements of evaluation were carried out rigorously and to programme. It proved difficult in an action research programme of this kind, with multiple objectives, to resource the comprehensive delivery of BEATL's demanding evaluation framework, while also providing the best possible support to module leaders carrying out their innovations.

CONCLUSION

BEATL's evaluation strategy is proving to be an effective tool for addressing the research questions posed in the project. It is felt by the research team that a case study method is not only the most appropriate but probably the only approach that would have proved productive in the BEATL context of real world innovation in 32 modules across three universities, where the nature of the innovations is not known at the beginning of the project and where the project team is meant to learn and modify processes in the course of project implementation.

A scientific approach with control and experimental groups would have been impractical in such a setting and would have missed out on the richness and diversity provided through the real world, more eclectic approach of the case study. However our BEATL experience also suggests that there are dangers in eclecticism dominating to the extent that the potential for generalization against research questions is undermined. There are obvious dangers also in a *non-scientific* approach to evaluation degenerating into a *non rigorous* methodology.

ACKNOWLEDGEMENTS

The authors wish to acknowledge their indebtedness to two colleagues: Dr Maria Avgerinou, Visiting Assistant Professor at the Northern Illinois University, Project Associate during the first year of BEATL and principal author of the project's initial evaluation strategy; and Dr Gaynor Attwood, Principal Lecturer, Faculty of Education, UWE, Bristol, for her invaluable contributions on the wider academic literature on pedagogic evaluation.

REFERENCES

Bhattacharya, B, Cowan, J and Weedon, E (2000) Action research: a means to more effective teaching and learning, *Innovations in Education and Training International*, **37** (4), pp 314–22, Routledge, London

Draper, S, Brown, M, Henderson, F and McAteer, E (1996) Integrative evaluation: an emerging role for classroom studies of CAL, *Computers and Education* (CAL 1995 Special Edition)

Elton, L and Laurillard, D (1979) Trends in research on student learning, *Studies in Higher Education*, **4** (1), pp 87–102

Gunn, C (2000) CAL evaluation: future directions, in *The Changing Face of Learning Technology*, ed D Squires, G Conole and G Jacobs, pp 59–67, University of Wales Press, London

Rogers, E M (1995) *Diffusion of Innovations*, Collier Macmillan, London
Yin, R (1994) *Case Study Research: Design and methods*, 2nd edn, Sage, Newbury Park, CA
Zuber-Skerritt, O (1992) *Professional Development in Higher Education*, Kogan Page, London

FURTHER READING

Avgerinou, M and Winter, J (1999) *BEATL Annual Report*, University of the West of England, Bristol
Bryman, A (1988) *Quantity and Quality in Social Research*, Unwin Hyman, London
Guba, E (1978) Toward a methodology of naturalistic enquiry in educational evaluation, *E Monograph Series in Evaluation no 8*, Center for the Study of Evaluation, University of California, Los Angeles, CA
Parlett, M and Hamilton, D (1972/77/87) *Evaluation As Illumination: A new approach to the study of innovatory programmes* (1972) workshop at Cambridge, and unpublished report Occasional paper 9, Centre for Research in the Educational Sciences, University of Edinburgh
Robson, C (1993) *Real World Research*, Blackwell, Oxford
Silverman, D (2000) *Doing Qualitative Research*, Sage, London

Part Two:
Supporting change within institutions and the wider environment

11

Developing research based learning using ICT in higher education curricula: the role of research and evaluation

Jacqueline A Dempster and Paul Blackmore

INTRODUCTION

The Technology-Enhanced Learning in Research Led Institutions (TELRI) project sought to explore and develop the relationship between teaching, learning and research through the use of technology. The project was located at the University of Warwick, with Oxford and Warwick working in partnership, joined at a later stage by Southampton, Durham and Birmingham. This chapter explores the role of research and evaluation in assisting that process, drawing on the implementation work of the TELRI project across a range of subject areas in a number of research led universities. The project team found a great deal to reflect on, about what they were attempting to achieve, the way they were approaching it and what happened, and some of the issues that arose are considered here.

EDUCATIONAL DEVELOPMENTS IN RESEARCH LED UNIVERSITIES

Over the last decade in the United Kingdom there has been growth in support for the use of technology within teaching and learning in higher education (HE). In particular, since 1993 the Teaching and Learning Technology Programme (TLTP) has promoted the creation of technology based materials for use across the HE sector. However, evaluations have shown that, in general, staff in research led universities have been reluctant to take up TLTP-like products. Programmes and teaching approaches are often strongly informed by staff research interests, and at their best may emphasize a research-like approach to learning, in which learners are encouraged to become researchers in their own right. Teaching processes may, therefore, concentrate on developing learners' capacity to be innovative, to work independently, to set and solve problems and to handle large quantities of information in a wide range of media.

The nature of the partner institutions meant that the project was located not only within the broader context of change, but also in a climate where, despite much persuasion as to its multiple benefits, the wider impact of educational technology has remained relatively low. Educational developers are successful when they help to deliver outcomes that are highly valued by the academic staff and students with whom they work. The TELRI project therefore sought to work with the grain of research orientated academics and turn it to advantage. The project aimed to enrich curricula by deploying technological solutions to develop the research capabilities of undergraduate students.

LINKING RESEARCH TO TEACHING AND LEARNING

A significant feature of a number of universities in the UK Higher Education sector is that they define themselves as 'research led'. Many of them claim that research informs teaching. Discussion concerning the nature of any link between staff research activity and the quality of student learning has become highly politicized. Despite the fact that studies have been generally inconclusive (Elton, 1986; Hattie and Marsh, 1996), a belief that research informs teaching persists.

Clearly any educational development project that makes tangible links is likely to attract and engage academic staff. However, the nature and effects of a research culture are hard to define (Blackmore, Roach and Dempster, 2001), and this is at odds with an increasing tendency to require explicitness in descriptions of learning processes and outcomes in the sector. Since the construction of new knowledge and understanding is inherently a part of research, we believed the most fruitful area to explore was that of the *processes* which research and student learning may have in common. Research activity by its nature fosters innovation and can therefore provide a valuable model for developing the higher cognitive skills that inform such capabilities. The research process can directly influence the nature of taught courses if these capabilities are emphasized and explicitly developed in the students. At present, the potential benefit of academics' research expertise as a model for student learning is not always exploited fully in course design and delivery, and this will only change if a conscious effort is made that it should do so. The TELRI project sought to do precisely this. It should be stressed that the improvements in students' learning that the project wished to bring about do not require a research led environment, and they are largely a re-expression of the goals that many would have for a higher education in general. However, it can be claimed that certain environments, of which research led institutions are an example (Boyer Commission, 1996), offer particularly valuable opportunities to enhance students' learning, in that the working processes of researchers may serve as a model for – and inspiration to – students.

RESEARCH AS PART OF DEVELOPMENT ACTIVITY

TLTP funding was intended for the support of educational development and not for research. This is, to an extent, understandable, given that such funding was intended directly to produce changes in practice. Further, the focus of the third phase of the TLTP programme was on implementation and not on production of materials, reflecting the quantity of software and related learning materials that had already been produced in earlier phases, and which in many cases had not been much used. Again, the focus is understandable. However, as a project team we realized that they were proposing to work in a field that was under-conceptualized and under-explored. We knew that if we were to do worthwhile work that acknowledged the complexity of what we were dealing with and took account of disciplinary differences, we would have to spend some time in research activity. The project devoted considerable time and effort to formulating a conceptual understanding of what the project was trying to achieve, since we believed the tendency to rush into implementation without laying the necessary methodological ground work would become a major barrier to progress.

Such research was approached through literature review and through evaluation of current practice. Specifically, we had coined a term 'research capability', which academic staff and the TELRI team found useful and engaging at a common-sense level. However, we needed to identify these capabilities, which required extensive exploration of accounts and analyses of relationships between research and teaching. We were also aware of a vast skills literature, which often appeared to be describing similar learning outcomes to those we were seeking to develop, but without reference to our chosen context. We also took into account a range of literature on student learning, particularly that which explores deep and surface approaches to learning (Boud, 1988; Bridges, 1994; Dreyfus and Dreyfus, 1986; Kolb, 1984; Kuhn, 1981; Marton and Säljö, 1984; Marton and Ramsden, 1988).

There are obvious challenges in doing such work within a funding approach that requires pre-specified 'deliverables' within a tight timescale. In the event we found a way through, and it may be that the pressure we felt was on us to produce concrete outcomes early on in the life of the project was a healthy discipline. However, there are certainly tensions produced when development funding precludes the level of preparatory research that is needed.

DEVELOPING A FRAMEWORK FOR COURSE DESIGN

TELRI's work was set against the background of the skills debate (Bridges, 1994), an attempt to clarify the purposes of higher education. At its heart is the concept of 'graduateness' and of employability as a desired outcome for students on degree programmes. There is a wish to identify and to develop through the curriculum those central capabilities that are transferable to a range of vocational and other situations and therefore have a wide application in both professional practice and lifelong learning.

In the TELRI framework, we focused on the cognitive processes of researchers and used this as a model for the development of students' capabilities (Roach, Blackmore and Dempster, 2001). We highlighted two complementary learning processes. The first, which we termed *adoptive learning*, is concerned with established knowledge and approaches and requires students to acquire and apply well-understood subject knowledge and the mastery of tools, techniques and procedures in bounded situations. The second, which we termed *adaptive learning*, is a creative, generative and reflective process, making use of higher order skills in more open situations. It is more difficult to define, especially across subject boundaries. The two forms of learning assist in the distinction between those adoptive skills and abilities which *may* be applied in particular contexts, and those adaptive capabilities which assist in transfer, facilitating the recognition of unfamiliar contexts and enabling understanding and innovation to be applied appropriately. Individuals whose professions require the rigorous application of a discipline, such as researchers, are, it is reasonable to suppose, highly effective in adaptive learning and are potentially well placed both to assist others in developing similar expertise and to assess the presence of such capabilities in others.

For such terms to be useful to academic staff in reviewing their curricula, the team believed that it was necessary to build them into a framework, and so one was designed to provide a generic, cross-curricular approach to the design and evaluation of courses that aim to facilitate the development of research orientated capabilities. Such frameworks can provide a means for institutions and individuals to make explicit what may currently be implicit, and therefore guide appropriate investment in teaching development and in ICT provision. In this case the framework led to the development of course design guidelines (Roach, Blackmore and Dempster, 2000) to support curriculum reflection and review and to guide the project intervention strategies.

EVALUATING THE EXISTING PRACTICE OF ACADEMIC STAFF

In the first stages of the project, the TELRI team consulted academic staff across a wide range of departments in research led universities. This took place alongside the literature review and resulting framework design and helped to inform it, particularly in relation to disciplinary differences. Discussions centred on what the development of research capabilities meant in academics' disciplines and in their own teaching approaches. By this means we gathered understanding of the learning processes a research based curriculum might help students to develop, across a range of disciplines, and how such courses might be delivered and supported more effectively using technology. There were clear similarities in the learning processes which academics in a range of disciplines described.

There were distinct differences between departments in how quickly the team was able to identify common ground and devise appropriate ways forward. On reflection, it is clear that a significant period of the initial discussions with lecturers was spent in establishing a common 'language' so that dialogue about teaching and learning approaches could be meaningful. The team needed to understand the unique aspects of each discipline. Similarly, lecturers needed to find ways of expressing their teaching objectives and desired student capabilities in generic terms as well as those embedded in their discipline.

For the initial appraisals, the value of a discussion based qualitative approach as opposed to a quantitative approach should not be underestimated. By this, we mean that arriving at useful conclusions is not always achieved by straightforward questions and answers. The most valuable and crucial information, particularly with respect to the specific discipline, is often derived from an iterative process involving probing, negotiation, serendipity and observation of attitudes during the course of discussion. It reminds us of the importance of keeping an open mind when academic staff discuss what they are doing, what they want to do and what they need.

Discussion of possible new practice proceeded far more quickly in courses involving tutors from the humanities and social sciences. In general, science departments were concerned with developing approaches in the *delivery of factual information* while the humanities departments were predominantly interested in developing methods to enable student *interpretation* of and *insight* into subject related materials. It may be that the nature of knowledge in those disciplines lends itself to more discursive approaches to learning. Perhaps ICT support for collaborative learning fits more easily here than in the curricula of the sciences. Furthermore, science based lecturers often wanted a 'total solution' for dealing with curriculum overload and marking and were generally less willing to engage in subject specific development and adaptation of approaches to teaching (with some refreshing exceptions).

It must be said the apparently overloaded curriculum of science subjects and the problems this brings to lecturers can seem a powerful reason not to alter teaching approaches at all. Scientific and other perceived 'content based' courses presented a particular challenge to TELRI. At present such courses are often seen by academic staff as primarily adoptive by nature, because of the quantity of propositional knowledge that they believe has to be mastered by the learner. Questions of relevance, and of the development of broader transferable capabilities, may be seen as secondary and in some ways 'not our problem'. Some staff felt they could incorporate the TELRI educational approaches into developing traditional modes of teaching and learning and that they might consider using ICT at a later stage.

ICT TOOLS

TELRI started with an educational idea rather than an ICT tool, and the team believe that this has been a major strength. In considering the potential value of ICT in supporting the development of research capabilities, TELRI has used the terms 'adoptive' and 'adaptive', learning to distinguish between uses of ICT tools. Some uses support adoptive learning by making research tools, data and information available, thus contributing to students' disciplinary techniques and knowledge. TELRI has not pursued these. Other uses, those in which TELRI has been concerned, support research *processes* and thus adaptive learning (Blackmore, Roach and Dempster, 2001).

TELRI approaches, therefore, could be used with a wide range of existing tools. There was no intention, at the start, to produce software. Ironically, because so many academic staff had no access to the ICT tools they needed, TELRI found itself obliged to produce a tool, a simple CGI script which enabled publication to the Web and critiquing of work. Without such a tool, many interested staff would have been unable to participate.

SUPPORTING LECTURERS IN DEVELOPING NEW PRACTICE

The TELRI framework is the common thread running through discipline based course approaches, providing a way of engaging with educational concepts in discussions with a wide variety of audiences and facilitating the exploration of case study examples across disciplines. Centred on the simple distinction between adoptive and adaptive learning, the course design framework assists academic staff in reviewing and clarifying their course purposes and approaches. Adoptive and adaptive learning engaged people in ways which detailed study of Bloom, Krathwohl and the post-Dearing lexicon of key skill terms did not!

Not all the departments initially selected for participation were in the end committed, and we did not attempt to negotiate what appeared after much effort to be immovable obstacles to progressing ideas and implementation. The initial show of interest came from two aspects of the project objectives: first the research focus, where academic staff wanted to make more explicit in their course descriptions and delivery their claimed research based approaches, and second the technology focus, where staff were keen to make more effective use of technology but were not sure how. A third factor was also apparent, namely that our intervention was not limited by cultural and policy barriers where staff or departments had control over the design, development and assessment of their courses, both in terms of planning and resources. Only in the cases where all three aspects came together did projects get under way, and progress was then quite rapid. Nevertheless, the value of the discussions at all stages for establishing lecturers who wish to be involved is not to be underestimated. This gave us a sound basis for setting out both the educational framework and identifying the change management factors in play.

The project team has often used the terms *'hassle'* and *'enthusiasm'* to describe the dynamics of implementing new teaching and learning practices, particularly apparent with respect to ICT based development. From our observations supporting educational development, there appears to be a cut-off point at which the 'enthusiasm' of the lecturer – even the most devoted convert – diminishes as the 'hassle' of teaching development rises. (This in turn negates staff development efforts.) However, there must be a point at which if you reduce the hassle to almost zero, even a low degree of enthusiasm or indifference might be sufficient to promote uptake and bring about change. (Were it possible to define such qualitative phenomena, exploring such relationships in a range of contexts would make an interesting study!)

In evaluation responses to our dissemination events, academic staff valued the simplicity of the educational ideas and the ICT tools. Staff and educational developers on the other hand were most interested in the evaluated case studies from subject based courses to use in their own activities.

The majority of lecturers we encountered were at ease discussing the ideas and making their own choices as to how they might inform their own teaching development. Most were interested to explore the TELRI approaches in relation to their own discipline and teaching culture, while the occasional individual was highly agitated by the ideas and even openly hostile. The innovative approach promoted by TELRI was seen by a few staff as unjustified experimenting with courses. There may also be significant resistance owing to the influence of validation and external subject bodies, particularly in vocational subjects, where academic staff may have power of assessment, but may feel that they do not have control in terms of purpose or external relevance.

The effective integration of technology assisted methods and materials into courses requires a rethinking of teaching and learning approaches which many lecturers find challenging. However, in the majority of cases, the main difficulties faced by lecturers are to do with lack of incentives to devote time away from research to teaching development, together with the formidable barrier presented by the often inadequate IT provision and support.

IMPLEMENTING NEW PRACTICE IN INSTITUTIONS

A strong tradition of central initiatives and support greatly assists projects such as TELRI. In such environments, there are likely to be more IT infrastructure, local technical support, and suitable ICT based materials and tools available to staff who wish to work with TELRI. A strong institutional initiative can bring problems, though, particularly when tools are chosen that do not do the jobs that need doing or are simply too complex for staff to engage with. TELRI took a different approach. It seemed desirable to test out ICT methods without having to buy expensive or complex software applications. The project therefore encouraged the use of simple ICT tools that provided the basic functionality of more sophisticated packages in order to pilot the educational methods. By starting in a small way, academic staff could gain experience of innovative methods that could usefully inform the ways in which institution-wide provision might be developed.

The team decided at an early stage to work through institutions' staff developers, and this meant an additional set of relationships which were problematic at times. The project's original intention had been to work one to one with academic staff early on, but thereafter to support institutional staff developers in implementing what was intended by then to be a well tried and documented approach. On reflection, this seems to have been unrealistic. It supposed that staff development units had time available to support the TELRI initiative, although the funding arrangements did not provide them with resources, and it required a high level of commitment to the ideas of the project. In general, the educational framework engaged academic staff in departments more readily than it did institutional staff developers. The resistance of some staff developers to the ideas (or the way they were presented) was surprising to us and provided a potential barrier to discussions with academic staff in those institutions. However, this is understandable, for staff development has a difficult status situation to maintain; it can be a difficult and diplomatic role involving relationships with lecturers which are hard to establish and easy to damage. External projects may propose alternative ideas to those offered by institution-based staff development.

While staff development units are in an excellent position to assist the development of established good practice, they may not be well positioned to promote experimental new practice except in their own teaching develop-ment programmes, since courses 'belong to' academic departments. Indeed, in some cases, staff/educational developers are seen solely as service providers rather than innovators. To promote new practice it is necessary to be well embedded into the academic culture across the institution, and in this case, to have an existing educational technology focus.

In the light of this experience, while retaining its staff development links, the project adopted an alternative strategy for working with institutions. Heads of department were contacted directly and the ideas and approaches were discussed directly with lecturers within a departmental setting. This resulted in a higher degree of interest and an improved level of imple-mentation of both the educational methods and the use of ICT to support them.

OUTCOMES

Implementation in courses across a range of disciplines was generally successful, and a large number of insightful case studies have been generated, although the extent to which the courses are 'finished products' varies. This depended on the complexity of what academic staff wished to do within TELRI. In some cases, implementation work has been highly intensive, involving considerable time with tutors to identify appropriate resource materials, so courses have yet to run. In others, course approaches required little modification, simple technologies were identified and implemented rapidly, and courses were running within weeks. The difficulties that the academic calendar and course schedules imposed on project work meant that some courses would not actually run until after the funded period of the project.

The team did not find it easy to evaluate each intervention in terms of learning gains. The sorts of capability we were seeking to develop are subtle and complex and therefore hard to measure. It could be argued that existing methods of assessment aim to measure these capabilities, but there is then difficulty in attributing any particular gain to the intervention. At the same time it was not feasible to seek to impose an additional burden on teaching staff by asking them to add further assessment points. We were, however, able to establish good correlations between the capabilities which courses intended to develop and the extent to which they were judged to be developed, through a triangulated evaluation approach that used TELRI team observation, tutor interviews and questionnaires, and student questionnaires.

SUCCESSFUL MODELS FOR CHANGING PRACTICE

The TELRI approaches seem to appeal to many academics willing to shift the practice or culture of their subject, but the operational context for teaching development and use of ICT is extremely restrictive for them. The difficulties for academic staff in changing approaches to teaching are substantial. Academics can change only if they are willing to take on every issue (validation, external bodies, IT issues, and so on), with little support. Reducing the hassle of uptake therefore seems vital, as the motivation to change is generally low. Therefore academic development requires incentives, support and accessibility.

The volume of implementation that can be achieved during the lifetime of funded projects depends on several factors. First, working in institutions will inevitably introduce uncertainties, because a project's work will to an extent depend upon the degree of assistance that the institution can offer its staff, both in access to appropriate hardware and software and in educational development incentive and support. Second, the successful integration of new practice in the longer term requires consideration of the culture of both specific disciplines and the institution. Short-term projects, particularly those funded externally, are not always well positioned to deal with this aspect of managing change.

In the TELRI project, we have been learning the central necessity of examining the purpose behind our implementations. From initial discussions with staff in the participating departments, it was apparent that the primary purpose of embedding research orientated learning into curricula was often overshadowed by secondary missions driven by political ('seen to be innovative') or technological ('we must use more IT') agendas. As TELRI developed its profile – hand in hand with a research orientated pedagogic framework – it was easier to communicate to academic staff and departments that we were offering to support them in using technology to achieve the educational ends they recognized and wanted. In particular, TELRI was seen by a number of staff, not only in those disciplines with which we worked, but also in medical education, management training and school based education, as a practical and sound way forward in the development of transferable skills.

In our strategic approach to institutional change we think we have certainly got something right. We chose to focus on research led teaching, something which was intrinsically of interest to academic staff and politically important for institutions. The changes we proposed were aligned with academics' sense of what they were doing (or felt they ought to be doing) and institutions' academic missions. We also, we believe, provided a simple means by which learning technologies could genuinely enhance educational quality. Offering a valid and explicit reason for change and showing a simple way in which technology could be used increased enthusiasm and engagement across several levels within the institutions.

FINAL THOUGHTS

In the early stages we had difficulty in communicating what we were trying to do. In part this was because we were still clarifying what we thought we were about. However, this stage was particularly difficult for us because, while most ICT related projects have a tool to sell or a specific product to offer, TELRI was offering an approach based on a set of ideas. We would argue that unless educational developers engage with educational purposes, they are unlikely to achieve anything useful. However, it made us vulnerable. Some academic staff were initially difficult to attract, for in some ways it is harder to engage busy people in a discussion of ideas than it is to sell them a tool (although considerably more fruitful if you succeed). Second, it could be claimed that the learning processes we were advocating were simply a re-statement of well-known good practice. This may be the case, but we also believed that much good educational practice is expressed in a language that many academic staff do not recognize or respect.

In summary, the project became most productive when we found an approach that was simple, clear, cost-effective and worked with the grain of the institution. The TELRI approach does seem to have struck a chord with a significant number of academic staff and to have resulted in uptake of ICT for carefully-focused educational ends.

REFERENCES

Blackmore, P, Roach, M P and Dempster, J A (2001) The use of ICT in education for research and development, in *Educational Development Through Information and Communication Technologies*, ed S Fallow and R Bhanot, Kogan Page, London

Boud, D (1988) *Developing Student Autonomy in Learning*, Kogan Page, London

Boyer Commission on Educating Undergraduates in the Research University (1996) *Reinventing Undergraduate Education: A blueprint for America's research universities*, Carnegie Foundation for the Advancement of Teaching, New York [online] http://naples/cc.sunysb.edu/Pres/boyer.nsf/ [accessed 28 January 2002]

Bridges, D (1994) *Transferable Skills in Higher Education*, University of East Anglia, Norwich

Dreyfus, L and Dreyfus, S E (1986) *Mind Over Machine: The power of human intuition and expertise in the era of the computer*, Blackwell, Oxford

Elton, L (1986) Research and teaching: symbiosis or conflict, *Higher Education*, **15**, pp 299–304

Hattie, J and Marsh, H W (1996) The relationship between research and teaching: a meta-analysis, *Review of Educational Research*, **66** (4), pp 507–42

Kolb, D (1984) *Experiential Learning: Experience as the source of learning and development*, Prentice-Hall, Englewood Cliffs, NJ

Kuhn, D (1981) The role of self-directed activity in cognitive development, in *New Directions in Piagetian Theory and Practice*, ed I Segel, D Brodzinsky and R M Golinkoff, Lawrence Erlbaum Associates, Hillsdale, NJ

Marton, F and Ramsden, P (1988) What does it take to improve learning? in *Improving Learning: New perspectives*, ed P Ramsden, pp 268–86, Kogan Page, London

Marton, F and Säljö, R (1984) Approaches to learning, in *The Experience of Learning*, ed F Marton, D Hounsell and N J Entwistle, Scottish Academic Press, Edinburgh

Roach, M, Blackmore, P and Dempster, J (2000) Supporting high level learning through research-based methods: guidelines for course design, *TELRI Project Publication* [online] http://www.telri.ac.uk/staffpack/ [accessed 28 January 2002]

Roach, M P, Blackmore, P and Dempster, J A (2001) Supporting high level learning through research-based methods: a framework for course development, *Innovations in Education and Teaching International*, **38** (4)

12

Implementing a virtual learning environment: a holistic framework for institutionalizing online learning

Gabi Diercks-O'Brien

THE ONLINE LEARNING PHENOMENON

As a result of the creation of the World Wide Web on the eve of the 21st century, growing numbers of higher education users have begun to 'do things online'. It is probably fair to say that the Web has now permeated most areas of higher education. Some observers see this new phenomenon as far more than just another technology whim in education, and new philosophical concepts of higher education are emerging, such as the 'e-campus' and 'e-learning'. Such interpretations of the online learning phenomenon are not surprising, as today's so-called 'knowledge society' seems to be intrinsically connected to the Web. The concepts of lifelong learning, access and participation, the globalization of education and the knowledge economy in the British educational context, also seem closely tied to the idea of Web based access and delivery (eg DfEE, 1999; DfEE, 2000; HEFCE, 2000; MacLeod, 2000; Moores, 2000).

Ever since its introduction into higher education, there has been confusion over the impact of the Web and its role in student learning. More often than not, online learning still comes in the guise of 'innovative projects', their main characteristics being that they are short-lived, over-funded and under-supported, with little or no positive impact on student learning. Readers may want to think about their own institution: how many successful examples of online learning are they familiar with? It would appear to be the case that many examples of so-called online innovations in day to day teaching practice across the globe are still largely experimental in nature.

There is not yet a theory of online learning, nor is there a new pedagogy, and it is debatable whether these will materialize. It seems unlikely that they ever will unless universities take a more coordinated and committed approach to the integration of these new technologies. However, despite all the problems, bad practice and hyperbole, online learning is likely to remain highly attractive, because it opens up entirely new opportunities for learning and teaching, such as:

- *Integration of different types of learning resources, media and activities.* For example, an engineering module delivered in a traditional lecture format could be supported with online learning resources. These could be lecture notes with interactive questions and feedback for summative assessment of students' understanding of the lecture content; a discussion group to provide students with the opportunity to learn collaboratively; and an interactive simulation model, allowing students to explore a difficult theoretical concept. In a virtual learning environment (VLE) these features are integrated and available through one single gateway.

- *Instant access* to resources, automated feedback and stored data on student learning progress but also integration with centrally held data to facilitate administration.

- *Flexibility of delivery*, such as on and off campus access, distance learning, mixed mode of delivery of classroom teaching and open access.

- *Flexibility of approaches to teaching and learning*, such as eclectic approaches to teaching, instructional design and constructivist approaches for different levels of tutor control and learner independence, and opportunities for collaborative learning.

- *Adaptability and flexibility* of resource creation and resource management via simple authoring tools that allow teaching staff to create, edit and update resources and reuse elements in other courses.

In order to understand the difficulties in institutionalizing online learning and adopting more appropriate strategies for its successful diffusion, this chapter is based on two propositions. First, a holistic and dynamic approach is required to understand how the institutionalization of online learning can be achieved. I would like to advocate a social systems approach which perceives online learning in relation to the entire system of a higher education institution. Ackoff and Emery describe social systems as organizations 'in which the state of the part can be determined only by reference to the state of the system. The effect of change in one part or another is mediated by changes in the state of the whole' (1972: 218). The problem so far with computer based learning innovation, and online learning in particular, has been that innovators lack a holistic understanding of the innovation and its interdependency with the system of their institution. Moreover, they often only vaguely understand their own role in relation to the innovation and the institution. (See for instance the British Open University's 'New Directions' Programme as described by Russell and Peters, 1998.) This lack of understanding (and consequently inappropriate action) has resulted in the inability of the system as a whole to cope with the demands placed on it by the new technology.

The second proposition is that online learning is very different from previous technology innovations in higher education. It should not be seen as simply another technology medium, such as paper or video, which did not have the same impact on learning and teaching and institutional systems. The relationship between online learning and the overall system of higher education is more complex than this, in part because it revolutionizes the way support systems have to be organized. The domains of learning and of infrastructures within a higher education institution can no longer be regarded as entirely separate entities (as reflected in the division between academia and administration). The way forward for the institutionalization of online learning will be to provide adequate infrastructures that recognize this interdependency between the institution and the teaching and learning, or in other words, learning infrastructures (Diercks-O'Brien, 2000a, b). Thinking in terms of learning infrastructures recognizes the dualist nature of online learning.

As it is highly dependent upon the institutional system, the institution will have to change dramatically to ensure its survival. Currently, however, online learning is at an impasse because most higher education institutions are inflexible and therefore are resisting the changes required for successful implementation. This is not a wilful resistance. Rather, it arises from a lack of understanding of the dualist nature of the online learning phenomenon. The institutionalization of online learning therefore means that considerable changes to the institution are necessary. The three most important factors are that university learning and teaching have to be rethought (eg Laurillard, 1993), organizational change is required at all levels (Ford *et al*, 1996), and finally and most importantly, entirely new approaches to support systems are needed (CSUP, 1992). The following discussion of the findings from the ELEN project evaluation will support these claims.

THE ELEN PROJECT

Description

In 1998 the Extended Learning Environment Network project (ELEN) received funding from the Teaching and Learning Technology Programme (TLTP) for a three-year period. Eight British universities joined in a collaborative partnership with the aim of implementing communication and information technology in a variety of subject areas and generic skills in their institutions. This was to be achieved through the integration into learning and teaching of computer based learning resources developed during the first two phases of TLTP, but also other suitable existing resources. The project began at a time when widespread interest in online learning and the integration of VLEs emerged. This meant that there would be a considerable shift in emphasis towards the form of delivery, in other words via the Web.

Since 1996 the University of Lincolnshire and Humberside had already been operating successfully an online undergraduate skills programme, the Effective Learning Programme, and utilizing an in-house developed VLE, the Virtual Campus, for the delivery. The consortium partners adopted this delivery platform for the implementation of online learning in their institutions. What followed was a unique experiment in which seven very different higher education institutions in Britain learnt how the introduction of a VLE and online learning impacted on their institution and how their institutional systems had to change in order to accommodate this innovation.

Project implementation was approached from several angles, but there were three main factors that determined the development process. First, there were 40 online learning projects across all consortium institutions (excluding the lead site team) with student numbers ranging from 30 to 1,200. The implementation of these individual projects made for a bottom-up approach to institutional change. Second, the role of the project management team and the function of institutional project managers as change agents in their own institution was vital to the implementation process. Thirdly, the positive impact of internal and external pressures in favour of online learning acted as levers for change.

Evaluation

Extensive internal and external evaluation was undertaken to assess the project development and the impact of online learning on the learning experience and on the institution. The internal evaluation focused on the effectiveness of online learning, the learning and teaching approaches taken and the success of the integration of this new mode of learning with the overall learning experience. Project leaders and students took part in this large-scale evaluation in which questionnaires, focus groups and interviews were used (Diercks-O'Brien, 2000a). An external evaluation was undertaken by Professor Harold Silver to evaluate the implementation of the project, in a way that was formative after year one and summative towards the end of the project (Silver, 2000; Keighley and Diercks-O'Brien, 2000). The external evaluation investigated the experiences of all stakeholders, apart from those students whose experiences were amply covered by the internal evaluation. Interviews and focus groups were conducted with representatives from the vice-chancellor's office and steering group members, institutional project managers, the project lead site team, staff in computer services and other support staff and the project leaders.

In addition to these formal internal and external evaluation activities, a reflective approach was used to monitor the project development informally. Issues brought up at project management team meetings and comments made by project leaders during visits were recorded. As the project evolved, the interdependency between online learning and a higher education institution became more evident. Consequently, the ELEN project evaluation activities moved more clearly towards system design evaluation (Jenks, 1998).

Findings

The results from the ELEN evaluation confirmed earlier hypotheses, such as:

1. Online learning requires a holistic approach to the learning environment.

2. The learning environment is highly dependent upon the provision of appropriate learning infrastructures and support systems.

3. Successful integration of online learning and institutionalization requires dramatic changes to the entire system of an institution of higher education, including the approaches to teaching and learning, the organizational systems and infrastructures and the provision of support.

4. The online learning phenomenon has specific features. These features require higher education institutions to change. While the features are generic, the required changes to an institution's system may take different forms, depending upon the institution.

5. Online learning has a greater impact than do previous technologies.

TRANSFORMATION PROCESSES: FROM LOCAL IMPLEMENTATION TO INSTITUTIONALIZATION

Rethinking university learning and teaching

The two major outcomes of the project evaluation in terms of higher education learning and teaching are that the learning environment has to be seen as an extended and networked learning environment and that this new learning environment requires new approaches to learning and teaching.

Compared with traditional classroom based teaching, online learning provides attractive opportunities for teaching and learning outside the classroom. Teaching staff direct students to resources that are available online, for working on the course outside formal contact time. While in practice the learning environment has always extended outside classroom boundaries, the difference in the new extended learning environment is that it is a far more complex learning environment. The two main characteristics are that students are presented with greater freedom in terms of choice of content and approaches to learning, while paradoxically they become more dependent upon university support with regard to the technology employed. Students are required to interact with a greater variety of new learning resources and learning activities, and this necessitates more adequate feedback, monitoring and support to ensure that they have employed appropriate strategies and have achieved the learning outcomes. The networked element means that students and teaching staff need to rely more heavily on the technology than they had to do with other technologies, in terms of training, access and support. Without changes to the institution's system in these areas, greater freedom and choice through online learning will remain a hope rather than a reality.

There has been much debate as to whether the new technologies are changing university learning and teaching. Some of the ELEN project partners and other experienced users of online learning in higher education have argued that online learning is no different from traditional forms of learning, contending that it only needs to be more carefully planned and executed and better supported. In other words, it is more dependent upon good teaching practice. Although no clear pedagogic models have yet emerged, it seems that teachers have to become more aware of instructional design issues when creating online learning resources and enabling computer mediated communication. It is not sufficient simply to create content without building into the design carefully planned learning activities and tasks. Moreover, online design has to include the learner's own learning styles and ways of interacting with the learning resources. Unlike in the classroom, students cannot easily check with the teacher or other students their understanding of a task, obtain feedback or gain an insight into their progress and performance. Online learning resources have to build such facilities into the design in order to become successful tools for learning.

New approaches to support systems

Technology dependency is a major concern for online learning innovation. It is easy to blame all failures of the new technologies on the technologies themselves. However, online learning technology represents an immense hurdle for all users. This hurdle is by no means insurmountable but it requires a real commitment to appropriate support systems on the part of the institution. The ELEN project evaluation has identified the concerns shown in Table 12.1 that students, teaching staff and institutional managers have had with regard to support systems.

From the table it can be seen that concerns vary considerably from one user group to another, although certain concerns are expressed by two or all three groups, such as access to technology. The main problem areas encountered in the ELEN project were:

- Uncertainties about responsibility for student IT training and support. This was usually left to individual lecturers who were often unable to provide adequate training owing to large student numbers and lack of facilities and resources.

Table 12.1   *Concerns about support systems*

User	Concern
Student	IT training and support, access on and off campus, integration of online learning, support for learning (relevance of the use of technology, task focus, learning outcomes, monitoring of progress, feedback).
Teacher	IT training and support, access on campus, technical and educational support with project development and design, administrative support in the extended learning environment, integration of online learning.
HE institution	Reliable networks, information integration and management, project management, learning and teaching strategy, IT strategy, access to support.

- Problems with student access due to inadequate technical and support infrastructures. Mostly there were no communication and liaison with central computing services.

- While most of the 40 online learning projects started off with clear aims and learning outcomes, the problems with IT training, support and access often led to a shift in priority as far as the integration of online learning was concerned. As a result, online learning was perceived to have a technology, rather than a task or learning, focus and it was seen as a burden rather than as an opportunity. Moreover, in many cases where the technology hurdle was experienced, students felt that the approaches to teaching with technology were inadequate and that they were not supported appropriately to work independently outside the classroom.

- Project leaders were initially unaware of the great amount of technical and pedagogical support needed in order to develop online learning projects. Almost all of the partner universities provided excellent support and project management to their project leaders.

- Project leaders were often unaware of the great administrative support needs and institutions were unable to provide adequate infrastructures in this area. However, in some cases new staff were employed and attempts were made to develop automated processes. Moreover, some partner universities have begun to consider new approaches to information integration and management.

- The partner institutions have begun to develop and implement an IT and a Teaching and Learning strategy and to provide central access to support through the development of educational development units and the creation of new dedicated posts.

Organizational change at all levels: from local implementation to institutionalization

There is a commonly held misconception that all use of new technologies in teaching and learning is 'innovative'. In fact, most new approaches are *ad hoc* localized approaches led by enthusiasts with no impact on the curriculum or on the ways in which universities operate. Innovation, however, has a fundamental impact, as Silver, Hannan and English point out:

> Fundamental to the notion of innovation and the boundaries of its operation and interpretation is the fact that it is not concerned purely with what teachers do and the procedures available to students. It is a 'planned process' which has to be interpreted in policy-related, structural and cultural terms as well as in its immediate, operational configuration.
>
> (Silver, Hannan and English, 1998: 11)

The institutionalization of a VLE and the integration of online learning into the curriculum are truly innovative, as they require fundamental changes to the strategies, systems and infrastructures of a university. The TALENT project, also funded through TLTP3, adapted a transformation model developed by the MIT's 90 Research Group in the form of a profiling matrix. According to TALENT, the original transformation model described the impact of the new technologies on a higher education institution in five stages, the stages ranging from localized to coordinated, transformative, embedded and finally innovative. The first stages are evolutionary and do not require structural changes; the latter stages are revolutionary and do require significant structural changes (TALENT, 1999; Black *et al*, 2000). The four case studies in the box exemplify how online learning created a considerable new problem in the ELEN consortium institutions, namely user administration, and how at the ground level of individual projects specific strategies were employed to overcome the problem.

While some universities in Britain have begun to implement new approaches to user administration, many are still a long way from adopting such innovative approaches. User administration was one of the major concerns in the implementation of the ELEN project. These case studies show that online learning has indeed a very powerful dynamic of its own and that it requires universities to adapt. If the institution is inflexible, institutionalization will not be achieved and the most that can be hoped for are coordinated approaches at department or faculty level. There is a distinct proportional relationship between online learning and scalability. Small, localized approaches to online learning can be fairly successful. Large-scale approaches,

Case studies: user administration of online learning

Localized: no user administration

The course used online learning resources outside the university Intranet, but protected through a generic password. Discussion tools which were freely available on the Web were used in addition, and students had their private e-mail addresses. While this approach released the department from user administration, user verification became a problematic issue and the department was unable to use computer aided summative assessment, which it would have liked to introduce. Due to financial constraints, the department later contemplated the introduction of printing costs. However, a printing quota system would have required user verification and the department faced the same user administration problem it had initially successfully avoided.

Localized: manual user administration through individual member of staff

In this case, an Intranet requiring user registration was used. The resultant administrative burden was placed upon one individual member of staff. Registering a few hundred students manually was time-consuming, even though semi-automated processes such as batch logons were used.

Coordinated: manual user administration through a dedicated administrator

The department used computer aided summative assessment on a large scale and was therefore dependent upon user verification. The administrative burden was recognized early in the implementation process and a dedicated administrator was employed to release academic staff from the burden of administering users.

Innovative: automated user administration through integration of the student management system

The administrative burden was reduced to its very minimum in this model. The centrally held student data could be accessed and uploaded through identification of the course code at the beginning of the new academic year, so that students were automatically registered. This model relied on the successful integration of centrally held university data into the VLE.

however, in terms of large user groups, great distances, multiple technologies and the management of large amounts of information, are far more dependent upon the flexibility and adaptability of the institutional system.

CONCLUSION

The discussions about the nature and the dynamics of online learning and the findings from the ELEN project evaluation indicate that universities need to adapt to make the online innovation work. The framework for the institutionalization of online learning and the integration of VLEs presented here is philosophical in nature. Users at all levels have to recognize that online learning is a new phenomenon with specific dynamics. Online learning is based on the concept of a new type of learning environment, an 'extended networked learning environment'. It requires new approaches to learning and teaching, support systems, and the overall flexibility and adaptability of the institutional system. The new technology and its new opportunities require users to think holistically and to see the innovation and their own role in the light of the overall institutional system. The system includes the people, their beliefs and actions, the infrastructures and subsystems. Users have to become more aware of the interdependency between their innovation and their institution. The findings of the ELEN project appeared to confirm the validity of this philosophical basis. The project represented an immense learning opportunity for the people and institutions involved. Towards the end of the second year of the ELEN project the consortium partners already felt much better equipped to deal with future online learning challenges, although it was acknowledged that some changes to their institutions would be less easy to implement than others, and that they would require considerable investment in terms of time, effort and resources.

The ELEN project did not aim to achieve the institutionalization of online learning during its three-year existence. This would have been over-ambitious and unrealistic. Nevertheless, the institutions made considerable progress towards the realization of such a goal. The project raised awareness within the team of the issues surrounding the introduction of online learning and the integration of a VLE. The partnership enabled individual team members at all levels to compare their experiences with those of others in the team; to identify similarities and differences in approaches; to reflect critically on these from a multitude of perspectives; and to modify their approaches accordingly.

ACKNOWLEDGEMENTS

I would like to thank the project managers and participating staff and students in the ELEN project consortium institutions for their contribution to the project. Without them the writing of this chapter would not have been possible. The consortium partners were the University of Lincolnshire and Humberside (lead site), the University of Huddersfield, De Montfort University, Loughborough University, the University of Manchester, Middlesex University, Thames Valley University and the University of Plymouth.

REFERENCES

Ackoff, R L and Emery, F G (1972) *On Purposeful Systems*, Aldine-Atherton, Chicago

Black, A *et al* (2000) Institutional readiness for implementing network technology, *Networked Learning 2000 Conference Proceedings*, Lancaster University, pp 38–48, Lancaster University and University of Sheffield

Committee of Scottish University Principals (CSUP) (1992) *Teaching and Learning in an Expanding Higher Education System* (MacFarlane Report), Polton House Press, Lasswade

Department for Education and Employment (DfEE) (1999) *The Learning Age: A Renaissance for a new Britain*, (Green Paper) February [online] http://www.lifelonglearning.co.uk/greenpaper/index.htm [accessed 28 January 2002]

DfEE (2000) David Blunkett's speech on higher education in the 21st century, 15 February, University of Greenwich, London [online] http://cms1.gre.ac.uk/dfee/ [accessed 28 January 2002]

Diercks-O'Brien, G (2000a) *Developing Learning Infrastructures for the Successful Integration of Online Learning in the Curriculum, ELEN Project Evaluation Report, Phase 1 Projects,* University of Lincolnshire and Humberside, Hull

Diercks-O'Brien, G (2000b) Approaches to the evaluation of networked learning, *International Journal for Academic Development*, **5** (2), pp 156–65

Ford, P *et al* (1996) *Managing Change in Higher Education: A learning environment architecture*, Society for Research into Higher Education/Open University Press, Buckingham

Higher Education Funding Council for England (HEFCE) (2000) [accessed April 2001] HEFCE launches e-university business model (press release), 10 October [online] http://www.hefce.ac.uk/Partners/euniv/default.asp [accessed 28 January 2002]

Jenks, C L (1998) Evaluating educational systems design, *Systems Research and Behavioral Science*, **15**, pp 209–15

Keighley, H and Diercks-O'Brien, G (2000) Embedding key skills into the curriculum through networked learning: an evaluation of implementation strategies, *Networked Learning Conference Proceedings*, Lancaster University, pp 163–69, Lancaster University and University of Sheffield

Laurillard, D (1993) *Rethinking University Teaching: A framework for the effective use of educational technology*, Routledge, London

MacLeod, D (2000) Clever business, *Guardian*, 28 November [online] http://education.guardian.co.uk/higher/story/0,5500,403535,00.html [accessed 28 January 2002]

Moores, S (2000) Bridging the digital divide, *Observer*, 22 October [online] http://www.observer.co.uk/business/story/0,6903,386061,00.html [accessed 28 January 2002]

Russell, C and Peters, G (1998) Chaos has no plural: trying out a holistic approach to organisational learning, *Systems Research and Behavioral Science*, **15**, pp 235–48

Silver, H (2000) ELEN: An evaluation, University of Lincolnshire and Humberside, Hull (unpublished report). A second internal evaluation report for 2001 will be completed by September 2001

Silver, H, Hannan, A and English, S (1998) 'Innovation': questions of boundary, Working Paper 2, *EducatiON-LINE* [online] http://www.leeds.ac.uk/educol [accessed 28 January 2002]

Teaching And Learning Using Network Technology (TALENT) (1999) *Book of TALENT* (Profiling Matrix), University of Leicester [online] http://www.le.ac.uk/TALENT/book/c2p5.htm [accessed 28 January 2002]

13

Spreading the word about pedagogic research: the virtual reading group

Paul Curzon and Judith Harding

INTRODUCTION

The higher education sector is moving towards requiring that all lecturers have teaching qualifications, with the aim that teaching should be built on a firm foundation of educational theory. All new staff would take a teaching certificate during their probation, as advocated by Ramsden (1992). However, the first year of a new lecturing job involves high workloads, preparing courses and learning the way the institution operates. Finding time to read pedagogic research literature is hard. Furthermore, new lecturers will typically have no educational background, which makes it difficult for them to target their reading. New lecturers are also likely to have more initial interest in the practical than the theoretical aspects of their teaching.

Experienced staff can have similar problems. Traditionally, ongoing staff development has concentrated on short course provision. This approach has many problems, not least that of low take-up. Increasing workloads can lead to development activities being dropped. Staff may also be sceptical about the benefits of teaching related development activities and favour their subject based work. One result is that pedagogic research has often been seen as having little relevance. An innovative approach to this problem has been to centre development activities round programme development (Knight, 1998). Even with this approach, lack of time is likely to be an issue and if development is to be built around a sound foundation of pedagogic research, then a process for supporting continuous awareness of that research is needed. To be successful the process must have a light touch, be embedded in a supportive environment and encourage reflection (Schön, 1983; Beaty, 1997; Brockbank and McGill, 1998).

Any educational development should be based on the theory of teaching it aims to encourage. Ramsden (1992) uses the classification: 1) Teaching as transmission, 2) Teaching as organizing student activity, 3) Teaching as making learning possible, arguing that research shows that the latter is most desirable and is associated with deep approaches to learning (Marton and Säljö, 1997; Prosser and Trigwell, 1999). It views teaching as a cooperative exercise, overcoming barriers to create a context where students can actively engage in learning. Evaluation and reflection are an integral part.

THE VIRTUAL READING GROUP

The aim of the 'virtual reading group' approach described here is to complement existing staff development initiatives, overcoming the problems outlined above and in particular to:

- increase the familiarity of staff with pedagogic research;

- share the benefits of development activities;

- encourage reflection on those development activities; and

- encourage participation in both formal and informal staff development activities such as discussing teaching related problems and solutions.

There are many periodicals, mailing lists and so on that provide abstracting services. For example, the journal *Research into Higher Education Abstracts*, edited by Ian McNay for the SRHE, 'exists to propagate knowledge about, and discussion of, significant research into higher education'. Primarily, abstracting services are 'teaching as transmission of knowledge'. In preparation for a literature review, PhD students may be encouraged to write their own summaries of important papers, creating an annotated bibliography. Rather than using the author's or the given abstract students write their own, so engaging more in the research. Writing is in itself an activity that facilitates learning (Riddle and Harris, 1997; Mitchell *et al*, 1998). Depending on the role of the supervisor, this might form a part of a 'teaching as organizing student activity' approach. A reading group takes this further, introducing a greater level of engagement with the subject. Here the student leads a group discussion of an influential paper in an environment that encourages evaluation and reflection. A context has been set up that *makes learning possible*.

Learning groups can provide a very effective learning environment (Jaques, 2000) but a physical gathering of people in a particular time and place is no longer needed. Technology has made possible other kinds of discussion groups, far more flexible in some ways and more limiting in others (Valley, Steeples and Hynes, 1996). Many online discussion groups such as Improving Student Learning (isl@jiscmail.ac.uk) are devoted to issues related to teaching and learning and have successfully brought people together from around the world. Such discussion groups can bring problems, such as mail overload. There are so many messages that subscribers sometimes read only a small fraction. Worse, it is difficult to filter out the interesting messages, though this can be relieved using separate discussion threads.

Moderated groups ensure that mailings are restricted to the topic of interest of the group. However on its own moderation does not overcome the mail overload problem. Digested newsgroups, such as the RISKS newsgroup on computer risks to the public (Neumann, 1985) are a digest variation on the online discussion group idea. Subscribers send summaries of incidents and comments on previous summaries to a moderator who digests them into issues sent to the newsgroup. The advantage of this approach is that it cuts the number of mailings and reduces overload problems.

We describe here a 'virtual reading group' approach to support understanding of pedagogic research. Technologically, it consists of a moderated mailing list and Web archive. In social terms it is a group of people who wish to share their experiences about teaching. Members write reflective summaries of development activities they take part in and send them to a moderator who forwards them to the group, at no more than one message per week to avoid overload problems. Discussion on previous summaries is added to the end of the weekly message (so can be ignored when time is short). The moderator is not just a filter but the teacher within the 'teaching as making learning possible' approach.

The virtual reading group differs from an abstracting service as summaries are written by readers, not authors. The aim of summarizers is to communicate their enthusiasm for the paper, or an indication of how it has influenced them based on personal reflection encouraged by the writing process. They are likely to highlight different things from the author: only one aspect of the paper might be seen as relevant or interesting, for example. Furthermore, the reading group has the potential to provide a social element which cannot be provided by an anonymous abstracting service. It is this social element together with the reflective writing aspect that makes the service more than just an information-feed.

Setting up a pilot virtual reading group

A pilot virtual reading group was set up at Middlesex University to test the idea. The main barriers we aimed to overcome were lack of time and doubts over the perceived relevance of pedagogic research. In many ways Middlesex is typical of a 'new' university. All new staff undertake an 18-month teaching certificate, and it has been recognized for effectiveness with an Investors in People award. There is thus a recognition of the importance of ongoing staff development at the organization's highest level. Workloads across many departments are high, especially among new staff. Staff are also spread over multiple sites, making meetings hard to arrange and time-consuming. E-mail is used widely. However, mail overload is considered a problem by many, as highlighted by staff surveys: 'My problem is that I receive too much information' and 'There is an e-mail blizzard' are typical responses quoted in Goulding (1999) where the importance of informal contact was also stressed.

There were four elements to the virtual reading group as implemented at Middlesex: a group of people, a moderator who administered the group, a moderated, digested mailing list, and a Web based archive. Members of the group wrote summaries of pedagogic related development activities. This could be something that they read or attended. However, they only wrote a summary if they found it useful, interesting or inspiring. Summaries were short, just a paragraph or two. They included a full reference of the paper or event and a short list of keywords. They also included the e-mail address of the author of the summary so that others could contact them directly. Summaries were submitted to the moderator who sent one or more summaries to the mailing list as a single message, at most once per week.

The virtual reading group aimed to overcome the problem of lack of time to take part in development activities, so it was important that it should not be time-consuming. The fact that there was only one message per week was therefore crucial. Originally no discussion was allowed on the mailing list, for the same reason. However after approximately six months, this was changed as a result of feedback from the group. Members were then encouraged to send comments about previous summaries to the moderator. Edited digests of comments were placed after the new summary so that those with little time could ignore the discussion, and just read the new summaries.

Recruitment

Recruitment to the pilot (aiming for 20 people) started in June 1998 with the group formally starting a month later. A 'first issue' handout was written by the moderator to illustrate the idea. This consisted of a dozen summaries of various staff development events and sources written in various styles. Four people who read widely on higher education research initially agreed to write summaries to seed the group.

The group was advertised in several ways. A Web page describing its aims and objectives was written, which contained a link to the pilot issue. Messages were sent to a variety of internal mailing lists, such as staff who had just completed the teaching certificate. The moderator also announced the group at staff development workshops and induction sessions for new lecturers. At these events paper copies of the pilot issue were distributed, together with a sign-up sheet, so that joining the group involved minimal effort. Members were encouraged to recruit others by word of mouth. After the group had been running for approximately four months, an article about the group appeared in the university weekly newspaper. The low volume nature of the reading group was emphasized in all advertising.

Between 50 and 60 people joined in the first month, greatly exceeding the target. This increased to 71 members after 10 months. The importance of personal contact was realized at an early stage, so recruitment was targeted in this way. Most joined using the sign-up sheet, while the remainder were recruited by personal contact with the moderator. No one responded to messages broadcast to mailing lists or to the article that appeared in the university newsletter.

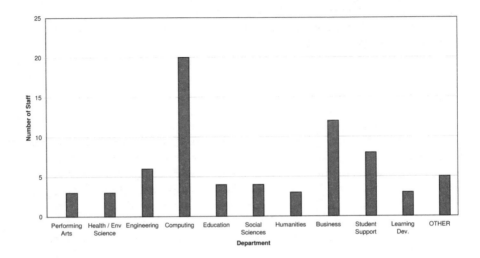

Figure 13.1   *Membership of the reading group by department*

The membership of the reading group was spread across the university (see Figure 13.1) and included new lecturers, existing lecturers from across the university, learning support staff and developers of resource based learning materials. All schools had at least three members. In addition, there was a large contingent from the student learning support services with eight members, and staff from the Centre for Learning Development with three members. Others were from the Quality Assurance Unit, the disability unit and a centre responsible for training for local industry. The school with the greatest membership was Computing Science with 20 members. The moderator was from Computing Science and over half of the group members from the Computing school were taking or had taken the teaching certificate. The familiarity of computing staff with the technology may also have been a factor. Other schools with a large group membership were the Business School with 12 members and Engineering with six. The schools with the smallest membership were Performing Arts, Health and Environmental Science, Education, Social Sciences and Humanities. Only 25 per cent of the total membership were taking or had taken the university's teaching certificate. Thus the group was of interest to experienced staff, and was being used as a form of continuous professional development. Group members held a variety of positions in the university.

It is clear that broadcast methods, while perhaps being useful as a way of raising the profile of the reading group, were not useful as a primary means of recruitment. Personal contact is of great importance and joining should be simple. Replying to a mail message was not simple enough; passing round sign-up sheets at meetings was. Many people joined after meeting the moderator and talking with him about it. Many of these people had previously received the broadcast mailings and thought the idea good, but had not joined. Factors that are of importance in recruitment to such a group are the enthusiasm of the moderator, the breadth of his or her personal contacts, and the ease of joining.

Submission of summaries

The moderator started the group by sending out an initial summary. Summaries were then submitted at the rate of approximately one per week (ignoring holiday periods) over the following year. The moderator wrote several which were used in weeks when submissions ran out to ensure that the momentum of the group was maintained. No summaries were submitted in the first six months by the staff recruited specifically to do so, due to lack of time on their part. However, they were not needed to the extent expected, since group members quickly started submitting their own. Submissions were spread across a range of schools, with three or more submissions from staff in Computing Science, Social Science, the Business School, Learning and Computing Support and the Centre for Learning Development (Figure 13.2). In each case the submissions were from at most two people from the department. The majority of summaries were written by experienced staff, with only one new staff member writing a summary. It should be noted that during the pilot, staff taking the teaching certificate were not explicitly encouraged to submit to the reading group as part of the course.

It was realized at an early stage that personal contact from, and reassurance by, the moderator was important to encourage people to make their first submission. The majority of submissions came after people met the moderator either by accident or at another meeting and discussed something they had read. People needed to be reassured that what they were considering writing was appropriate. This was confirmed by a survey (discussed below) where people were asked to indicate reasons why they had not submitted summaries to the group. The moderator therefore made a point of chatting informally about the group to members he met.

A wide range of sources was used as the basis of summaries including books, chapters in books, journal articles, workshops attended, technical reports, Web pages, newspaper articles and popular magazine articles. Summaries were also written on a wide range of subjects related to higher education including peer tutoring, resource based learning, multimedia based learning, assessment, student cheating, student writing, gender issues,

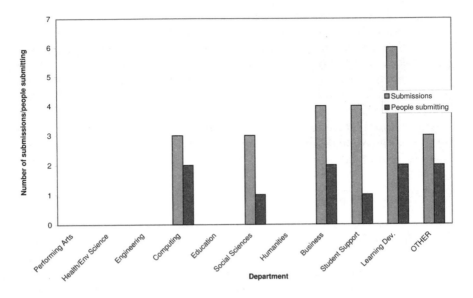

Figure 13.2   *Submission of summaries to the group by department*

and management in higher education. The moderator noticed that sub-missions were often simple summaries rather than reflective in nature, so he emphasized the importance of reflection in subsequent messages. On several occasions summaries submitted by one person led to threads where others were then prompted to submit summaries on related topics.

Feedback from group members

Early anecdotal feedback was generally good. For example, the following (paraphrased) quotes were communicated to the moderator.

> I hadn't thought there was any point reading educational literature, as I have so much experience teaching, but the group has led me to read more.
>
> (An experienced lecturer)

> I read the summaries but I just do not have time to write them myself.

> The group is provoking discussion – I overheard some people discussing one of the articles summarized.

This feedback was backed up by a questionnaire based survey conducted after the group had been active for six months. The questionnaire asked about the background of the respondents together with their views on the reading group and its effect on them. A total of 38 people returned the questionnaire out of 71 members of the group at the time: a 53.5 per cent return rate. The following percentages refer to the respondents of the survey rather than the whole group.

Fifty-five per cent of the respondents were female. The members of the group had a very wide range of experience in higher education. Roughly half had less than 10 years' experience and a quarter had less than five. The members also had a wide range of qualifications. Thirty-seven per cent had a teaching qualification (in most cases a PGCE) and a further 21 per cent were currently studying for one (in all but one case the university's teaching certificate). The members also had a wide range of roles within the university, and several people even gave more than one primary role. Sixty-eight per cent gave teaching as their primary role, with over a fifth giving management and another fifth giving research. Other primary roles included staff development, student support, administration and programme development. Sixty-eight per cent had read 'most' or 'all' of the summaries, with the remainder saying they had read some or a few.

Members were asked to rate the reading group on a five-point scale for the categories: how useful the group was; how interesting it was; how enjoyable it was; and how informative it was (see Figure 13.3). The responses to all these questions were generally positive. Fifty per cent said the reading group was useful, with only 24 per cent saying it was not. The remainder were neutral. Sixty per cent thought it was interesting with only 9 per cent indicating it was not. Sixty-seven per cent said it was informative and only 11 per cent that it was not. Thirty-nine per cent thought it was enjoyable and only 13 per cent thought not. After all the questionnaires had been returned, all members of the group were told at the start of the next weekly message how to unsubscribe from the group by replying to the message. None did. In fact throughout the year of the pilot no one asked to leave the group. Thus everyone was positive to the extent that they did not think it worth leaving the group.

In a further question, members were asked whether they felt the group had had any impact on their job. Eleven per cent gave a positive response and 71 per cent a negative response. This is perhaps unsurprising given that the survey was conducted after the group had only been running for six months. Other responses, however, suggested that the reading group had had some tangible effect. Sixty per cent said that the reading group had encouraged them to discuss teaching and learning issues with other members of staff. Forty-three per cent said the group had encouraged them to read more. Eight per cent had contacted the author of a summary to discuss it.

Only a quarter of the group had up to that point written summaries. However, 46 per cent said they were definitely willing to write summaries, with a further 11 per cent possibly willing. The reasons given for not submitting were various. The overriding reason (84 per cent) appeared to be the lack of time. Nearly a quarter of respondents thought they had not

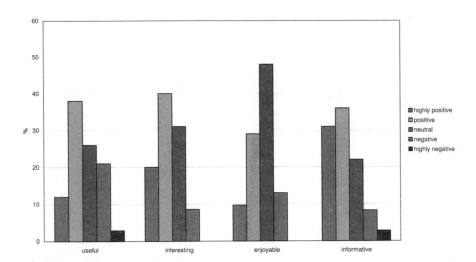

Figure 13.3   *Feedback about the group*

read anything of interest. Sixteen per cent had not submitted anything due to lack of confidence. This agrees with the informal finding that people needed personal encouragement by the moderator to actually submit their first summary. Anonymity was not an issue. Other reasons given for non-submission were 'finding things I want to communicate to the group', 'knowing what keywords to use', 'being able to do justice to what I have read', 'not sure of breadth of remit', and 'having nothing to say'. Even though only one person mentioned keywords, this was an issue as a majority of the actual submissions did not include them: the moderator had to add them.

People had only been allowed to comment on previous summaries for a few weeks before the survey was conducted. Only a couple of comments had been submitted up to that point. However the group was overwhelmingly positive about the idea (91 per cent). Given the issues raised about time and mail overload, it seems likely that had the group started with discussion that some people might have been put off joining. Starting the group as a non-discussion forum therefore may have been useful.

Only a quarter of the group had accessed the Web archive. Several people mentioned that they archived all the messages themselves. Initially a termly digest service was also offered. However this was not popular and so was dropped.

At the end of the pilot, the group continued for a further year and a half. However, the amount of networking done by the administrator decreased over this time, as did the effort he was able to put into the group due to new responsibilities. Submissions to the group tailed off correspondingly over the period.

CONCLUSIONS

The virtual reading group pilot was very popular and it achieved many of its aims for both new and experienced staff. Feedback confirming the informative nature of the group and that it encouraged staff to read more, for example, suggests that it helped to increase the familiarity of staff with the literature. The large group membership means that it increased the participation in development activities. Feedback also suggested that it encouraged informal staff development to occur.

During the pilot study only a small proportion of the membership wrote summaries: though those that did tended to submit more than once. As summaries were mainly written by experienced staff, one result was support from old to new. The lack of contributions from new lecturers was disappointing. Perhaps this could be overcome by tying the group more closely with the teaching certificate. Lack of time is clearly an issue that prevents staff from undertaking staff development activities, and this was a major motivation for setting up the group. A large proportion of the group indicated they had not written summaries due to lack of time. Many people also included informal comments on the questionnaire suggesting that they felt that lack of time was preventing them getting as much out of the group as they would have liked. However, of those mentioning time as a factor for not writing summaries, 58 per cent had read most or all of the summaries submitted. Thus the reading group overcame the barrier of time at least with respect to dissemination of information for these people. The Web archive and termly digest components proved less important than initially expected.

Personal contact was the most important issue both in recruitment and in encouraging people to write summaries, fitting the idea of the moderator as a teacher in the 'teaching as making learning possible' model. The moderator must be someone who naturally does a great deal of networking with a wide variety of contacts throughout the university and who regularly meets new staff. This was only partially the case in the pilot where the moderator had only been at the university for two years and had no formal staff development role. The way the submissions dwindled as the moderator ceased to network reinforces this conclusion. The moderator must be enthusiastic about the group and must be willing to write summaries. Ideally several people should be recruited to help maintain momentum during slack periods. However such people must be truly committed to the project and also have the time both to read material and to write reflective summaries.

We used a range of methods to evaluate the reading group and so allow the way the group was run to evolve. We collected anecdotal evidence by informally networking with the members of the group. This suggested to us that the group was having some effect on the way participants thought about educational literature and was leading to increased discussion. We also used formal questionnaires, which for example determined that the participants felt the group was useful, as well as a direct question to the group on a specific issue about the idea of allowing discussion. Furthermore, we analysed the activity on the reading group itself. By noting who made submissions and when, and the moderator changing the amount of effort invested, we were able to determine the importance of the moderator in the process.

The above evaluation approaches evaluate the extent to which the group is being used and is perceived to be useful. Such evaluation does not necessarily mean educational change is really occurring as a result of the group, however. Has the reading group really had any long-term effect on the individual members or the establishment as a whole? This is hard to determine for many reasons, not least that it was one of many initiatives being undertaken at the time it was started. Ways that we could use (though which at the time of writing we have not) include more detailed interviews with individual members of the group. A more effective approach would be to combine such interviews with evaluations (perhaps using SOLO style questionnaires) of the members both before they joined and at intervals thereafter. A control group of individuals not taking part in the reading group should be used. Such a study would need to be designed with care, however, if the effects of different initiatives were to be untangled. Most likely it is the combined effect of many different such lightweight educational initiatives in parallel that alters the institutional culture and so raises the level of educational development occurring.

ACKNOWLEDGEMENTS

This work was funded by a SEDA small grant and the Centre for Learning Development and School of Computing Science of Middlesex University. We are also grateful for the help of Ann Blandford, Kay Dudman and Di Parker.

REFERENCES

Beaty, L (1997) *Developing Your Teaching Through Reflective Practice*, SEDA Special no 5, Staff and Educational Development Association (SEDA), London
Brockbank, A and McGill, I (1998) *Facilitating Reflective Learning in Higher Education*, Open University Press/SRHE, Buckingham
Goulding, K *et al* (1999) *Final Report of the Communications Strategy Group*, June, Middlesex University
Jaques, D (2000) *Learning in Groups*, 3rd edn, Kogan Page, London
Knight, P (1998) Professional obsolescence and continuous professional development in higher education, *Innovations in Education and Training International*, **35** (3), September, Routledge, London

Marton, F and Säljö, R (1997) Approaches to learning, in *The Experience of Learning: Implications for teaching and learning in higher education*, ed F Marton, D Hounsell and N J Entwhistle, Scottish Academic Press, Edinburgh

Mitchell, S *et al* (1998) *Improving the Quality of Argument: Trial materials*, Middlesex University

Neumann, P (1985) Forum on Risks to the Public in the Use of Computers and Related Systems (RISKS), comp.risks online newsgroup

Prosser, M and Trigwell, K (1999) *Understanding Learning and Teaching: The experience in higher education*, Open University Press/SRHE, Buckingham

Ramsden, P (1992) *Learning to Teach in Higher Education*, Routledge, London

Riddle, M and Harris, R (1997) Literacy through written argument in higher education, in *The Quality of Argument*, ed M Riddle, Middlesex University

Schön, D (1983) *The Reflective Practitioner: How professionals think in action*, Basic Books, New York

Valley, K, Steeples, C and Hynes, P (1996) Information technology and flexible learning in *The Management of Independent Learning*, ed J Tait and P Knight, pp 74–86, Kogan Page, London

14

Professional development for organizational change

Helen Beetham and Paul Bailey

BACKGROUND AND RATIONALE

Higher education (HE) has played a pivotal role in the development of networked computing and the accumulation of global information resources (Brown and Duguid, 1998) and the UK HE sector has been among the world leaders in this field (NCIHE, 1997; JISC, 2001). Individually, many UK institutions have responded to the strategic imperative of the Dearing Report, 'to harness both the communications infrastructure and the growing and developing collections of high quality learning materials' (NCIHE, 1997) in support of their own students' learning needs. Responses have included the creation of new management roles, investment in information and communications technology (ICT) infrastructure, and strategic funding (Gibbs, 2000). Nevertheless, the current JISC five-year plan (JISC, 2001) reports that the provision of technology infrastructure and resources has outstripped the capacity of the academic community to exploit it. This concern is echoed in the latest Campus Computing Survey from the United States (Green, 2000), which found that:

> Two decades after the first desktop computers arrived on college campuses, we have come to recognize that the campus community's major technology challenges involve human factors – assisting students and faculty to make effective use of new technologies in ways that support teaching, learning, instruction and scholarship.

The literature on these 'human factors' tends to focus on Rogers' categorization of individuals as 'early' or 'late' adopters and to wonder at the apparent 'resistance to change' of the majority (Rogers, 1995). However, it should not be any surprise that academic staff have viewed the learning technology revolution with a degree of scepticism. While it has opened up higher learning to a global student body, it has also challenged the traditional activities, roles and cultures of people working in the sector (Schank, 1994; Goodyear, 1997; MacAleese, 1998; Somekh, 1998; Kewell, Oliver and Conole, 1999). There remains the vexed question of whether these changes actually make for a better learning experience for the students, in whose name they have been so vigorously promoted (see for example Noble, 1999). To what extent are new technical systems being used to substitute for contact time between students and tutors? Is there any evidence that students learn as effectively via computer mediated interaction? Is it an undiluted blessing for students to spend their college years in front of a computer screen in preparation for e-jobs in the information economy?

The agenda for using ICT in higher education is not a simple matter of encouraging teachers to adopt new tools and techniques. Learning techno-logies threaten to change us, as learners and teachers, as well as promising to help us cope with changes taking place around us. To some extent the experience of the UK's nationally funded Teaching and Learning Techno-logy Programme can be seen as confirmation of these observations. After fairly significant investment in the development of new computer based materials during phases 1 and 2, the programme's funders were distressed at the low level of take-up (Atkins, 1998). The challenge for UK HE was to embed new technologies into the curriculum in ways which enhanced students' learning, promoted whole-organization development, and left staff feeling empowered rather than threatened by the process of change. The EFFECTS project came about as a response to this challenge.

Methodology and model

The aim of EFFECTS, established under the third round of TLTP funding in 1998, was to develop a framework that could be adopted in a wide range of institutions to support staff in embedding the use of new learning technologies into the curriculum. The framework has been piloted at five consortium institutions, and the process has also been cascaded to a second tier of 'partner' institutions where further programmes have been developed. Programmes are institutionally validated, usually in the context of a post-graduate certificate or diploma in education. In addition to academic credit, participants can now also achieve a professional award in Embedding Learning Technologies, recognized through the Staff and Educational Development Association's Professional Development Accreditation Frame-work and providing a transferable qualification. This inter-institutional dimension, along with the EFFECTS consortium itself, provides a mutually supportive network of practitioners working as change agents in their own local contexts.

The EFFECTS approach has addressed the challenges outlined above by working at a number of different levels. At the level of student learning, the approach has been to involve staff as action researchers in investigating how their students can learn effectively with the technologies available.

Programmes have set out not to promote specific technical solutions but to encourage staff to articulate their own agenda for student learning, to develop a considered intervention (via a learning programme, activity or set of materials) and to evaluate the outcomes. Frameworks for understanding student learning with technology have been offered, but ultimately it has been the role of the practitioner/participant to translate these into practice in his or her own local context. Participants have also been introduced to a range of evaluation methodologies.

At the level of curriculum development, it was understood that the transformation of learning and teaching demanded new ways of working, especially of working with staff from outside the subject area: educational developers, resource developers and managers, learning skills advisers and other categories of learning professional. At this level, all five of the original EFFECTS consortium members had a history of support for small-scale development projects and of providing staff development opportunities to interested individuals. There were few examples of joined-up thinking, however: projects were funded with no requirement to evaluate or report on the lessons learned; workshops were held with no follow-on support for staff to apply new ideas in practice; there were few attempts to move beyond the immediate, practical concerns of implementation. Above all there were no mechanisms to recognize and reward staff with skills in this area. Longerterm support, development and recognition have been confirmed as priority needs by staff in a number of recent studies (Beetham, 2000; Ramsden and Martin, 1996).

The EFFECTS project addressed the integration of technology at both student and curriculum level through its seven *learning outcomes*, designed to follow a professional development cycle but with an overarching concern for student learning. Participants on all EFFECTS programmes had to demonstrate that they had met all of these outcomes, though this might be evidenced in a wide variety of ways.

> Outcome 1: Conduct a review of ICT in learning and teaching and show an understanding of the underlying educational processes
> Outcome 2: Analyse opportunities and constraints in using ICT and select ICT appropriate to the learning situation
> Outcome 3: Design and plan a strategy for integrating appropriate ICT
> Outcome 4: Implement a developed strategy
> Outcome 5: Evaluate the impact on student learning
> Outcome 6: Disseminate the findings of the evaluation
> Outcome 7: Review, plan and undertake appropriate continuing professional development.

From Figure 14.1 it can be seen that outcomes 1 to 5 describe a process of curriculum development through action research. Action research, as defined by Kemmis and McTaggart (1988), 'is carried out by practitioners

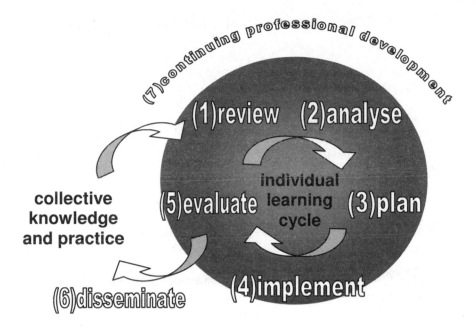

Figure 14.1   *The EFFECTS generic learning outcomes*

seeking to improve their understanding of events, situations and problems so as to increase the effectiveness of their practice'. The rationale behind the action research model was to encourage participants to develop their practice in a conscious, scholarly fashion in which they retained ownership of the process and its results. Outcome 6 provided an essential link between individual development and the collective experience of practitioners in learning and teaching. The rationale behind this outcome was to ensure that new findings, concepts, methods and learning tools were cascaded to other members of academic staff. In one sense this outcome was the counterpart to outcome 1 (review), through which participants drew on the existing knowledge and expertise of the community to help meet their own development objectives. Participants were expected to meet outcome 7 in the course of their work towards the other outcomes, for example by keeping a reflective diary of critical incidents, or by attending a training course in a specific technical application. Five professional values reinforced the focus on student learning and on the process of development:

1. A commitment to scholarship in teaching, both generally and in the discipline.

2. A respect for individual learners and for their development and empowerment.

3. A commitment to collegiality.

4. A commitment to ensuring equality of educational opportunity.

5. A commitment to continued reflection and consequent improvements to practice.

At the level of organizational development, there was a clear need to move on from *ad hoc* innovation to long-term strategies for embedding learning technologies across a range of institutional structures, cultures and processes. The project team were concerned that the focus on individual professional development might lead to unrealistic demands being made of EFFECTS participants. Surveys of organizational development in higher education (Wright and O'Neil, 1995; Lueddeke, 1997; Hart, Ryan and Bagdon, 1999) had shown that it required – in addition to staff with appropriate expertise – leadership commitment, a favourable departmental climate, good knowledge management and interpersonal networks, appropriate reward structures, and of course available infrastructure and resources. The project team therefore developed *guidelines for institutions*, based on lessons learned by the consortium members, to inform the development and embedding of EFFECTS programmes. There were three central requirements: participants must have access to appropriate support and expertise; the experience of individual practitioners must be used to inform institutional strategic development; and there must be a commitment to ongoing collaboration with other institutions, both in the development of programmes and in the sharing of practitioner expertise. The rationale behind the guidelines has now been incorporated into the recognition process for the SEDA Embedding Learning Technologies award.

Evaluation strategy

Ongoing evaluation and analysis of project outcomes was built in to the EFFECTS approach from the start. Like the project itself, the evaluation strategy needed to operate at the levels of student learning, curriculum development and organizational change. This meant that three types of information needed to be collected: the educational impact of the projects undertaken by programme participants; the resource implications of the programmes and of participants' work within programmes; and the transferability of the EFFECTS model within and across institutions. The intention was to analyse this information analysis against the criteria of 'intended use by intended users' (Patton, 1996).

Formative evaluation data was collected by structured quarterly reports from each of the project sites and was supported by an annual evaluation meeting of the entire project team. Summative data was collected during the final year by three external evaluators, using surveys and structured interviews with a range of project stakeholders. However, these two evaluation

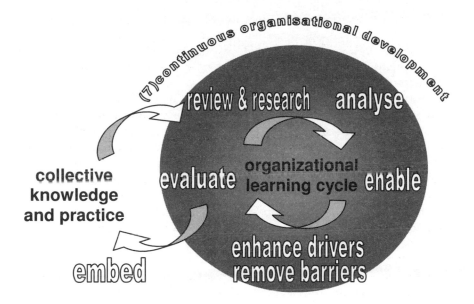

Figure 14.2 *Outcomes for organizational change*

processes were far from distinct. From the outset the project was intended partly as a research exercise to assess the impact of learning technology programmes in different institutional contexts. Information was collected and interpreted iteratively, allowing the project to respond to emerging trends. One unforeseen outcome of this process was the convergence of originally very different institutional programmes towards a more similar model, as lessons were learnt from each other's experience. It was also important that the external evaluators were involved as members of the project team, sharing the overall goals of the project, and that members of the project team were in turn involved in analysing and making sense of the information generated.

The EFFECTS evaluation strategy has been reported in more detail elsewhere (Oliver, Phelps and Beetham, 1999; Harvey and Oliver, 2001). The remainder of this chapter considers how curriculum, programme and institutional development were informed by outcomes at the various levels of project evaluation.

Evaluating the impact on student learning

Each of the many projects undertaken by EFFECTS participants (over 120 to date) set out with different aims in respect of student learning outcomes; therefore no single approach to evaluation was possible. Indeed, the aim of the project was for participants to develop evaluation skills appropriate to their own practice, rather than imposing a uniform framework. As a result, some learning outcomes have been formally evaluated, analysed and published, while others have been assessed through informal feedback mechanisms and shared only locally with members of the participant's department.

Some general trends have been noticed during the course of the project, however. There has been less interest than formerly in the use of structured courseware, with participants more likely to create their own learning materials using Web authoring tools and/or online learning environments such as WebCT. Computer assisted assessment packages are relatively widely used, particularly for formative assessment. Computer mediated communication has also become very popular as a means of introducing discursive activities and small group work into large student cohorts, as well as providing support to off campus students. The student learning issues of greatest concern centre around access and information literacy. There is a sense that students are relatively willing to engage with online resources but lack critical awareness and the skills of selection, analysis and evaluation. A related concern is the rise of online plagiarism, both deliberate and inadvertent. There is also disquiet over the difficulty of engaging students with online learning activities, and a growing belief (rightly or wrongly) that this is only possible where students have no alternative to online study, or among students with very high motivation and strong communication skills.

Evaluating the professional development of staff

An analysis of the individual EFFECTS programmes found that they had contributed to the development of groups of learning technology experts and change agents within each institution, many of whom reported that their professional role had changed as a result. Considerable benefits had been gained from the process of collaboration among programme teams, and the profile of learning technologies had often been enhanced within the institution. The very different programme formats demonstrated that the generic framework was flexible enough to adapt to local staff needs, strategic agendas and institutional opportunities.

A number of key issues were highlighted, however, which needed to be addressed in taking forward the work of the project. Academic credit proved to be of little incentive to the majority of academic staff, who already had PhDs and increasingly also had professional qualifications in learning and teaching (such as SEDA or ILT membership). Later in the project lifespan the learning outcomes were used to support professional development through less formal and non-accredited routes such as one-off workshops and semi-structured consultancy to projects, and these have offered further proof of the flexibility of the original framework. Some participating institutions have also focused on supporting participants to write up their projects for publication or presentation at conferences, as this was a more recognized route to recognition. By the end of the project some twenty had done so successfully.

The problem of academic workload was endemic. Although many participants expected learning technologies to help them manage their teaching load, they struggled to find time for the personal and professional development this involved. Face to face workshops were reasonably well attended if they were provided in a block during less busy periods such as the summer vacation, and participants clearly benefited from these at the outset of their projects. Ongoing workshops to support the process of development, however, were not. To ensure support during the crucial period of implementation and evaluation, most programme teams developed online materials that could be accessed by participants at any time. These, however, were poorly used. Overall, the most highly valued form of support was the one-to-one 'tutorial' or 'consultancy' session with an expert member of the programme team, a labour-intensive scenario that the EFFECTS project had hoped to replace with more peer learning. In future the situation may improve as EFFECTS graduates become sources of expertise in their own right, and as institutions recognize the value of setting aside staff time for personal and professional development.

From the end of year evaluation reports it emerged that most participants had worked successfully through EFFECTS learning outcomes 1–3 (review, analysis and planning) and gone on to implement the technology in a learning context (outcome 4). In other words, the programmes had been successful in getting participants to engage with relevant ideas, models, approaches and examples of best practice in learning technologies, and to actually embed ICT into their learning and teaching. There was far less evidence of participants successfully evaluating and writing up their work. Useful outcomes had been achieved, but generally through one to one support and collaboration with an expert member of the educational technology team. We hypothesize that there is a lack of expertise among academic staff in educational evaluation, reflection on practice and writing for learning and teaching publications. This is perhaps unsurprising given the prevailing culture of subject research. With few real career opportunities in learning and teaching development, there is also an understandable reluctance to commit further time to this process once participants have met their immediate objectives.

The process of co-constructive evaluation allowed potential tensions in the project philosophy to be articulated. Some of these centred on the difficulty of reconciling the individual and the collective interest in professional development. Because of the need to draw down institutional resources for continuation, EFFECTS programmes were often closely allied with management initiatives. There was also an overarching agenda to produce case studies of learning technology practice as a key deliverable for the project's funders. Against these collective interests, however, the underlying philosophy was to encourage individual exploration and development. Again, the conflict was most visible once participants had received sufficient support to get their own development projects off the ground, when their interest in evaluation and dissemination fell away.

Potential difficulties also emerged in reconciling the professional and academic demands of EFFECTS courses, although these are problems shared with other vocational courses that are accredited within an academic framework. In four of the accrediting institutions, the action learning cycle has been used to help resolve this conflict. Participants are required to develop a wider range of skills and concepts than are needed to deal with immediate professional problems, which equips them to respond to a wider repertoire of situations in future and also enhances the academic credibility and intellectual rigour of the programme.

Evaluating institutional development

The institutional impact of the EFFECTS project was evaluated longitudinally through baseline assessments and structured reporting, leading to a final case study from each participating institution. In a complex and rapidly changing organizational environment, it has proved impossible to distinguish the impact of EFFECTS from that of other initiatives and forces taking place in the same timeframe. There are many examples, however, of specific local benefits.

Institution A used the EFFECTS programme to prepare staff for working in a new learning centre, which included large, open plan areas given over to computer based learning. The first cohorts were chosen to attend by their line managers, but at the end of the course over 80 per cent said they would recommend a colleague to attend and 83 per cent would recommend a colleague to use ICT in their teaching.

Institution B had a culture that was resistant to large centralized initiatives, so the EFFECTS programme was targeted at 'cognate groups' of staff. The first group worked in a single subject area, and so formed a natural learning set to support one another through their learning technology projects. A second group shared a common interest in implementing a new learning environment. Participants followed a common development process and were able to share their experience across departmental boundaries.

Institution C found that professional accreditation was not highly valued by staff. Instead, the programme developers secured funding for a number of small-scale learning technology development projects. Successful bidders to the fund were supported through the project development cycle using the generic learning outcomes as a guide. Funding was dependent on participants producing a final evaluation report, a condition which helped to ensure that the lessons learnt in the course of implementation were made available to other parts of the institution and beyond.

At Institution D the EFFECTS project coincided with a new initiative to encourage a more student centred approach to learning. This provided an incentive to attend the programme and bid for initiative funding at the same time. Participants completing the institution's widely respected learning and teaching course were also keen to undertake further professional development. The demand for the EFFECTS programme led to the development of further masters modules – based on the EFFECTS learning outcomes – in embedding keys skills and workplace links.

A range of other institutions now have or are working towards their own recognized programmes, informed by the experience gained at the original institutions. On the whole, programme developers have been successful where they have built on existing strengths or piggy-backed on other institutional agendas, particularly by tying programmes of staff development and support into the funding of small-scale learning technology development projects. Institutional timing has also been shown to be crucial. Some educational developers who have attended EFFECTS national workshops have gone on to implement EFFECTS programmes, while others have tried and failed to make progress due to a range of factors which are summarized below.

At each institution, the EFFECTS project showed that the expertise to embed learning technologies could emerge through small-scale development projects, providing there was central support and a structured programme of professional development. Credible professional incentives (that is, career enhancement) were the strongest factors motivating staff to develop their skills, while lack of time and high workloads were the strongest disincentives. A common finding was that professional development initiatives should be integrated with other learning technology initiatives, particularly around the institutional learning and teaching strategy, and with sources of funding for curriculum development.

Learning technology was embedded into the curriculum most readily where the *department* had a supportive culture, but institutional commitment was also essential, whether this was manifested through funding awards, career progression or time off for development. Communication networks and opportunities to share experience with other practitioners were also essential. Technical infrastructure usually lagged well behind the ambitions of the most forward-thinking staff, and EFFECTS participants were often able to influence decisions on software purchasing and support, either by reporting on their own experience or by becoming members of working parties and committees.

At institutional level it emerged that professional development for academic staff was *increasing* the demand for qualified, educationally aware support staff, at least in the short term. Academic staff with the relevant skills were becoming sources of support for others in their department, and while this was one of the key aims of EFFECTS, these early adopters were often dealing with greater workloads with no accompanying rise in status.

Connecting personal, professional and institutional development: participants' stories

Connecting the different cycles of development was not a generic, one size fits all operation. Rather it depended on the use of a range of evaluative approaches to identify opportunities for intervention and change. This approach is illustrated through the stories of some individual participants.

Alan had an interest in using computer assisted assessment (CAA) to run formative tests with colleagues in his department. During the course of his review and analysis, he realized the greatest benefits of a CAA system would be for summative examinations. This would require integration of the CAA system across the institution, in collaboration with key areas of central IT and administrative services. To achieve this he started with a pilot in his own department which demonstrated the benefits of CAA, followed by an institutional audit which found widespread interest from academics. This careful information gathering allowed him to win senior management support for the purchase and integration of an institution-wide system.

Bill took over a large final-year module in computing and information science which had received poor feedback from students in previous years. He wanted to try some new methods of teaching while also showing that creative use of technology could improve student learning. He redesigned the module assessment around group research projects, asked groups to produce their own Web based resources, encouraged collaborative online learning activities and provided online support materials. Feedback showed that tutors spent more time supporting individuals, students developed new skills and the module was considered far more relevant to their overall degree. To highlight the issues identified in the project, Bill produced an institutional paper concerning the use of the Web for learning and teaching.

Carole was redeveloping an existing module for delivery via a new online learning environment. Her initial analysis identified a management team concerned more with the constraints of funding than with learning and teaching issues, and a team of staff without the skills to convert materials for online delivery. Through consultation with the EFFECTS team, templates were produced which allowed the existing staff easily to author consistent standard materials. However, standardization also allowed the management team to follow developments, and they soon offered inappropriate criticism which clearly showed their lack of understanding of the learning process. This demonstrated the need for professional development to be extended to the programme managers as well as the innovators.

Emil began on the EFFECTS programme as a lecturer with an interest in learning technologies and ended up Learning Technology Coordinator for the university. Through his personal reflection he identified that '[his] new role [was] built on a combination of skills and experience including teaching, research and the development and use of learning technologies. [He] must aim to remain up-to-date in all three areas and this will require considerable investment in continuing professional development'.

Many other accounts reveal how participation in an EFFECTS programme has had an impact beyond the individual most directly involved, at the level of the department, faculty, subject area or institution. Embedding learning technology is still largely the preserve of the early adopters or pioneers, and it is these individuals who are best placed to map out the difficulties which lie ahead. Providing institutional decision makers are willing to receive their reports from the front line, changes can be put in place which make the going less difficult for those who follow on behind. Without an EFFECTS programme, however, encouraging reflection and evaluation of the experience, it is possible that these pioneers may simply have continued thrashing through the jungle on their own.

CONCLUSIONS

The EFFECTS project has worked with other TLTP3 projects across institutional boundaries to build a community of common practice and understanding around the academic embedding of learning technologies in UK HE. There is a growing number of academics with experience of and interest in learning technology innovation. This is evidenced, for example, in the numbers presenting technology related developments at the ILT-AC conference (June 2000, June 2001) and in the national interest generated by EFFECTS workshops. However, the status of this kind of work remains contested, and the position of learning technology specialists remains even more precarious than that of their academic counterparts. The work of community building is hampered by the continued low priority of learning and teaching development in relation to other areas of academic practice, by the lack of a culture of CPD and an expectation of evidence-based practice in academic teaching and learning, and by the difficulty of achieving academic recognition (for example, through the RAE) for theoretical or evaluated work relating to learning technologies. The long-term impact of EFFECTS will depend on how these generic cultural issues are resolved. Our work in supporting participants to develop their practice will only have been valuable if that practice itself comes to be more widely recognized and valued.

REFERENCES

Atkins, M (1998) *An evaluation of the Computers in Teaching Initiative and Teaching and Learning Technology Support Network*, HEFCE [online] http://www.hefce. ac.uk/pubs/hefce/2001/ [accessed 28 January 2002]

Beetham, H (2000) Learning Technology Scoping Study: lessons for educational developers, *Educational Developments*, 1 (4)

Brown, J S and Duguid, P (1998) Universities in the digital age, in *The Mirage of Continuity: Reconfiguring academic resources for the 21st century*, ed B L Hawkins and P Battin, Council on Library and Information Resources, Washington

Gibbs, G (2000) *Learning and Teaching Strategies: Developments in English higher education institutions 1998–2000*, Centre for Higher Education Practice/Higher Education Funding Council for England

Goodyear, P (1997) *Ergonomics of Learning Environments*, paper to EduTech 97, Universidad de Málaga

Green, K (2000) *The 1999 National Survey of IT in Higher Education*, Center for Educational Studies of Claremont Graduate, University in Claremont, CA

Green, M F (1997) Leadership and institutional change: a comparative view, *Higher Education Management*, **9** (2), pp 135–47

Hart, G, Ryan, Y and Bagdon, K (1999) Supporting organizational change: fostering a more flexible approach to course delivery, *Association for Learning Technology Journal*, **7** (1)

Harvey, J and Oliver, M (2001) *EFFECTS Final Evaluation Report*, available from P Bailey, ILRT, 8-10 Berkeley Square, University of Bristol, Bristol BS8 1HH

Joint Information Systems Committee (JISC) (2001) *Five Year Strategy: 2001–2006* [online] http://www.jisc.ac.uk/curriss/general/#g1 [accessed 28 January 2002]

Kemmis, S and McTaggart, R (eds) (1988) *The Action Research Planner*, Deakin University Press

Kewell, E, Oliver, M and Conole, G (1999) *Assessing the Organisational Capabilities of Embedding Learning Technologies into the Undergraduate Curriculum*, ELT working papers no 2, University of North London

Lueddeke, G (1997) Emerging learning environments in HE: implications for institutional change and academic developers, *International Journal of Academic Development*, **2** (2)

MacAleese, R (1998) Comment: the coming tornado?, *ALT-J* **6** (2)

National Committee of Inquiry into Higher Education (NCIHE) (1997) *Higher Education in the Learning Society* (the Dearing Report), HMSO, London

Noble, D F (1999) *Digital Diploma Mills IV: Rehearsal for the revolution* [online] http://www.tao.ca/writing/archives/rre/0802.html [accessed 28 January 2002]

Oliver, M, Phelps, J and Beetham, H (1999) Implementing and evaluating a national programme of professional development in C&IT use, *Innovations in Education and Training International*, **37**

Patton, M Q (1996) *Utilization-Focused Evaluation: The new century text*, Sage

Ramsden, P and Martin, E (1996) Recognition of good university teaching: policies from an Australian study, *Studies in Higher Education*, **21**, pp 299–315

Rogers, E M (1995) *Diffusion of Innovations*, 4th edn, Free Press, New York

Schank, R C (1994) Active learning through multimedia, *IEE Multimedia*, **1** (1), pp 69–79

Somekh, B (1998) Designing software to maximise learning, *ALT-J*, **4** (3)

Wright, Q and O'Neil, C (1995) Teaching improvement practices: successful strategies for HE, in *Teaching Improvement Practices: International perspectives*, ed Q Wright *et al*, Anker Publishing, Bolton

15

Integrating learning technologies to support the acquisition of foreign languages for specific disciplines

Alison Kennard and Juliet Laxton

> We believe that the successful exploitation of Communication &
> Information Technologies (C&IT) is pivotal to the success and health
> of higher education in the future... What will be required... is a
> fundamental rethink of institutional priorities, an equally essential
> change of culture, and well-informed leadership. Above all, there
> remains an urgent need for institutions to understand better and
> respond to the challenges and opportunities of the emerging inform-
> ation age.
>
> (National Commission of Inquiry into Higher Education,
> *Higher Education in the Learning Society*, 1997, ch 13,
> 'Communications and information technology')

INTRODUCTION

The last decade has witnessed an important reconsideration of the role of
the university teacher. This involves a move away from the model of the
lecturer as transmitter of knowledge towards that of lecturer as facilitator
of learning. The effects of this change are particularly in evidence within
foreign languages provision, where communicative and task based methodologies are now commonplace and classroom practice is increasingly
motivated by the twin concerns of teaching what and teaching how.

One issue that has yet to receive sufficient attention within the literature
is the role of institutional contexts and learning environments on the
implementation of information and communications technology (ICT). This
chapter attempts to redress this. We use our experience on the ALLADIN
(Autonomous Language Learning in Art and Design using Interactive

Networks) project to demonstrate the influence of contextual factors on ICT implementation among art and design students learning a foreign language. While some of the issues raised are specific to art and design, others such as the consequences of casualization in terms of professional IT development, as well as training needs of full-time staff, have much wider implications.

THE ALLADIN PROJECT

The remit of the ALLADIN project was shaped in response to the HEFCE/ DENI Languages Subject Overviews (QAA, 1996) which pointed to the under-exploitation of language learning resources due to inadequate integration into teaching and learning programmes. It was supported by the Dearing Report (NCIHE, 1997) which highlighted the need for institutional strategies to guide and enable the student in the learning process.

Foreign languages delivery within the art and design sector attempts to meet these needs through the use of independent learning programmes and computer based resources. The scope for individual interest and flexibility which these strategies offer is of central importance to students of art and design, who are often committed to lengthy sessions of studio work, and demonstrate an above average level of learning difficulties and an idio-syncratic learning style. ALLADIN's findings confirm the value of a focus on the specific needs of learners from art, design and media disciplines, while reinforcing the general arguments in favour of ICT and independent learning for students of any undergraduate subject area.

Our research began by identifying how ICTs were being used in language delivery for specific disciplines. Our data reflected current practice and experience in the rest of the British HE community and supports what Laurillard (1994) defines as 'predictable findings'. These so-called 'replic-ations' include uneven uptake, a lack of subject specific materials and resources, the frequent grouping of art, design and media students within generic language provision, and uneven ICT competence of language tutors and their students. Staff development and student induction are therefore required here in order to maximize the use of available resources. As well as these common, generic issues, further considerations arose regarding curriculum design and the ability to apply ICT use to specific subjects that have been neglected in the past. In the case of ALLADIN, this involved the multifaceted HE provision of art, design and media disciplines.

THE LEARNING CONTEXT

If informed observation and evaluation are crucial steps on the road to change, there are many obstacles that lie in the way for the action researcher. Laurillard posits learner context and all its attendant ramifications as the central factor in evaluating the effectiveness of ICTs for educational purposes. In doing so, she offers the following caveat:

> When we ask, 'do learning technologies improve learning?' we have to remember the complexity of the system that can conspire against them working at all. When we aim to optimize the conditions for learning technologies to work, we must remember how complex the learning context is and how little control we have over any of it.

> (Laurillard, 1994)

The learning context of the art and design student is an interesting illustration of this 'complexity' of the system, due to the number and nature of the factors which influence their learning experience. For example, the art and design learning environment is characterized by lengthy periods of studio or location work which may be solitary and may contrast sharply with the more collaborative, classroom base common to those students majoring in foreign language disciplines. Moreover, art and design students from certain disciplines may display reticence about collaboration with their peers in view of the individualistic nature of artistic composition, where originality of expression is inextricably bound up with personal achievement. Although this is particularly marked for art and design students, clearly the competitive ethos of higher education can undermine efforts at collaboration in all disciplines.

On a more pragmatic level, the lengthy periods spent working in the studio or using block-booked technical equipment can present timetabling difficulties for the art and design undergraduate studying a language. This can make for frequent absences from class when the learner's priorities are more firmly attached to his or her major degree subject. ICT based independent learning can go some way to compensating for this lost learning time, as we shall outline further. The practical problems posed by lengthy timetable blocks also arise in other discipline areas such as the natural sciences, where half day laboratory sessions may take precedence over a one-hour language class.

A further major feature of the complexity of the art and design system is both a learning style and a learning need. Defined now as a learning difference, dyslexia accounts for 10 per cent of the art and design student population (compared to the UK national average of 4 per cent). Dyslexia is generally attributed to the predominance of the right hemisphere and 'visual' side of the brain, as opposed to the 'symbolic', text-based left hemisphere which is the seat of literacy or linear thought. Thomas West characterizes dyslexics as creative and visual thinkers who are particularly disposed to 'global thinking' and problem solving (West, 1991: 21–22). They are perhaps therefore well situated for exploiting the interconnectivity or possibilities for information selection which hypertext has to offer, compared to their greater difficulties in apprehending linear text on paper.

Allan Paivio (1986) provides a further illustration of the potential advantages that ICT can offer to the dyslexic learner in his description of dyslexia in terms of a dual-coded model of cognition. Here, non-verbal objects and events are represented in the form of 'imagens' (akin to West's notion of 'visual thinking'), as opposed to 'logogens' or verbal objects. According to this theory, recognition and recall are enhanced through the presentation of phenomena in both verbal and visual form. This has implications for ICT in terms of its support for multi-sensory teaching through textual, pictorial and audio representations. It should also be noted that the impact of Paivio and West's work touches the non-dyslexic learner in art and design too.

There is evidence to suggest that the learning culture in some art and design institutions has the potential to conspire against the successful implementation of learning technologies, particularly in 'complementary study' areas. This is in part due to basic practical considerations such as the timetabling incompatibilities mentioned earlier. More significantly, however, the nature of the relationship between art and design programme administration and the minor subject programme, in tandem with the academic support services, determines whether ICT-based learning is effectively embedded. Another factor is the employment status of minor programme (here, languages) teaching staff. This has implications across the board, since a recent report suggests that up to 50 per cent of all undergraduate teaching in the United Kingdom is conducted by hourly paid postgraduate tutors (Harris, 2001). A British lecturers' union, the Association of University Teachers, suggests that the level of casualization is higher in academia than in the catering industry. As a consequence, any model of ICT implementation that assumes a preponderance of full-time lecturing staff able and willing to undergo the requisite staff development is likely to be found wanting.

A brief overview of the art and design institutional context is therefore required here. British art and design undergraduates study within either an independent institution or an autonomous school or faculty within a university. Each art and design establishment brings with it its own global learning culture and its own pedagogical priorities. Prior knowledge of the individual art and design culture in question therefore has a direct impact on the possibility of bringing about change. In most cases, the language component of an art and design programme will form only a minor part of the overall curriculum. Thus dialogue and mutual support between major and minor programme component staff are essential to the process of embedding new practices and technologies into a learning environment.

The relationship between art and design staff and minor study area staff can prove to be a contentious issue. Communication and cooperation is not always easy to achieve between the two parties, particularly in cases where art and design tutors appear to need persuading of the role and value of their students' minor curriculum study area. This may manifest itself in the breakdown of previously negotiated timetabling agreements, or in a lack of knowledge of what is achieved in language classes in terms of key and transferable skills, through combining creative practice, language work and ICT.

This situation points to the need for active senior management support in order to ensure that when it comes to supporting the integration of ICT-based resources in a language curriculum, or any other component of a programme, it is more than simply a question of committing funds to the task. Engineering a fundamental acceptance through the learning culture is achieved through practical mechanisms for use, training, changing expectations, and policy.

THE ALLADIN MODEL

ICT offers a flexible learning model which maximizes opportunities for language acquisition in an art and design curriculum subject to certain constraints. The major challenge it faces at the level of implementation is institutional scepticism towards, or ignorance about, the broader pedagogic value of ICT provision, and the decisions this gives rise to. These include: an unwillingness to allocate anything other than language contact hours to ICT; a limited view of what art and design education comprises; a lack of investment in ICT skills and training for staff; and a tendency to regard ICT provision as a pragmatic rather than a pedagogical choice.

Then promoting the integration of ICT into a 'minor' curriculum subject, it is vital not to present it as an overwhelming task. When depicted as in the ALLADIN representation (see Figure 15.1), the process can look far more demanding and forbidding than it actually is. The proposed course design model is derived from practical experience of developing and delivering language programmes for art, design and media students which incorporate ICT-based activities. It offers an overview of an entire process, which can guide those departments wishing to set up language provision that integrates ICT for subject specialists. Our findings show that very few dedicated products exist to support language learning in these discipline areas and consequently it does not presuppose resource commitments over and above the institution's facilities and selected basic software.

The model represents the contextual features of the language learning experience and the place of ICT within it. The different elements of the process it illustrates can be investigated selectively or iteratively to take into consideration: maximum use of institutional resources and facilities; effective use of teaching and learning time; learner styles and strategies; and level of language learning and ICT ability. Our course design model comprises needs analysis, course re-evaluation, and staff development and student induction. It also presupposes transferability of learning through cross-referencing between discipline and language context, as well as the

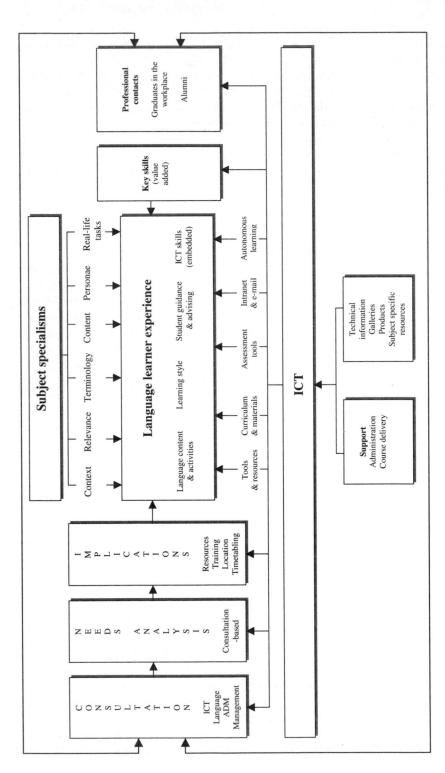

Figure 15.1 *ALLADIN course design model*

application of teaching and learning strategies to support learner difference (for example, through dyslexia support).

The model represents an idealized scenario. Few institutions will have the opportunity to start from scratch and include every element depicted. Feedback from industry which can be used to shape the course design process or influence content is also harder to achieve than is desirable. To date, professional evaluations of second language activity in the art and design workplace are typically made by enthusiasts, or those who have a relationship with the programme in question, and cannot be counted on to be entirely objective.

THE MODEL IN USE

Any stage of the model can be used to initiate discussion about changing practice in order to embed the use of ICTs in the art and design language curriculum. Project fieldwork activities revealed a number of points of interest to users of the model. In some cases, a prime objective was consultation and needs analysis as a means of starting a review of provision, followed by staff development workshops. In others, a major concern has been specific skills deficits, such as Web use by art history students learning French, or enabling learners to critically evaluate Web sites. The model also lends itself to adaptation and rescaling, depending on whether institutions wish to offer languages for specific purposes (LSP) or generic language courses available to non-specialists within an institution-wide language programme (IWLP). The model can also be used by non-art and design language providers.

In terms of teaching and learning methodology, the model attempts to clarify the relationship between course content and delivery media, while highlighting the opportunities for dialogue with the subject specialism. How far those relationships are intertwined becomes a matter of institutional or programme preference and raises the following questions. How far can art and design contexts be drawn upon in a multidisciplinary group without alienating specific groups of learners? How far do tasks cross over between disciplines in order to make meaningful, real-life language learning possible? Can ICT be a pedagogically effective means to support these activities, as opposed to something undertaken for its own sake? To what extent can we integrate learners from main and elective programmes if disparities of level exist in terms of language study and undergraduate study?

The student as autonomous or semi-autonomous learner and focal point of the learning process lies at the heart of these questions and relationships. Fostering learner motivation and independence in the use of ICT is therefore vital. Learners have to become aware of how they learn and of how tools and tasks can be matched most effectively. The student's own programme interests and creativity have to be brought to bear on the learning experience.

The tutor facilitates and guides every stage of this process. In an art and design context, major differences exist between the learning experience in the main programme and the language classes. An understanding of these differences is therefore crucial.

Our study of ICT implementation within the language curriculum has offered us the opportunity to review art and design language learners and consider whether or how far they differ from other discipline based learners. While we have focused on applying the ALLADIN model to create hypothetical profiles of art and design language students, the same model can be transferred to a range of other learners. Consideration of art and design students' primary learning environment therefore leads us to a greater understanding of their learning styles and expectations. Use of learning styles questionnaires or activities enable us to identify learning strengths (for example, visual and auditory), and inform our use of ICT to support their language acquisition.

Nevertheless, we must also ask what the limitations of ICT are in this area, and at what point we might encounter resistance from learner, tutor or department. In the project's experience, new users of ICT adapt fairly readily to using ICT-based grammar exercises and can see the usefulness of accessing subject related resources through the Internet. However, work on learner styles and learning strategies within independent or classroom based learning opens up the danger of resource fatigue. In staff workshops, recommendations for improving independent learning through the use of ICTs have met with mixed responses. Many teachers regarded ICT in the classroom as a diversion from 'proper teaching', which seems to imply that being a teacher precludes enabling autonomous learning. Similarly, the student may feel that such work is inconsequential and divorced from 'real tasks' such as report writing or project planning.

An important aim of the learning process must therefore be to ensure that using ICT-based tools and support materials renders the learning process more effective and achieves better results for the learner. This will be the learner's and the tutor's bottom line. Integrating ICTs with assessment instruments is one way to monitor the effectiveness of use.

EVALUATION

There are two ways of viewing the evaluation process. Roughly speaking, one can take a positivist-realist or a constructivist view. The traditional positivist-realist approach sees the evaluator's task as that of investigating a process or event as a set of data to be discovered or revealed by the evaluation instrument. A more radical approach has been proposed by Guba and Lincoln (1989) who offer a constructivist theory of evaluation. For a constructivist, the evaluation process seeks to investigate the created realities of the participants that:

exist outside of the persons who create and hold them; they are not part of some 'objective' world that exists apart from their constructors. They consist of certain available information configured in some 'sense-making' formulation whose character depends upon the level of information and sophistication (in the sense of ability to appreciate/understand/apply the information) of the constructors.

(Guba and Lincoln, 1989: 143)

The upshot of this theoretical framework is that evaluation does not proceed with the evaluator passive and disengaged, discovering the facts of the matter. Such a view is both philosophically naïve (Rorty, 1980) and empirically dubious. We endorse the 'fourth generation' approach to evaluation suggested by Guba and Lincoln. Our experience of the evaluation process during the project suggests that evaluation is very much an active process which involves a great deal of reflection in, and on, action.

A range of evaluative processes was incorporated into each stage of the ALLADIN project. Initially, traditional methods were envisaged, such as questionnaires and mail shots. It soon became apparent that a more proactive method of creating involvement in the project and generating feedback was required. As a result, the project team shifted their activities to running workshops with inbuilt evaluation, thereby gathering more spontaneous feedback.

Internal evaluation

Internal evaluation took place concurrently through the use of pre- and post-questionnaires at project workshops and reports from fieldwork institutions, on the experience and outcomes of working with ALLADIN, and the ways in which these could shape further dissemination and embedding activities. As a result, in-depth reflection has led to:

- the confirmation of workshop content;
- the evaluation of student attitudes and competences in using ICTs;
- the identification of staff and student training needs;
- shifts in project emphasis and direction;
- institutional needs analyses;
- the review of exemplar materials;
- the evaluation of existing resources;
- the creation of evaluative tools for both software and Internet information.

More specifically, evaluation enabled the project team to adjust direction by increasing the range of deliverables produced during the project. A significant example of this includes a move from solely IT-based tools (such as software packages and attendant evaluation tools) to communications technologies (such as online target language communities) which offered more flexibility for and relevance to the individual learner. In addition, we directed our focus toward staff development needs, rather than the mere creation of sample ICT-based activities intended as stimulus to further thought. The need to attract attention to the project's work through more light-hearted means also became clear. An example of this was running an online prize draw with guaranteed entry in return for feedback on the Web site and deliverables. This achieved its goal of attracting more detailed commentary from new sources.

A significant case of illuminative evaluation and reflective practice emerged during a training event for new users of ICT in art and design language provision. These tutors regarded ICT as a technology based route to resources that had already been available in printed form, rather than a qualitatively different learning opportunity. Certain tutors misunderstood the scope offered by ICT resources today, believing them to be largely confined to grammar-based drill exercises or ready-made packages, rather than raw material to be manipulated to suit one's own purposes. Experimenting with the possibilities of virtual learning environments, chat rooms and electronic discussion groups proved more of a challenge for low competence IT users than for those who were already creating word-processed teaching materials.

Resistance, or a lack of open-mindedness, was also a factor on these occasions. Communications technologies, including virtual learning environments such as MOOs (technically speaking, multi-user domain, object-oriented) often work on the basis of analogy or metaphor. Any unwillingness or inability on the part of the new user to 'enter into the spirit of the game' can block the capability of the tutor or learner to proceed with the use of these technologies. This led us to the conclusion that we should not assume even basic levels of familiarity with ICT on the part of staff. Such a conclusion was counter-intuitive since we had presumed that tutors would have a greater facility in using ICT than students. Thus we might propose that a major obstacle to ICT implementation may be staff unfamiliarity with new learning technologies. In certain cases, substantial staff orientation and training may therefore be required prior to implementing a curriculum with an ICT component.

External evaluation

External evaluators have been involved at several crucial stages in the three-year life span of the project:

- Formative:

  - at the start of year one: mapping use of ICT for language learning in the art and design community;

  - at the start of year two: identifying key areas for fieldwork, such as the development and testing of project tools and training opportunities;

  - at the end of year two: detailed assessment of project deliverables including the Web site and exemplar materials.

- Summative:

  - during year three: considering lessons learned and feedback on the usefulness of project deliverables.

Evaluation was originally proposed to form two cycles in the second and third years of the project. Each cycle was to involve six institutions as the basis for case studies to test out the integration of ICT resources and approaches to teaching and learning. As the project evolved, however, it became clear that a more broad-ranging approach in terms of potential audience and users would generate considerably more feedback and fieldwork opportunities than a 12-user method. The original evaluation plan was therefore replaced by a more diverse programme which allowed for both fixed, thematic workshops organized in a range of venues and staff development events organized for particular institutions.

Formative evaluation was carried out by a linguist/software developer at the end of the second year to encourage reflection on project deliverables such as exemplar materials and Web site. Summative evaluation was performed by a languages/educational consultant whose methodology incorporated structured discussions, monitoring of the Web site, observation of workshops, e-mail interviews with workshop participants, analysis of feedback questionnaires, and examination of records of activities.

It was agreed with these colleagues that any understanding of the project's impact on the educational sectors in question would be impossible to ascertain as early as the end of the project's initial life span. This agreement was based on the breadth of the project audience, and the time and effort required to plan, disseminate and embed learning opportunities for users who were harder to reach than originally thought. It was also due to the diversity of what the project had to offer and the equally diverse profiles of its potential users. This also influenced the decision of the summative evaluator to focus in detail on qualitative evidence as part of her activities.

CONCLUSIONS: A WAY FORWARD

By way of conclusion to our discussion, we will consider some of the major outcomes, lessons and policy implications that the ALLADIN project observed over the course of the last three years. To recall Dearing's recommendations on the use of ICT in HE with which we opened this chapter, these findings can be couched in terms of three basic areas:

A rethink of institutional priorities

- The implications of casual employment status of language teachers within specialist art and design institutions. While some sessional staff may be motivated by the opportunity for training irrespective of whether they are in full-time and permanent posts, others will be reluctant to undertake any additional training unless it is obligatory or remunerated.

- The need for senior management support in the embedding of ICT for post-project take-up and longevity.

A change of culture

- Users were sometimes surprised by the place of language learning in art and design education or the place of ICT in the language curriculum. Increased value can be offered through awareness of ICT possibilities.

- Assumptions about ICT ability, understanding and practice were over-estimated.

Better understanding of and response to the information age

- The role of the Internet and CMCs (computer mediated communications, such as e-mail and chat rooms) emerged as critical in embedding new technologies in art and design learning.

- Parity in terms of delivery and availability of resources for different student groups on the same module/course is required.

- A shift in teaching and learning methods is needed when using ICTs compared to using traditional media.

Thus, any attempt at ICT implementation must take into account a wide range of contextual factors and be sensitive in dealing with all the parties involved. Moreover, one can only work with the materials at hand. No successful ICT project can be based upon unrealistic expectations about levels of staff training and motivation, the amount of institutional support or the willingness of students to devote extra time to ICT. ICT implementation calls upon us to negotiate the subtle and sometimes frustrating dialectic of reality and expectations.

REFERENCES

Guba, E G and Lincoln, Y S (1989) *Fourth Generation Evaluation*, Sage, Newbury Park, CA

Harris, T (2001) Wanna study? Start teaching, *Guardian*, 3 April, p 45

Laurillard, D (1994) How can learning technologies improve learning?, *Law Technology Journal*, **3** (2) [online] http://www.law.warwick.ac.uk/ltj/3-2j.html [accessed 28 January 2002]

National Committee of Inquiry into Higher Education (1997) *Higher Education in the Learning Society* (the Dearing Report), HMSO, London. Ch 13, Communications and information technology [online] http://www.leeds.ac.uk/educol/ncihe/nr_202.htm [accessed 28 January 2002]

Paivio, A (1986) *Mental Representations: A dual coding approach*, Oxford University Press, Oxford

Quality Assurance Agency (QAA) (1996) *Subject Overview Reports: Languages (various)*, QAA for Higher Education, Gloucester

Rorty, R (1980) *Philosophy and the Mirror of Nature*, Blackwell, Oxford

West, T (1991) *In The Mind's Eye: Visual thinkers, gifted people with learning difficulties, computer images, and the ironies of creativity*, Prometheus, Buffalo, NY

Structures for facilitating play and creativity in learning: a psychoanalytical perspective

Mary Caddick and Dave O'Reilly

INTRODUCTION

This chapter originated in the Fund for the Development of Teaching and Learning project at the University of East London to disseminate 'The Atelier Principle in Teaching'. During that project, the current author worked closely with the Deputy Head of the School of Architecture, Nick Weaver, and an educational developer, Dave O'Reilly, to investigate and articulate the processes of learning and teaching in the atelier (or design studio or unit). Each of us brought a distinctive perspective to that task. Nick was best placed to conceptualize the atelier principle from within the discipline (Weaver, 1999). Dave introduced problem based learning as a bridge to wider debates about active learning in groups (O'Reilly, Weaver and Caddick, 1999). My own contributions were to bring a perspective from my training in psychoanalytical observation of infants and children at the Tavistock Clinic in London and a professional background in art practice, art education and art therapy. As well as presenting a series of papers together at national and international conferences, we explored the possibilities of capturing the atelier process on video, which I draw upon in this account (Caddick, 1998). Mention is also made of the tutor training programme which we established as a mode of dissemination, discussed in greater detail elsewhere (Weaver, O'Reilly and Caddick, 2000).

Essentially, the atelier method of teaching involves a group of students (usually 10 to 20) working with one or two tutors, who are often practising architects teaching part-time, through a year-long cycle of design. In this chapter the focus is on what a psychoanalytical perspective might tell us about the psycho-dynamics of the atelier process, particularly in relation to creativity. Beyond that I make some tentative extrapolations to learning and teaching in higher education generally and how creative learning may be inhibited in massified and modular institutional cultures. To justify the wider implications of studying the atelier method, we might note that both Donald Schön and Ernest Boyer have extolled its virtues as a model of learning and teaching that other disciplines might adopt or adapt (Schön, 1987; Boyer and Mitgang, 1996). Yet, as Ochsner has written:

> Other than the work of Schön and a few other, there seems to have been surprisingly little examination in depth of the design studio as an educational environment. In particular, there seems to have been almost complete silence on two inter-related questions: (1) the precise nature of the creative processes in which students are asked to engage in the design studio; and (2) the character of the interaction between students and faculty that might enhance this interaction.
>
> (Ochsner, 2000)

Like Ochsner I will seek to address these two questions from a psycho-analytical perspective, though my preoccupation is more with the group experience and the atelier as a container, whereas Ochsner focuses more on the tutor–student interaction, in analogy with the therapist–client inter-action in analysis.

PLAY, CREATIVITY AND EDUCATION

Before we consider the findings in the atelier itself, it would seem useful to draw some boundaries around the key terms of play, creativity and education. With regard to play and creativity of infants and children, Sylva explains that skills are gained and development takes place because 'play increases self esteem, opens the mind to new possibilities and teaches problem solving skills' (Sylva, 1984). This is no less important for students: indeed, Stephenson's research on independent study students shows the growth of self-esteem as a key factor underpinning the capability of independent learning (Stephenson, 1988). One of our graduating tutor trainees offers the following reflection on her education and the value of play:

> The kindergarten was surely one of my most favourite institutions I passed through during my educational career. For three years I went every day to go and play. In my view playing is the perfect way to learn since it follows one's own curiosity. I see education as something that should develop the whole person not just a narrow academic training. . . education is the building of character and not the accumulation of knowledge.
>
> (Ulrike Steven, July 2000, Reflection on my education)

Yet definitions of education can be as ambiguous as definitions of art, play and creativity:

> The word art – a word as ambiguous as the word education. . . when I speak of art I mean an education process, a process of upbringing: and when I speak of education I mean an artistic process, a process of self-creation. As educators, we look at the process from the outside; as artists, we look at the same process from the inside; and both processes, integrated, make a complete man [or woman].

> (Read, 1970)

But what is needed to support this process of 'self-creation'? How do play and creativity develop?

Psychotherapists and psychologists recognize that play is essential to development. Play starts from the very beginning and has been observed *in utero*. Twins have been observed following each other's hands on either side of the membrane that separated them in the womb, and as toddlers these same twins were observed playing in a similar way with a curtain between their hands. From the very beginning play is interpersonal, a social process. Play is not vital for the biological survival of the body, as are eating and sleeping, but it is vital for psychological survival in society. 'What all analytic orientations have in common, however, is a belief that play has meaning, and that even play of the most meaningless kind has meaning' (Alvarez, 1992).

Infants gain many life skills through the experience of play. Skills are gained and development takes place. Playing in a safe playground encourages exploration and discovery and 'one of the objectives of play in general is to give the child opportunity to explore the boundary between the 'real' and the "make-believe"' (Bruner and Sherwood, 1976). But playgrounds can become danger-grounds and the players may freeze or get blocked, their learning, development and enjoyment damaged. Playing and sociability may have innate beginnings, but it seems it is the quality of the early environment that develops or inhibits this potential. As Robertson observed, the under-stimulation of one infant resulted in retarded development, his potential being left unrealized. The infant 'did not have the incentive to perfect and practise his skills or to explore his surroundings' (Robertson, 1965). The implications for care givers and educators are far-reaching. As many educators recognize, a slow child/student is not necessarily born that way, and reparative care which involves guided stimulating play may be literally life-transforming.

In complementary play with the mothering person, the infant gains symbolic functioning in which 'self' and 'other' come to be perceived as distinct. Vygotsky argues that 'a child does not behave in purely symbolic fashion in play; rather he wishes and realizes his wishes by letting the basic categories of reality pass through his experience. The child in wishing carries out his wishes. In thinking he acts' (Vygotsky, 1978).

With this development children are no longer held hostage to the meanings of objects; they can experience possessing an object and can come at the world creatively; an exciting, empowering and efficacious experience. As Alvarez explains, 'In play the emphasis changes from the question of "what does this object do?" to "what can I do with this object?"' (Alvarez, 1992). Winnicott sums this up very simply, 'playing is doing' (Winnicott, 1971).

The shift from 'what is the object?' to 'what can I do with it?' is clearly visible in art and design subjects and forms a core educational aim. The art/design student is creating a thing that has not existed before. Aristotle had three separate modalities of thinking, *theoria*, *praxis* and *poiesis*, each with its distinct form of knowledge and realm of applicability (Squires, 1999). *Theoria* is concerned with *episteme*, the immutable knowledge relating to the underlying order of things, which has become the ideal model of (theoretical) knowledge in the university. *Praxis* in contrast is concerned with *phronesis*, the ability to engage in human/social affairs and is more akin to practical savvy or professional competence. However, art and design subjects make particular use of the third way of thinking, *poiesis*, which is concerned with *techne*, the making of things. This shift to 'what can I do with the object', from expectant passivity to informed activity, is surely the prime aim of problem based learning and, one hopes, the aim of education.

THE ATELIER AS A CONTAINER FOR CREATIVITY

How does the School of Architecture at the University of East London contain or hold the uncertainty, creativity and serious play involved in art and design? How does it support staff and students in generating solutions to the open-ended problems of design?

It seems helpful to pursue the analogy of children in the family in considering how the school works. The school itself is like a family and each unit within the school has the feel of a family, with all the ups and downs of family life. The units are run by part-time practitioner tutors, and these tutors are like siblings, with the small core of full-time staff in the role of the parents, aunts and uncles. The head of school is the figurehead and gives the architectural direction, while the deputy head gives the educational direction. The deputy head is in school all the time, keeping the place running with his ear to the ground, making sure the tutors and students are treated respectfully, thoughtfully; that their physical space is respected and maintained as a safe playground, both the private space of their unit room/home and of the shared public spaces – no mean feat in a university with a culture of mixed use and continuous use rooms. This quiet work, underpinned by principles of care and respect, has much to do with the school's success and yet often goes unnoticed, not unlike the work of mothers and housewives.

The dynamic of the individual units in the school have features which resemble family life. The unit is a container for the activities, interactions and development of its individual members, just as in a healthy family. Each unit has its own identity and way of doing things. One unit might study greenwood in Dorset, which involves construction using unseasoned wood, and another investigates the 'hinges' between wealthy and poor areas of London, just as some families recreate themselves in city amusement arcades, while others walk in the countryside. One tutor made the following reflection:

> The unit is really a working relationship among a group of people and at its best is a kind of family. Families need to sit down together at tables and discuss things and work together and make joint decisions about things. In the studio we always make each year a big table basically big enough for everyone to sit around.

> (Deckker, 1998)

Families have a common culture, and each unit has the year's project and tutor's culture at its centre. Each student is respected as an individual and can approach the project differently. Sometimes students will join up to work together, other times they work alone. Mixed years in the units (years two and three together, and years four and five together) add to a family feeling of older and younger siblings. But just as the siblings/students can help each other, for example the second years often help the third years before the final assessment, so too there can be a struggle to have their different needs met. Second years will see what will be demanded of them in the third year, and third years can be provoked into action by the strong work of the second years.

Families and units have a home that is their own with a door that locks, as well as public spaces where they can spread out. Just as families meet up and compare parenting and the offspring's development, so too students and teachers meet at reviews, juries and assessment to discuss educational development from the experience of both the teachers and the students. Children from different families meet in social playgrounds, while students from different units meet at lectures, workshops and in open work spaces or the canteen. Families have different cultures strongly influenced by the parents. Unit tutors are expected to develop and research their interests with the students, creating a unit culture. Some units work together around a communal table, listening in to conversations and tutorials, whereas in others the students disperse around the school and meet in private to talk to the teachers. Some parents are at home more than others, and some tutors are in school often, while others less so, some extending their contact through e-mail and tutorials in their office. Occasionally there are one-tutor units, one-parent families which stay together, like the others, 'for better for worse' for one academic year.

To extend the family metaphor, some other methods of teaching in higher education can be viewed more like a series of foster homes with broken or lost continuity of contact, forgotten names and unknown students. This evidently frustrates and disappoints both students and tutors. Tutors miss seeing how students progress through the year, but also find that with too many students to be able to hold in mind, teaching enjoyment turns into more of a strain. Just as broken homes can disrupt development, perhaps the equivalent in higher education disrupts educational development.

A common phrase heard in psychoanalytic circles is that the health of the family depends on the health of the mother or mothering person. This rings true in higher education. In some schools many tutors feel that they are not bringing to their teaching what really interests them, their own research, firing the students up with this while benefiting from the challenge themselves. Rather, they become a form of technical support or they repeat lessons time and again. This evidently dismays tutors and students alike, and engagement and enthusiasm wane on both sides. As one of the school's tutors explains:

> I think the unit system has advantages for both sides. For me it has the advantage that I can pursue research into ideas which I am not able to do in practice. For the students it has the advantage of working with a good architect who can show them how ideas and interests influence the design of buildings and the perception of buildings.

> (Deckker, 1998)

In the rest of the university, which follows the modular system, time and money is being spent on a system to track students because students get lost. Tracking offers a short-term remedy but does not address the cause or prevention of the problem. In the School of Architecture, because of the engagement and shared responsibility between the tutors and students in each unit and because students are known and seen every week by the same tutor in his or her own room, they quickly have a sense of belonging. It is just about impossible for a student to disappear without this being noticed after a few days.

Because the units stay together for a whole year, storms have to be lived through by both tutors and students and disappearing is not an option. Observing the units in the school I have often been reminded of aspects of psychotherapy. In therapy the ups and downs of the therapeutic relationship have to be lived through as part of the process of successful therapy. Clients in therapy, not unlike students in the units, learn to take a share in the responsibility of the work being undertaken. Students are challenged in their relationships with the authority figures, their tutors, and how this relates to their experience of authority in their family lives. In therapy the client often works through expectations of the perfect therapist in order to reach an understanding of the 'good enough' therapist. In therapy the careful and disciplined protection of the time and place for the therapy work, and the continuity of regular contact between the therapist and client, are necessary structures, and this paper argues that similar structures are valuable in the facilitation of play and creativity in teaching and learning in higher education.

Creativity has been described as 'to be and to dare'. Just as infants need a play partner to feed back/reflect back to help them play through something that they cannot talk through, so the student benefits from finding a play partner in the teacher. The play partner, teacher or mothering person has to satisfy many requirements to fulfil the role, but the most important of these is that she too can play and reflect back what is happening in the successes and failures of the playing and creativity. In this way and vitally, an infant or learner experiences that it is safe and permissible to make mistakes, to be imperfect and that it can be valuable to make mistakes as a way of learning.

Many times in the atelier I observed how students become quiet and disappointed in a discussion on why their work has not been 'successful', especially when the work is the result of beginning to take risks. We the teacher/facilitator know that the discussion may be the most informing and developmental of the day, more exciting and educational than the 'well done' commentary, but the students' disappointment reduces their confidence which in turn reduces their openness. It is thrilling when students and teachers alike realize that it is in the engagement and even the struggle of the problem solving, rather than only in the correct solution, that lie excitement, enjoyment and value, that to get it wrong can be the best way to learn, and trying only to get it right can retard. This is the confidence that comes through play and fuels creativity, the confidence 'to be and to dare'. Some infants, some students (and indeed some tutors) lack the confidence and ability to play. Psychoanalytic ideas on the reasons for this may help us to find ways of supporting students (and tutors) with these difficulties.

LESSONS LEARNT

The School of Architecture at UEL is by no means perfect, and there are difficulties and complaints. The school takes risks, which is why it is so alive, but that too brings failures as well as successes. As we all know, the family is not always a healthy place. Families can smother, neglect, abuse, dominate, imprison and so on. Similar problems can take place in units behind shut doors. Unlike families, however, the units are watched over and discreetly managed to make sure such problems are minimized. Good management is essential. Training for the tutors, and educational development and support for them, will also help, not least in making space for reflection on their own experiences of learning and giving opportunities to explore their own creative process. And of course students are not children dependent on their tutors.

The more that governments cut teaching hours, the greater the need for well trained teachers. So also is the need for conditions that contain the students and support their educational engagement even in the absence of teaching staff. Institutions are challenged to find creative ways to ensure real educational experiences. The School of Architecture at UEL illustrates the value of small groups of students having a space they can call their own in which they can work, remain in regular contact and share responsibility with each other and with their teachers. Just as in therapy much of the work happens between sessions, so too much educational work happens between the periods of organized teaching. The school's physical and interpersonal structures go some way to contain the student and facilitate learning, limiting possible damage by an untrained, weak or preoccupied tutor and supporting the students' learning processes in the absence of the tutor.

Play is a powerful process, a tool to be handled with care. Teachers need to be aware that students may come into higher education with disturbed experiences of play and the playground and will react accordingly when brought into the arena of play. On the other hand many art and design students are offered what appears to be a very open playground, but find that it is not safe or conducive to play because the ground rules – boundaries of the educational process, including assessment – are unclear or even invisible. Because art and design draw very much on the individual and what the individual brings, the results of their play can feel very personal, and a rejection of the work can be experienced as a rejection of the whole of their being. The person and the work produced need to be disentangled. The assessment criteria need to be clear to help the students do this, and the language used in teaching needs to support a safe place to play.

Care for the other on a fundamental level is very important to good teaching and learning, care that holds and contains. This care is not sentimental, a projection of the teacher's own needs, nor to be confused with weakness, but care that is grounded in awareness and insight of oneself and towards others. Some psychotherapists believe that successful therapy involves the act of love. Research into 'How six outstanding math professors view teaching and learning: the importance of caring' found, 'The most compelling finding of this study is the caring and concern for students expressed by all six of these math professors. Clearly they view caring as one of the most important characteristics of good university teaching' (Weston and McAlpine, 1998).

Care in teaching which comes from awareness and insight endorses the human scale, interpersonal learning structures which will support and contain play, the taking of risks and creativity. But the institution's physical and management structures need to support this care, and once established these caring physical structures can aid a good enough teaching and learning experience even in the absence of caring or 'good' teaching.

CODA: OBSERVING WITHIN THE ATELIER

It is not within the remit of this paper to discuss in detail the influence of the observer on the observed. Such a discussion would be fascinating but would demand another paper in its own right. Before my work at the university I had experienced observing a baby for one hour, one day a week in the home for two years as part of my training at the Tavistock Clinic. We were very carefully instructed in our observer role and discussed the role of the observer and the possible effect on the observed on many occasions. I approached my role in the university very differently, but informed my work with the understanding and sensitivity I had learnt from my Tavistock experience. At the university I became something akin to an explorer reporting on my experience. I became a member of the atelier for a year, but I was neither a teacher nor a student, something in-between observing both parties at work. I became friends with the students and the tutors. I went away for two weeks with them on their unit trip. I tried to be very clear about my role, aims and objectives and was experienced as a benevolent member of the group, spared the responsibility for the teaching and learning and nearly free of anxieties regarding the outcome of the atelier's year. As I reflect now on the work I undertook in the atelier I wonder whether I was perhaps somewhat naïve in not going about problematizing the business of being an observer, but perhaps in this context my approach was appropriate.

REFERENCES

Alvarez, A (1992) *Live Company: Psychoanalytic psychotherapy with autistic, borderline, deprived and abused children*, Tavistock/Routledge, London

Boyer, E L and Mitgang, L D (1996) *Building Community: A new future for architectural education and practice*, Carnegie Foundation for the Advancement of Learning, Princeton, NJ

Bruner, J and Sherwood, V (1976) *Play, Its Role in Development and Evaluation*, Penguin, Harmondsworth

Caddick, M (1998) *The Atelier Principle in Teaching: The experience*, videotape available in VHS or PAL format from the School of Architecture, University of East London

Deckker, T (1998) Interviewed in Caddick (1998) *The Atelier Principle in Teaching: The experience*, videotape available in VHS or PAL format from the School of Architecture, University of East London

Ochsner, J K (2000) Behind the mask: a psychoanalytic perspective on interaction in the design studio, *Journal of Architectural Education*, May, pp 53–54

O'Reilly, D, Weaver, N and Caddick, M (1999) Developing and delivering a tutor training programme for problem based learning: a case study in architecture, in *Research and Development in Problem Based Learning*, ed J Conway, D Melville and A Williams, 5

Read, H (1970) *The Redemption of the Robot*, p viii, Faber and Faber, London

Robertson, J (1965) Mother–infant interactions from birth to twelve months: two case studies, in *Determinants of Infant Behaviour*, vol 3, ed B M Foss, Methuen, London

Schön, D A (1987) *Educating the Reflective Practitioner: Towards a new design for teaching and education in the professions*, Jossey-Bass, San Francisco, CA

Squires, G (1999) *Teaching as a Professional Discipline*, Falmer, London

Stephenson, J (1988) The experience of independent study at North East London Polytechnic, in *Developing Student Autonomy in Learning*, 3rd edn, ed D Boud, pp 211–27, Kogan Page, London

Sylva, K (1984) A hard-headed look at the fruits of play, *Early Child Development and Care*, **15**, pp 171–83

Vygotsky, L S (1978) The role of play in development, in *Mind in Society: The development of higher psychological processes*, ed M Cole *et al*, pp 92–104, Harvard University Press, Cambridge, MA

Weaver, N (1999) The atelier principle in teaching, in *Project Studies: A late modern university reform?*, ed H S Olesen and J H Jensen, pp 220–32, Roskilde University Press, Roskilde

Weaver, N, O'Reilly, D and Caddick, M (2000) Preparation and support of part time teachers: designing a tutor training programme fit for architects, in *Changing Architectural Education*, ed S Pilling and D Nichol, pp 265–74, E and F N Spon, London

Weston, C and McAlpine, L (1998) How six outstanding math professors view teaching and learning: the importance of caring, *International Journal for Academic Development*, November, pp 146–55

Winnicott, D W (1990 (1971)) *Playing and Reality*, Tavistock, New York

17

Integrating skills development with academic content in the changing curriculum

Andrew Honeybone, Jennifer Blumhof and Marianne Hall

INTRODUCTION

The incorporation of skills development within the higher education (HE) curriculum has been heavily promoted in recent years. From the predominantly economic arguments of the Thatcher government to the wider ranging social, individual and economic purposes advocated by Dearing, there has been a perceived need to ensure that all students acquire not just a thorough knowledge of the subject they are studying but also the skills needed to be socially active and fulfilled citizens who are capable of contributing effectively to the economic prosperity of the country. These skills range from the intellectual skills that are more familiar to higher education to the practical and so-called key or transferable skills. The emphasis has been on making the skills development explicit in the curriculum. This has led both to concerns that such developments might be at the expense of academic content/rigour and to some questioning by HE staff themselves as to whether they have the necessary skills to teach skills.

In addition to this external rationale for skills development, the argument for the inclusion of skills in the HE curriculum can be advanced from another perspective, based on the nature of learning within HE. If learning is viewed as an active process, engaging learners in the construction of their own meanings, then students will need to use a wide range of skills – communication, intellectual and practical – in developing their individual understandings. This internal perspective need not be in conflict with the external pressures for skills development. Seeing skills as an immediate aid to learning can help to improve student motivation (they are likely to get better marks if they improve their skills) while in the longer term the acquisition of skills can aid lifelong learning in the wider economy and society.

It is in the context of these two perspectives that the present chapter will consider the contribution that has been made to this process of curriculum change by one funded project, the Hertfordshire Integrated Learning Project. The origins of the project will be outlined before the pedagogic rationale and components of the integrated learning model are described, including the action research approach underlying much of the project. Attention will then be focused on the use of problem based case studies as a principal means of integrating skills with academic content, before some conclusions are drawn about the success of this approach both pedagogically and as an agent of change.

ORIGINS OF THE HERTFORDSHIRE INTEGRATED LEARNING PROJECT

The Hertfordshire Integrated Learning Project (HILP) was established at the University of Hertfordshire in 1996 to promote good practice in skills development in higher education, and more particularly to explore ways in which such development could be integrated successfully with academic content. The project received its initial funding from HEFCE's Fund for the Development of Teaching and Learning (FDTL) and has subsequently received further funding from a variety of sources inside and outside the University of Hertfordshire (UH). Currently, although FDTL funding has finished, HILP's work continues internally through the implementation of aspects of the university's learning and teaching strategy and externally in the wider dissemination and discussion of skills in higher education through workshops and conferences.

Before the start of HILP, the Enterprise in Higher Education Initiative at UH had been successful in encouraging different departments at the university to introduce elements of skills teaching within their courses. Also, there was a tradition of skills development within the limited number of BTEC courses. However, there was no university-wide policy on the place of skills in the curriculum, and for most undergraduate programmes of study skills development remained a peripheral activity, outside the mainstream process of academic curriculum design. For most academics, skills were not a central concern and in certain quarters were seen as an unwelcome diversion from the desired concentration on the academic discipline.

It was against this background that HILP sought to engage more people in the debate and to move the argument forward by seeing skills development as part of the overall process of curriculum design. The intention was to explore ways of integrating skills with academic content within each part of a degree programme. A model, the so-called integrated learning model, was developed that offered a generic approach to skills development in the curriculum which could then be adapted for use within any particular discipline. Thus right from the start of the project the intention was to involve a wide range of subjects, including both arts and sciences and more academic as well as professional subjects. The areas included at the outset were environmental studies, applied social work, business and management studies, chemistry, computer science, English, geology, history, law, mechanical engineering and music.

THE PEDAGOGIC RATIONALE FOR THE INTEGRATED LEARNING MODEL

The generic integrated learning model was intended to provide an overall framework and pedagogic rationale for the HILP approach to skills development. It was based on a view of learning in higher education that placed the emphasis on students constructing their own critical understanding of their chosen area of study rather than on reproducing propositional knowledge based content which had been transmitted by the lecturer to the student (Gibbs, 1992). In Prosser and Trigwell's terminology (1999: 153–57) it is a conceptual change/student focused approach to learning and teaching rather than an information transmission/teacher focused view. Laurillard (1990) makes a similar distinction between a communication and a didactic model of learning.

In the HILP approach, communication and construction go hand in hand: the constructivist notion of students developing their own meanings is brought about through the process of communication. In other words, it is a form of social constructivism as expounded by Gergen (1995) that underlies the work of HILP, rather than the individual constructivism of von Glaserfield (1995). While individual students are indeed involved in the construction of their own meaning, that meaning is both assisted and constrained by the nature of the communication within the particular social and intellectual context of the subject, institution and society in which the student is studying. Thus in developing a supportive learning environment for students, account needs to be taken of this overall context of the student's study and of the skills that the student needs to be a successful active, interactive (Salmon, 1998) and reflective learner (Boud, Keogh and Walker, 1985). Using Barnett's terminology (1997), the student needs to be encouraged to move between the more traditional academic world of critical reason and the world of critical action with that movement being articulated by critical self-reflection.

It is on the basis of this thinking that the HILP integrated learning model (as illustrated in Figure 17.1) seeks to provide a framework that will assist both staff and students in developing a constructive and communicative environment for their teaching and learning. Whilst the integration that is of central importance to the project is that of skills development with academic content, that integration is itself set within a broader integration of curriculum development, staff development and influences on policy

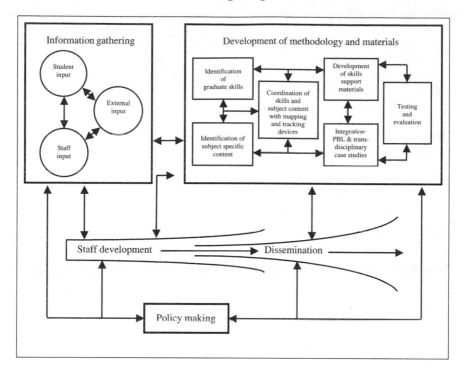

Figure 17.1   *The HILP integrated learning model*

making both inside and outside higher education. That is why the model includes information gathering, staff development and policy-making components as well as the central focus on the development of a methodology and materials for curriculum design.

In other words, effective curriculum design must be set in the context not only of the needs of students and other stakeholders such as their future employers, but also in terms of what is deliverable from an academic staff point of view. Staff are after all themselves major stakeholders in higher education, and any successful change must involve both their willing cooperation and investment in staff development. Thus at the outset HILP adopted a grassroots, bottom-up approach to project implementation with the emphasis on staff development through participation in the process of curriculum change. Essentially it was an action research approach with staff implementing an initial round of changes to the way in which they taught their courses before evaluating those changes in the light of student learning and then moving on to another round of revisions. This involved a significant shift in the balance of curriculum design from what was taught to how it was taught and how students learnt.

Within the constructivist approach to learning outlined above, this meant that staff needed to design a curriculum that encouraged students to acquire the skills needed to be active learners. HILP argued that this could best be done by integrating skills with academic content through the adoption of an explicit/embedded approach to skills development (Hodgkinson, 1996) with problem based learning (Margetson, 1994) being used as one key means of bringing about such integration.

THE COMPONENTS OF THE INTEGRATED LEARNING MODEL

Information gathering

A literature review of HE curriculum developments with regard to skills development and associated methods of teaching and learning such as problem based learning (PBL) and case studies was undertaken at the beginning of the project. This was followed by a round of semi-structured interviews with staff from the above disciplines to clarify perceptions of skills and their relevance to different disciplines. Staff were also asked whether, and how, problem based learning and case studies were used.

Most staff recognized the arguments in favour of skills development, but there was concern that the introduction of skills development into the higher education curriculum might be at the expense of the disciplinary content. Skills were of greatest interest to staff when they were being used within the highly dependent context of their own discipline.

For HILP this reinforced the idea (referred to below) that skills should be seen primarily as an aid to learning within the subject. Therefore attempts were made to incorporate a strong subject specific element within HILP's skills categorization and to ensure that the more generic skills were placed very firmly in their disciplinary setting. Communication and research were the skills most frequently mentioned by staff, with the former being perceived as rooted as firmly in the discipline as the latter.

Regarding PBL, most staff confirmed that problems were used in their disciplines but they did not necessarily describe this as PBL. For example social work and law refer to 'case work'; business and environmental sciences refer to 'case studies' and computer science and chemistry refer to 'problem solving'. There was general agreement that through problem based activities students could develop a range of skills such as research, information gathering and handling, information technology, problem solving and (as students invariably worked in groups on problems) teamwork. There was also widespread agreement that, for level 1 students, problems are reasonably simple and tutors usually provide a substantial amount of scaffolding (structured support and background information) and guidance. During subsequent years problems may increase in complexity and tutor scaffolding decreases, with a student's final year project being a fairly independent piece of research. These in-house PBL experiences, together with those experienced directly by members of the HILP team, began the formulation of a 'hybridized' PBL which will be discussed later.

Development of methods and materials

Despite the clear imperative for skills development, defining the HE skills and categorizing them was highly problematic. HILP decided to adopt a wide and inclusive approach after a review of previous skills work. The graduate skills menu evolved with five main categories of skills (see Figure 17.2). The first three (communications, interpersonal and self-management skills) approximated to previous definitions of key or transferable skills which were then supplemented by the additional categories of intellectual and practical/applied skills. Within each of these categories, individual skills were identified and a descriptor provided as an aid towards the establishment of a common language for skills or at least a means of facilitating a translation into alternative languages.

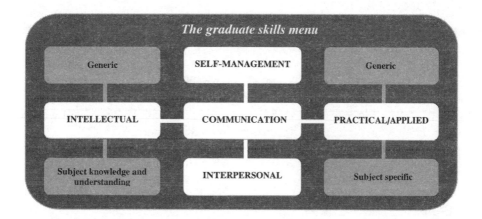

Figure 17.2   *The graduate skills menu*

However, HILP saw the main value of the menu as lying not so much in the definition of individual skills, which could be argued over ad infinitum, but in the notion of the menu and the processes involved in selecting, adapting and applying skills from the menu. The analogy of the menu was seen to be appropriate for a problem based constructivist view of learning where staff and students needed to be able to select a range of 'food' (that is, skills) from different parts of the menu so as to provide a balanced diet of skills to sustain the particular learning task in hand. Having selected such a range of skills from the generalized descriptors in the menu, there was then a need to adapt those skills to the particular disciplinary context in which they were to be used (for example, the skill of presentation would take on very different forms for the lawyer and the social worker). The selected and adapted skills then had to be applied in combination to complete the learning task.

These processes of selection, adaptation and application can themselves be seen, using Bridges' terminology (1994), as meta-skills, and HILP argued that that is where the focus of skills development in higher education should lie. What is required is a holistic approach to skills rather than a reductionist and mechanistic use of pre-determined skills in isolation and weakly related to a specific context. With this view, the skills identified in the present menu can be seen as provisional, with the menu being continually modified to suit the requirements of the diverse communities of cooks and diners in the different disciplines.

Within the constructivist approach to learning outlined above, staff needed to design a curriculum that encouraged students to acquire the skills needed to be active, deep learners. For most students, interest in learning lies largely in gaining knowledge and understanding of the subject they are studying, and to be acceptable, therefore, skills development needs to be embedded within the subject. However, Hodgkinson's (1996: 61) study found that 'total embedding may mean that the. . . skills disappear without trace, leaving the student unaware of the skills they are developing, and thus potentially less able to use the skills in new contexts'. HILP therefore, as previously mentioned, explored an explicit/embedded approach to integrating skills development with academic content, keeping the skills work embedded within the subject content but making them visible with the aim of encouraging the 3As: awareness, articulation and advancement.

Margetson (1994) suggests PBL is an effective means of integrating content and process (with 'process' being broadly translated as 'skills'). PBL can be considered to be both a philosophy and a process. The underpinning PBL philosophy is that problems drive a 'deep' learning process which starts from an understanding of how students learn. It encourages the development and application of problem working strategies and the acquisition of disciplinary knowledge bases and skills by placing students in the role of problem workers. As a process, PBL has been strongly associated with a 'medical school model' subscribing to a highly structured learning process. It is delivered through problem based tutorials, facilitated by a tutor, where small groups of students are introduced and encouraged to work through a problem, often supported with a wide range of resources specially developed for the process.

Because of the more diverse student intake that we were dealing with at Hertfordshire and the huge pressure on resources, particularly staff time and availability, HILP developed a 'hybridized' form of PBL. The 'hybrid' retains the philosophy but modifies the process. Transdisciplinary case studies are developed which are resource effective as they can be used by a range of disciplines. While resource constraints generally preclude the use of small group tutorials, which are considered by some to be the hallmark of PBL (see Macdonald's comments on this issue (2001)), tutors do provide 'floating facilitation' of small group work by moving between groups within a larger class. In addition to the tutorial support, staff guidance is given through initial 'framework' lectures that set the scene for the students by familiarizing them with the structure of the case study, the nature of the assessed coursework and some description of the problem area. The skills are supported through workshops and surgeries and the provision of resources covering both skills and academic content, so that elements of resource or material based learning are also incorporated in the PBL process (Rowntree, 1997). Students are encouraged to reflect on their learning and on their skills development in particular through self-evaluation exercises at the beginning and end of the case studies.

Staff development

At the outset HILP adopted a grassroots, bottom-up approach to project implementation with the emphasis on staff development through particip-ation in the process of curriculum change. Effective curriculum design must be set in the context not only of the needs of students and other stakeholders such as their future employers, but also in terms of what is deliverable from an academic staff point of view. Staff are after all themselves major stake-holders in higher education, and any successful change must involve both their willing cooperation and investment in staff development. Essentially it was an action research approach, with staff implementing an initial round of changes to the way in which they taught their courses, before evaluating those changes in the light of student learning and then moving on to another round of revisions. This involved a significant shift in the balance of curriculum design, from what was taught to how it was taught and how students learnt.

Dissemination

HILP has had a very tangible affect on curriculum design within UH through the development of transdisciplinary case studies, and continues its develop-mental work within UH by supporting the implementation of skills related aspects of the university's learning and teaching strategy. Externally, HILP has acquired a disseminating role in the wider discussion of skills in higher education by organizing workshops and conferences (for example, two national skills conferences and a regional workshop) and through the work of project members in national projects such as subject benchmarking and European curriculum design initiatives such as ESSENCE.

Policy making

As previously noted, HILP initially adopted a grassroots, bottom-up approach to project development and implementation. However, through a combin-ation of encouragement from the FDTL National Co-ordination Team and the fortuitous coincidence of the university's preparation of a learning and teaching strategy, the integrated learning model was amended to include a policy-making component. In adding this component the intention was that the bottom-up approach within participating disciplines would dovetail with a top-down approach which in time would help to achieve the institution-wide implementation of skills development. The HILP approach has now become institutionalized through its incorporation not just in the UH learning and teaching strategy but also in the university's policies and regulations (UPR) on General Educational Aims of Programmes of Study. Through the incorporation of HILP work in this way, it has become possible to extend the contracts of project staff to ensure the continuing implementation of skills development. This has been done through the use of some of the Teaching Quality Enhancement Fund institutional strand funding.

THE INTEGRATED LEARNING MODEL IN PRACTICE: THE EXAMPLE OF THE BROADLAND PROBLEM BASED CASE STUDY

To show how the elements of the model work in practice, the Broadland case study (a transdisciplinary problem based case study trialled with students from different disciplines) will now be described. This case study illustrates how the HILP 'hybrid' approach to PBL attempts to deepen learning by drawing students through a problem working exercise and assignment. The case study adopts an explicit embedded approach to skills development, integrating the carefully crafted skills work (and skills resources) with academic content, also supported with background resources. It also had an impact on staff development through team teaching and curriculum design, and was and is used as an exemplar to disseminate and illustrate curriculum design issues in action, warts and all. As for policy making, the Broadland case study work informed the thinking of the UH Managed Learning Environment initiative, now known as Studynet. The various iterations of the case study have led to the current position in which the students experience a combination of face to face and computer mediated learning which incorporates CCASE*notes*, that is a collaborative computer articulated study environment based on Lotus Notes software, hence the name CCASE*notes*.

A particular concept that is being explored in the development of CCASE*notes* is that of 'near distance learning'. This can be defined as an approach to learning that combines computer mediated learning with strategic personal contact for students attending university courses in which, although geographical proximity remains, traditional levels of face to face contact, particularly for small groups and individual students, are no longer possible. Thus CCASE*notes* seeks to achieve the pedagogic aim of providing a supportive environment for collaborative student learning by creating a composite learning environment, part actual, part virtual, incorporating face to face contact, computer based information, computer mediated interaction and some elements of computer based assessment. It has similarities with courses in the middle of Rowntree's continuum from face to face learning to materials based (or resource based) learning (Rowntree, 1997), but with one important difference: the staff–student and student–student interaction can be both face to face and computer mediated.

So far, the case study has been used by students in law, business studies, music and environmental studies, with students in the different disciplines focusing on a relevant aspect of the central problem of the sustainable development of part of Broadland for tourism and recreation. Law students concentrated on issues of access, business students looked at the provision of tourist facilities, music students composed short works to express the qualities of the area, while environmental studies students had to formulate an overall approach to sustainable development, together with some site specific examples. The details that follow describe the development of the environmental studies version of the case study which comprises a six-week block of a second-year course.

The case study begins with a short series of framework lectures which set the scene for the students by familiarizing them with the structure of the case study, the nature of the assessed coursework (a videoed presentation) and some description of the Broadland area, though there is an ongoing debate among the course team about how much factual material should be provided in the introductory lectures, particularly in the context of improved online access to such materials.

The scene setting is supported by a field visit, then the staff–student contact time is split between two types of workshop: subject specific workshops during which students, working in groups of four or five, prepare material for their presentations; and skills workshops in which the development of the skills required for the successful completion of the assignment task (such as creative thinking) are explicitly addressed. In the workshops students are expected to take responsibility for their own learning and discuss among themselves how best to complete the task, with the tutors acting as facilitators.

The face to face contact is then supplemented by two linked online areas, the student guidance and discussion area and the resources area. Both of these areas are accessed via the Broadland case study home page. The address of this home page is http://www.herts.ac.uk/ltdu/projects/hilp/broads.html.

The student guidance and discussion area provides three main facilities. First, via the noticeboard, students are able to obtain all the basic information about the requirements and structure of the case study.

Second, the area provides an additional means of student–student, student–staff and staff–staff two-way communication. In addition to interaction within their own group discussion area, students can contribute to the whole class discussion area and, more informally, to the student chat area. The present structure of CCASE*notes* provides for up to 20 groups of students to work in small groups within their own discussion areas. Members of staff can communicate with students either through the noticeboard facility or more interactively through the group and class discussion areas. There is also the provision of a private area for staff discussion.

Third, a means of recording parts of the assessment and evaluation of the course is provided. Peer and tutor assessment marks can be entered and students can receive their group marks through CCASE*notes*. There is also a graduate skills self-evaluation form for the self-assessment of levels of skills development at the start and end of the case study, as well as a final case study evaluation form.

The resources area provides an improved source of support materials for the case study. Two types of online material are included in this area: case study resources specifically related to Broadland plus links to related Web sites, and skills resources to aid skills development during the case study.

Evaluation of the Broadland case study is continuing, with two cohorts of students having completed the CCASE*notes* version just described. Feedback has been obtained from class discussion, course evaluation forms, analysis of usage levels of the site and staff discussion. Therefore what follows is only some limited interim reflection.

Overall the student response has been favourable, with high levels of usage of both the resources area and the student guidance and discussion area. The switch to online resources has been welcomed and has apparently overcome the previous limitations on access to paper-based materials. Whether or not many students have been deterred from seeking out their own additional sources of information because of the range of materials available online is not yet clear, but one student did comment that the resources 'highlighted everything you needed to know about the topic we were covering'. This comment was made even though we had pointed out in the initial briefing session that the materials in the resources area should be regarded as the starting point for wider investigations.

The response to the student guidance and discussion area was also good. The preliminary returns indicate that a large majority of students (over 80 per cent) found CCASE*notes* useful and easy to use. Similar proportions (or higher) found the noticeboard, instructions, group work and class discussion areas useful. A typical comment was:

> In the group work and class discussion we were able to keep in touch with what was happening. Members of the group were sometimes absent and this was the ideal way to impart information. The instructions were concise and easy to follow and hopefully meant that the operation went smoothly enough.

Also there were some indications that the online communication was helping to provide some of the 'social glue' (Rowntree, 1997) which is important for collaborative learning. One student commented that 'I didn't know everyone in the class, seeing their comments on the class discussion broke down that barrier.'

However, although these favourable comments represented the majority view, contrary opinions were expressed. For example, one group did not find the group discussion area useful and commented that 'we found it a lot better and easier to just sit and talk to each other in an actual meeting rather than a virtual one'. One group, because of the requirement to hold a virtual meeting, even sat in a row in front of five adjacent computers and communicated online. Perhaps this gives us a salutary reminder: students learn in different ways and their personal needs vary. Thus computer mediated communication in the context of near distance learning can contribute to the 'enriched classroom' (Retalis *et al*, 1998) and provide a useful extension of choice in the means of communication. It need not become the only means. In our enthusiasm for promoting the use of CCASE*notes*, we may have been guilty of implying this.

Somewhat to our surprise, the surgery facility was not used even though messages were posted to remind students of the facility. Three reasons for this lack of use may be offered. First, students still had regular opportunities to consult with members of staff in class; second, the surgery facility was only a sub-category within the group discussion areas and was thus not readily visible; and third, staff responses could not be made to an individual student: they could only be made to the individual's group or to the whole class. The few students who did seek individual advice online (other than from members of their own group) tended to divide their messages between the class discussion area and their own group discussion area, without making it clear that they were seeking a response from a member of staff. This made it more difficult (and therefore time-consuming) for staff to identify when individual responses were needed. Thus in terms of the three modes of interaction identified by Holland and Odin (1998), the learner–teacher mode of interaction in CCASE*notes* could be improved, while on the evidence so far available, the other two modes of interaction, learner–learner and learner–content, have been facilitated by CCASE*notes*.

As far as skills development is concerned, the student self-assessment forms indicate that most students felt that their level of skills had been improved by the case study. This conclusion is borne out by the generally good quality of the assignments, as such successful outcomes could not have been achieved if students had not effectively developed and used the appropriate range of skills. If anything, there is some evidence that the numeric scores that the students gave to themselves may underestimate the degree of actual improvement. The reason for this is that some students awarded themselves lower scores at the end of the case study than at the beginning, not because they thought that their skills had actually decreased, but because they felt their initial lack of understanding of the skills had caused them to overestimate their ability at the outset. This would indicate that these students have become more reflective learners.

CONCLUSION

Linking the findings from the individual case studies to the overall aims of the HILP project, there is evidence to support the view that problem based case studies can be an effective means of encouraging students to develop their skills. However, it is a major step from individual examples of skills development to an institution-wide progressive development of skills throughout the curriculum. Thus it was essential in HILP that the initial bottom-up approach was supplemented by some top-down policy changes, linked to further staff development, that encouraged the wider uptake of the HILP approach. What is being attempted is a fundamental change in the approach to curriculum design, akin to what Biggs has referred to as 'constructive alignment' with PBL 'being alignment itself' (or at least an example thereof) (Biggs, 1999: 64, 71). All parts of the learning environment and of the curriculum are seen as mutually supporting elements designed to encourage students to adopt a constructivist approach to their learning and achieve the intended outcomes of their courses. This thinking is very similar to that behind the HILP integrated learning model: all the components affecting student learning must be related specifically so that the methods employed in the design and delivery of the curriculum are consistent with the stated aims and needs of students, staff and the wider community.

REFERENCES

Barnett, R (1997) *Higher Education: A critical business*, Society for Research in Higher Education (SRHE)/Open University Press, Buckingham

Biggs, J (1999) What the student does: teaching for enhanced learning, *Higher Education Research and Development*, **18** (1)

Boud, D, Keogh, R and Walker, D (eds) (1985) *Reflection: Turning reflection into learning*, Kogan Page, London

Bridges, D (1994) Transferable skills: a philosophical perspective, in *Transferable Skills in Higher Education*, ed D Bridges, University of East Anglia, Norwich

Gergen, K J (1995) Social construction and the educational process, in *Constructivism in Education*, ed L P Steffe and J Gale, Lawrence Erlbaum, Hillsdale, NJ

Gibbs, G (1992) *Improving the Quality of Student Learning*, Technical and Educational Services, Bristol

Hodgkinson, L (1996) *Changing the Higher Education Curriculum: Towards a systematic approach to skills development*, **61**, Open University Vocational Qualifications Centre, Milton Keynes

Holland, J and Odin, J K (1998) Distance learning using ALNs: broader implementation and specific pedagogical issues, *Active Learning*, **9**

Laurillard, D (1990) Computers and the emancipation of students: giving control to the learner, in *Computers and Learning: A reader*, ed O Boyd-Barrett and E Scanlon, Open University, Milton Keynes

Macdonald, R (2001) Problem-based learning: implications for educational developers, *Educational Developments*, **2** (2)

Margetson, D (1994) Current educational reform and the significance of problem-based learning, in *Studies in Higher Education*, **19** (1)

Prosser, M and Trigwell, K (1999) *Understanding Learning and Teaching: The experience in higher education*, SRHE/Open University Press, Buckingham

Retalis, S, Makrakis, V, Papaspyrou, N and Skordalakis, M (1998) A case study of an enriched classroom model based on the World Wide Web, *Active Learning*, **8**

Rowntree, D (1997) *Making Materials-Based Learning Work: Principles, policies and practicalities*, Kogan Page, London

Salmon, G (1998) Developing learning through effective online moderation, *Active Learning*, **9**

von Glaserfeld, E (1995) A constructivist approach to teaching, in *Constructivism in Education*, ed L P Steffe and J Gale, Lawrence Erlbaum, Hillsdale, NJ

Conclusions

18

Towards a culture of evaluation

James Wisdom

INTRODUCTION

In the introductory chapter, Ranald Macdonald wrote of how the developing approaches to evaluation were blurring the distinction with research. In this concluding chapter we need to consider what can be drawn from these examples of current experience and what guidance they give educational developers in the next phase of their practice.

It is not my intention merely to summarize the contributions: they are too rich and diverse to deserve such treatment. There are, however, some themes which can be drawn from the material and which we can use to guide our thoughts about the directions educational development might take in its next phase. How is our practice changing? In particular, are we developing the capacity to make good decisions about the design, delivery and effectiveness of educational development work?

CHANGING PRACTICE

Although there are some interesting examples of work resulting from lecturers approaching educational developers for collaboration, much of the work in this volume has been designed – by academics within each discipline – in the expectation that working with mainstream lecturers might not be easy or straightforward. We are clearly still in the era when academic staff perception is that change is being effected in higher education by the direct application of pressure on themselves. While lecturers can respond by turning for assistance to the educational development community, another strategy has been simply to continue to work in the traditional pattern, but harder. Tradition has, after all, produced a higher education sector which is the envy of the world. These chapters show the ways in which educational developers and project designers have created a whole raft of strategies and approaches with which they could collaborate with their colleagues: using regulation and policy, establishing networks, collaborating in research, devising models and strategies, valuing the emotional component of education, or challenging pedagogic tradition with new technology.

Despite the difficulties higher education has had in harvesting the apparent benefits of the new information technologies, we still have faith that this is a development which will bring deep changes, though we think we might have to work hard to ensure these changes are for the better. The sector has learnt that if the predominant pedagogy is 'teacher-focused information transmission' (Prosser and Trigwell, 1999) then the use of information and communications technology (ICT) as a technology allowing for substitution is unlikely to be particularly successful. The approach that predominates in this volume is that effective working with ICT very rapidly compels lecturers to reconsider their pedagogy, and that from that questioning process a whole design solution will emerge. Although the first contact may be made in terms of ICT, the driver of change is now pedagogic reform.

There are a number of chapters in which teams have devised a model, a framework, a protocol or a process which effectively enables lecturers to interrogate themselves, to think through their priorities and purposes, to bring the major variables into the equation, and to align their teaching, the students' learning, the assessments and outcomes, all within a framework of student numbers, staff time and realistic resource support. It is clear that these approaches, while effective and useful for individuals, are particularly powerful when they are engaged by groups of lecturers together. One emerging theme has been the tendency to identify the critical importance of senior management activity.

There has been, of course, one sector-wide model which was designed to stimulate questioning and consideration for local application. In every phase of its development, including the current incorporation of bench-marking standards, the rhetoric of UK quality assurance has been of templates for local design, prompts for self-description, questions which lead to enhancement as well as assurance. Where that questioning process has been converted into prescription and where instructional formulae have generated 'correct' replies, the enhancement value of the activity has been subverted. Educational developers, among others, must ensure we preserve the value of the development that arises from the questioning processes outlined in this volume.

Some of the work described in this volume set out to shift the culture of its discipline. The UK's Quality Assurance Agency's Subject Review process generated examples of good practice, and if deemed excellent, applicants were invited to collaborate and disseminate through consortia. Working across a whole discipline is not easy, especially where the Subject Review has had a weak impact. What we can see is that projects put together many of the same elements in different proportions: generating material, examples, case studies; growing a network – of awareness and general involvement – across the discipline; growing a cadre of colleagues more closely involved;

seminars, conferences, regional and departmental workshops; publishing and using the Web. In some cases, an equivalent to the review process was required to generate the really pressing educational issues and examples. The phrase 'raising the profile' is the one most used, but really what is happening is the further development of the discipline's conversation about education – more participants, new ideas, wider use of language, greater energy and enthusiasm. Some chapters show that one of the critical moves in this process has been locking in senior management involvement, often through the professional or accrediting bodies.

One of the perennial disappointments for those involved in improving the quality of student learning is when examples of good practice are not taken up. It all seems so straightforward. The threnody of anguish in each staff room suggests that colleagues are eager for change, there are many ways of discovering good ideas, the Web is now an excellent distribution medium, great activity appears to occur, perhaps the number of active experimenters increases, but the problems seem to stay the same. Worse, the enthusiasts are 'yes-butted' out of the scene (yes, it is a good idea, but, there are very particular reasons why it would never work here). Although early Teaching and Learning Technology Programme (TLTP) and Fund for the Development of Teaching and Learning (FDTL) projects put strong emphasis on dissemination, the sector is learning that take-up, implementation and embedding are different orders of difficulty. One response has been an exploration of the power of action research as a methodology which can match the scale of this challenge, and the evidence of some of the chapters shows how fruitful this can be. There are implications here for the newly-established UK Subject Centres, which may find that they need to invest as much effort into the processes of making educational change in their discipline as into the products and ideas which they are making available for their colleagues.

What is also clear from the work described in these chapters is that educational development is likely to be quite slow. We have moved on from the model of discovery, dissemination, acceptance and application which held out the promise of rapid change, to more realistic processes of implementation. These sometimes compel us to refocus from the lecturer in the classroom to the systems and structures which operate the programmes and then on to the institutional frameworks which in some places are running to catch up. These issues have been recognized, and for the first time there are policy and funding frameworks that encourage innovation, or at least reduce its discouragement. As a result we are now able to see more clearly the new challenges, such as the need for people experienced in real transfer, staff priorities which are still focused elsewhere, the inherent problems in project funding, and the development of a management culture with the skills to implement educational reform. Although at all stages there are systems to fix, the real work is still about changing people.

THE CONTEXT OF EVALUATION

One of the significant features of many of these chapters is the evaluation culture which predominated during the period of their creation. The FDTL followed the outcomes of the assessment of teaching quality. That activity had been designed around the philosophy of self-assessment and peer review, with a strong emphasis on the audit of processes, managed within each discipline and relying on what institutions were already doing and were capable of developing within a year or two. It was not a process explicitly driven by the outcomes of educational research, nor was the fund itself for research – it was explicitly to disseminate the good practice revealed by the quality assessment process.

Therefore to understand what is reported in some of these chapters we would need to explore what applicants to the fund (deemed to be excellent in some dimension) could turn to for measures of educational effectiveness, remembering that these applicants were mainstream discipline staff, not educational professionals. There had been for some time a wide acceptance of the value of active learning, and also of the intention that education should develop a critical and analytical approach. Many academics would have felt that, from their experience, they could recognize active learning and measure its increase. Similarly, estimating the quality of the critical and analytical skills of students has long been part of most lecturers' assessment practices. There had also been a growing acceptance of the importance of skills development, though whether those were study, generic, transferable or enterprise and how they might be assessed were (and are) still in debate. Nevertheless, measuring changes to the skills components of courses does not, on the surface, appear contentious. Staff who had embraced the value of explicit learning outcomes were developing a language with which they could discuss educational effectiveness, in particular because of the analytical work which had been done in defining levels (see, for example, Moon, 1996). Although often without the original dimension of 'approaches to learning', the language of deep and surface learning had been spreading and there had been some influential work which had shown how such approaches might be measured (Gibbs, 1992a).

More traditional measurements were changes in examination and other assessment outcomes, the noting of variations in progression and non-completion rates, and the use of information from student feedback question-naires and discussions. Less specific but just as traditional were changes in the feelings of the staff, from recalling what it was like to have the time to take pleasure in reading students' work, to recognizing that students were being better prepared for second and final year study, to the personal satisfaction of coping successfully with a large class, and reckoning that the expenditure of time and effort in changing the course had been worthwhile. There was a culture of qualitative evaluation within some disciplines, and familiar to some educational developers, as was some experience of educational research techniques. Both these factors will be discussed later in this chapter, but their present significance is that they were not widely used at the time much of the work reported in this volume was being designed.

EDUCATIONAL EFFECTIVENESS

It is a commonplace in higher education that the sector invests far less in research and development to support organizational change than its competitors within the knowledge economy. Much of the work referred to in this volume has been supported with direct funding and has in part depended on an HEI infrastructure of staffing and expertise. It is not surprising, therefore, that there are stakeholders who are interested in whether it represents value for money, sometimes based on an attempt to measure educational effectiveness.

The educational effectiveness approach was used explicitly within the third phase of the TLTP. The annual reports of these projects show them tackling the question. (Some of these are published on project Web sites, a list of which can be found on the Teaching Quality Enhancement Fund's National Coordination Team Web site, www.ncteam.ac.uk.) A synthesis of the reports, prepared by the Tavistock Institute for the Higher Education Funding Council for England (HEFCE) (Sommerlad and Ramsden, 2001), discusses the outcomes in uncompromising terms:

> Despite the level of programme learning that has occurred and is evident in the evolution of the TLTP over successive phases, (this report) suggests there are some areas of systemic weakness... The particular areas we identify as problematic in this way include: the frameworks and intellectual depth of thinking about pedagogic issues; the conceptualization of cost effectiveness and the paucity of meaningful data; and disciplinary/subject understanding and analysis.
>
> There are limits to what can reasonably be expected of TLTP projects in these areas, given the past serious neglect of pedagogy in HE as a focus of serious study and global recognition of the paucity of good R&D on new learning technologies; the poor 'state of the art' of financial costing of pedagogic activities in universities generally (including lack of comparable data on traditional teaching methods); and the hitherto lack of support for disciplinary networks as key agents of innovation diffusion.
>
> (Executive summary)

And later, in their discussion of educational and cost effectiveness, they write:

Understanding educational effectiveness in its fullest sense calls for interdisciplinary perspectives that transcend existing domain assumptions. It takes time for professionals coming from different worlds of practice and educational background, with their distinctive discourses, orientations, workstyles and disciplinary perspectives, to arrive at some shared concepts, terms and theories which make sense of their different experiences. We should not be surprised, given the short timeframe of the TLTP, that these shared understandings are still being worked through.

(Sommerlad and Ramsden, 2001: 49)

One of the conclusions we may draw is that, while it appears initially to be a straightforward project responsibility to evaluate for effectiveness, projects have been unable to engage successfully with a cost-effectiveness model and so some have worked on notions of educational effectiveness while many have located their evaluation in terms of project effectiveness.

EVALUATION WITHIN PROJECT WORK

One approach to evaluation can arise from the nature of project work itself. In many cases projects are based on a proposal or bid which has been agreed by programme managers and then allocated time and a budget. Once the project has been converted into a plan with allocated expenditure and reporting moments, sometimes the project managers decide the need for evaluation can be satisfied with an audit approach (responsibility for funding) or a reporting approach (reasons for variations from timetable and budget). Audit and reporting can be minimal or extensive, but both are associated with compliance within a contract. In this model the emphasis is more on monitoring than evaluation, and the educational effectiveness is derived from the quality of the original idea and how well it was converted into a plan.

While it is possible to evaluate within the lifetime of a project, projects do come to an end. Project staff can tell a community about their work and disseminate their outcomes; they can work closely with colleagues to implement their outcomes into practice, testing perhaps if local variations influence their acceptability; they might perhaps be funded for sufficiently long to implement, evaluate, redesign, implement and evaluate again (in a semestered modular programme this can take two years); they may even be able to move to embedding –the incorporation of new developments into validated course design, well taught by staff who were never part of the project team; but in all these models it is beyond the project to evaluate long-term impact. Projects therefore look for evaluation approaches within their time-limited existence which can meet their and their stakeholders' needs.

If higher education ever was a simple process (it is one of those worlds where most of its inhabitants locate their golden age in the past), there surely must be few practitioners for whom each year of teaching is so similar that the impact of one significant variation can be easily identified. There is little evidence of them in the chapters of this book. The world of higher education is dynamic and multi-dimensional, and as yet only partially equipped with quantitative research tools that match the demands of that environment. It is hardly remarkable that so many of the present authors have looked to qualitative evaluation processes for the capacity to work successfully within an unstable world.

Although learning from difficulty or even failure is one of the most powerful educational experiences, it is sometimes hard to find in higher education practice. Many students now find themselves on programmes in which every piece of work they do is intended for summative assessment, with little or no chance to re-do work to improve it. Similarly in funded project based development work, there is learning to be had at programme level which relies on understandings gathered at project level. One example of this approach comes from the guidelines prepared for the evaluation of the Electronic Libraries (eLib) programme:

> First, the primary purpose of evaluation is to contribute to the collective learning of all those involved in the programme or having a stake in it. Such is the experimental, open-ended nature of the programme that we do not know what is going to work and thus participants should be open to the idea of learning from failures and difficulties of implementation as much as from achievements and successes. As a developmental programme, evaluation should contribute to the building of future scenarios and the gathering of information to inform future choices.
>
> (Kelleher, Sommerlad and Stern, 1996)

Though this approach acknowledges learning at programme level, much the same dynamic applies to discipline based projects which are hoping to have a wide application, generic projects working on sector-wide processes and institutional projects which are contributing to the learning of the organization. Given that part of the cultural background of modern higher education includes competition as well as collaboration, personal and career prestige as well as learning from difficulty, and high profile dissemination as part of project strategy, it is important to recognize the multiple pressures experienced by designers of evaluation processes.

MODELS AND METHODS OF EVALUATION

The eLib guidelines offered this framework of elements in the design of suitable project evaluation:

- What are the main purposes of the evaluation?

- Who are different actors who have a stake in the project and its evaluation?

- What evaluation activities are appropriate at different stages of the project lifecycle?

- How will evaluation be integrated into the project?

- How will users be involved in the evaluation?

- What kinds of evaluation questions will be asked and what assessment methods are appropriate?

While frameworks such as this and the example of the monitoring and evaluation briefing from the National Coordination Team given in Macdonald's chapter encourage developers to consider what approaches would most suit their needs, it is clear from the evidence in this volume that there were no standard, off-the-peg approaches which were being used across a number of projects. The authors report a wide range of methods, even putting to different uses approaches which appear superficially similar.

It is interesting to note how some of the projects have moved away from large-scale and distributed forms of information gathering towards smaller-scale, more personal but richer activities. Widely distributed questionnaires – now even more tempting via e-mail – have not always generated the quality of data their users had anticipated. Questionnaires developed through interviews and focus groups, adapted from recognized models, used regularly over a period or used to generate commentaries for further analysis, are all examples of the precise use of what is a ubiquitous but sometimes clumsy device.

Many project teams have made extensive use of focus groups and structured meetings. Equally popular have been interviews, either structured or semi-structured, in some cases using telephone and e-mail to extend their range. Observation of staff and students was a widespread method, in some cases listening to a user's commentary for even more precision. Particularly valuable has been the delivery and full evaluation of workshop activities. And many projects have made extensive use of their steering groups and often an external evaluator or critical friend.

Perhaps more important than the methods adopted by the authors of these chapters has been the framework of reflection within which so many of them have located their evaluative and developmental activity.

QUALITATIVE EVALUATION

Educational development work can have many purposes and those working with it can have many motives. Their approaches to evaluation can sometimes be best understood by considering some of the political contexts around them. A prime concern has been to establish or retain a credibility with their colleagues, the discipline-based academic staff. While some projects focused closely on the needs of their consortium, others had the ambition to influence and reform across the discipline. To grow interest beyond an immediate circle of enthusiasts, at a pace and in a style which ensures doors (and minds) remain open, requires a complex and subtle range of skills. Even a simple awareness test of a project's name might, of itself, have been sufficient to close a few doors; in some cases this, if repeated at stages throughout a project, would have been surprisingly counter-productive. Many teams came to see qualitative evaluation as offering more effective and holistic approaches than the simple but apparently scientifically respectable methods they originally contemplated.

This has not been an easy development. The relationship between research and teaching has been under continuous review in recent years, in part because of new understandings of the relationship between teaching and students' learning. Where academics have come to define themselves (through political and funding pressures) as primarily research-focused, sometimes a research-based approach to changing pedagogic practice can appear attractive. Simple, apparently scientifically respectable methods might appeal to academics who are moving beyond their traditional discipline, but it is important for all parties to acknowledge that they are moving into an area which has already developed effective and appropriate practice.

Particularly influential in the thinking of some of the authors in this volume has been the work of Denzin, Lincoln, Guba and Yin. In *Fourth Generation Evaluation*, Guba and Lincoln (1989) set out a process of collaborative enquiry which takes evaluative work beyond measurement, description and judgement. In *Case Study Research: Design and methods*, Yin (1994) has been able to offer an approach which can discuss the richness of the experience of educational change within a dynamic and sometimes unexpected environment. In the two editions of the *Handbook of Qualitative Research*, Denzin and Lincoln (2000) have brought together a battery of authors whose work can offer insights and guidance to practitioners researching their practice. They offer this definition:

Qualitative research is a situated activity that locates the observer in the world. It consists of a set of interpretative, material practices that make the world visible. These practices transform the world.

(Introduction: 3)

Lecturers and educational developers designing research and evaluation processes from within their work recognize the value of Denzin and Lincoln's perspective:

> although the field of qualitative research is defined by constant breaks and ruptures, there is a shifting centre to the project: the avowed humanistic commitment to study the social world from the perspective of the interacting individual.
>
> (Preface)

It is evident within many of the chapters that their authors brought the scepticism employed within their prime discipline into their work of designing and evaluating their educational development work, and that it has rarely been unproblematic to incorporate the easily available research methods into an acceptable framework. Often it is helpful to recognize the historical context in which we work:

> Qualitative inquiry is the name for a reformist movement that began in the early 1970s in the academy. The movement encompassed multiple epistemological, methodological, political and ethical criticisms of social scientific research in fields and disciplines that favoured experimental, quasi-experimental, correlational, and survey research strategies. Immanent criticism of these methodologies within these disciplines and fields as well as insights from external debates in philosophy of science and social science fuelled the opposition.
>
> (Schwandt, 2000)

RESEARCH INTO PRACTICE

Among the most important initiatives for educational developers in recent years have been the Improving Student Learning symposia. Introducing the first volume of papers, Graham Gibbs reported that:

> Most of the papers reported here are by lecturers who were using research frameworks and research tools to make sense of their own teaching and their own courses. This represents a sea change in attitudes and behaviour and is a remarkable testimony to the development of what Boyer has called the 'scholarship of teaching'.
>
> (Gibbs, 1994)

Introducing the third volume of papers, Gibbs picks up this theme:

As before, the emphasis has been on practitioners researching their practice rather than on either researchers describing their research or on practitioners describing their practice. As before the work by 'full-time' researchers has provided research tools for practitioners to use, designs of studies for practitioners to follow, findings to replicate and concepts to apply. But it is the use of research by practitioners which best characterizes these proceedings. Their studies are perhaps less extensive and sophisticated than those of the professional educational research community, but they are embedded in contexts in which they practise, and directly inform decisions they take to improve practice. This is the future of using research to improve student learning.

(Gibbs, 1996)

What then are the research tools, the designs and the findings which Gibbs is urging practitioners to use? A key passage comes from the introduction to the first volume:

The [research framework dominant in the ISL symposium], based originally on work in the 1970s by Ferenc Marton in Sweden and John Biggs in Australia, is founded on four key observations. First, students go about learning in qualitatively different ways. The approach students take to their studies can be seen to involve either an intention to make sense (a deep approach) or an attempt to reproduce (a surface approach). Second, the outcomes of student learning are not just quantitatively different, they are also qualitatively different – students understand different kinds of things, structured in different ways, not just more or less. Third, students understand what learning itself is, what knowledge is, and what they are doing when learning, in profoundly different ways, seeming to develop over time in the sophistication of their conceptions of learning. Fourth, teachers understand what teaching and learning consist of, and therefore what 'good teaching' should consist of, in qualitatively different ways. These factors interact . . . so that all learning phenomena can be seen to take place in a context mediated by the perceptions of students and their teachers involving their conceptions and approaches.

The most important research tools associated with this framework are first, categories of descriptions of approach, conception of learning and conception of teaching, allowing interview data to be categorized reliably and meaningfully. Second, the SOLO taxonomy, enabling easy categorization of the structural qualities of learning outcomes. Third, questionnaires (such as the ASI or Approaches to Studying Inventory) allowing easy measurement of the extent to which students generally take a surface or deep approach. And fourth, questionnaires (such as the CEQ or Course Experience Questionnaire) allowing easy measurement of students' perceptions of key features of courses which are known to influence students' approach.

Some of the research tools which have animated the nine ISL symposia are becoming more widely known and appreciated through the educational development community. Lecturers' conceptions of students' learning, for example, have been categorized in the following way:

- a quantitative increase in knowledge;
- memorizing;
- the acquisition, for subsequent utilization, of facts, methods, etc;
- the abstraction of meaning;
- an interpretative process aimed at understanding reality;
- developing as a person.

(Marton and Säljö, 1997; Marton, Dall'Alba and Beaty, 1993; in Prosser and Trigwell, 1999, which reports how these and other studies have been further elaborated.)

Prosser and Trigwell, working from Dall'Alba (1991) and others, have also developed five conceptions with which lecturers describe teaching:

- as transmitting concepts of the syllabus;
- as transmitting the teacher's knowledge;
- as helping students acquire concepts of the syllabus;
- as helping students to acquire teacher's knowledge;
- as helping students develop conceptions.

This has led them to develop (see Prosser and Trigwell, 1999) an Approaches to Teaching Inventory, a 16-question instrument through which lecturers can explore their own course-related intentions and strategies according to two orientations:

- conceptual change/student focused;
- information transmission/teacher focused.

The Structure of Observed Learning Outcomes (SOLO) taxonomy can be drawn from Biggs and Collis (1982) or from Biggs (1999). It uses five categories to analyse students' work – prestructural, unistructural, multistructural, relational and extended abstract – and has been applied to estimate development in students' learning as well as the quality of assessment tasks (see, for example, Olsson, 2000).

Since the emergence of a set of understandings about students' approaches to learning and the description of concepts of 'surface' and 'deep' approaches, there has been an elaboration and a refinement of the instruments available to researchers and practitioners (for the early Approaches To Study Inventory, see Entwistle and Ramsden, 1983). The Approaches and Study Skills Inventory For Students (ASSIST) (Entwistle, Tait and McCune, 1998, and Tait, Entwistle and McCune, 1998) is the most recent, and is shaped to explore, first, students' conceptions of learning (using Marton and Säljö's categories set out above). It tests students' reasons for entering higher education in terms of intrinsic or extrinsic interests, or perhaps having no clear goals. In its analysis of approaches to studying, the questions about seeking meaning, relating ideas, the use of evidence and having an interest in ideas are used to signify a deep approach. Questions about organized studying, time management, alertness to assessment demands, achievement and the monitoring of effectiveness are used to characterize a strategic approach to learning. The surface approach to learning is explored with questions about lack of purpose, unrelated memorizing, syllabus-boundness and students' fear of failure. Finally the students are asked for their preferences for different types of course and teaching in terms of supporting understanding or transmitting information.

The Course Experience Questionnaire is sufficiently flexible to be used at individual unit or module level, at year level for a course, and also for whole named programmes of study. It is widely used in educational development and educational research and has even formed one of the components of Australian HE national quality assurance processes. It is described in Ramsden (1992) and in Wilson, Lizzio and Ramsden (1997). In its most extended form it asks 37 questions and reliably reports on students' experience of learning in terms of good teaching, clear goals and standards, generic skills, appropriate assessment, appropriate workload and the course's emphasis on independence.

While not strictly research tools, there are two other approaches to identifying good teaching and learning which have therefore been influential in the design of educational development projects. The first is John Biggs' four contexts which support good learning:

- a well-structured knowledge base;
- an appropriate motivational context;
- learner activity;
- interaction with others.

A good teaching system aligns teaching method and assessment to the learning activities stated in the objectives, so that all aspects of this system are in accord in supporting appropriate student learning. This system is called *constructive alignment*, based as it is on the twin principles of constructivism in learning and alignment in teaching.

(Biggs, 1999)

A comparable model, used in Cross (1996), is the finding from the Study Group on the Conditions of Excellence in American Higher Education (1984) which noted that colleges must:

1. Hold high expectations for student performance.

2. Encourage active student involvement in learning.

3. Provide useful assessment and feedback.

The second is the nine strategies devised by Graham Gibbs for improving the quality of student learning (Gibbs, 1992b):

● independent learning;

● personal development;

● problem based learning;

● reflection;

● independent group work;

● learning by doing;

● developing learning skills;

● project work;

● fine tuning existing models.

Finally in this section it is important to note the influence of the work of Angelo and Cross, whose *Classroom Assessment Techniques* (1993) is a compendium of techniques which lecturers have been using to evaluate their teaching, where the word 'assessment' referred to what staff in the UK would know as feedback from students, or measurements of effectiveness in teaching. Knowledge of these approaches was spreading through the educational development community, though the intended readership for their work was also the subject lecturer. Cross (1996) maintains that the use of these techniques is likely to raise questions which can best be tackled by classroom research, in which students should play a part. A process which can replace the use of the ubiquitous and often ineffective end-of-module questionnaire as the main form of student feedback can be found in Wisdom (1995), and George and Cowan (1999) have offered us a recent and valuable discussion of this field.

TOWARDS A CULTURE OF EVALUATION

The stresses and strains resulting from the work of developing universities and colleges to be able to offer the best possible modern higher education to all our citizens are teaching lecturers, stakeholders and political leaders some important lessons. For educational developers, perhaps the most important has been that people and structures have to change together, and the HEFCE is assembling a strategy for enhancement which is funded to operate at some of the key points simultaneously. Educational development now has to contribute to teaching and learning policy formation at departmental, institutional and national level, as well as recognizing the significance of, managing the impact of and influencing the creation of policies covering other key areas of higher education.

It is beyond the scope of this chapter to determine the appropriate relationship between quantitative and qualitative approaches to practitioner research into educational change, but it is important to explore whether the emphasis on action research effectively debars educational developers from using their work to contribute to policy formation. The evidence from the chapters is that, in different ways, the learning from the work has made contributions sometimes far beyond the bounds of the projects, even though few made use of any of the research tools outlined above. Correspondingly, as the discussions over UK quality assurance have shown, the shift to understanding the processes of student learning has still to make its impact in the face of the tenacious enthusiasm for peer reviewed teacher performance and institutional wealth as the focus for attention.

One analysis of this issue which may have resonance for educational developers has been offered by Ray C Rist, the Head of the Evaluation and Scholarship Unit within the World Bank Institute. In writing about the formation of public policy, he notes that:

> Research can contribute to informed decision making, but the manner in which this is done needs to be reformulated. We are well past the time when it is possible to argue that good research will, because it is good, influence the policy process. This kind of linear relation of research to action simply is not a viable way in which to think about how knowledge can inform decision-making. The relation is both more subtle and more tenuous.
>
> (Rist, 2000)

Because Rist sees policy making as a process that evolves through cycles and rejects decision making as a single event, he is able to describe qualitative policy research as having an enlightenment function, not an engineering one. By analysing the policy cycle in terms of three stages – formulation, implementation and accountability – he is able to show that qualitative research can focus its influence on all three stages through such elements as offering speed and timeliness, providing the concepts and language, bringing experience and feedback, responding flexibly and using continuous evaluation. In departments, disciplines, institutions and even nationally, the quality of some of the action research described in this volume's chapters fits very comfortably with this approach and is contributing to the development of policy on enhancement, even during the process of the work itself.

The emphasis on action research matches one of the key understandings of pedagogy, which is that good teaching involves a continuous engagement with our own personal values. They are acknowledged as much within an action research project as they are in a classroom. In the same way, recognizing and making explicit the intrinsic has been a powerful force in two aspects of modern pedagogy: assessment criteria and feedback from students. In both cases, to fully engage with the students in these areas is not merely a cosmetic device which by chance benefits student learning; it is central to any student's personal development. They are two sites where power, control and ownership in education are negotiated and sometimes contested. Students are more than merely the subjects or the beneficiaries of educational research. The same values would surely lead us to concur with Cross that students could and should be engaged as practitioners in research and reform.

While the challenges of wider participation, globalization and e-learning may in the end require a new structural response, current policy in many countries is to use the existing institutions as the foundation for the new developments. Therefore the task for educational developers is to support their practitioner colleagues in collaborative developmental work to manage the processes of change. The systems are not yet (if ever they even might or should be) sufficiently uniform to enable policy-driven implementation of standardized change, so we are likely to need a variety of change mechanisms. At the heart of many of these will be opportunities for personal and professional growth. Bringing understanding of how students learn, knowledge of effective research tools and experience of action research and project development processes, the educational developer has a great deal to offer to the partnership with students, subject lecturers, policy developers, institutional managers and other colleagues.

REFERENCES

Angelo, T A and Cross, K P (1993) *Classroom Assessment Techniques: A handbook for college teachers,* 2nd edn, Jossey-Bass, San Francisco, CA

Biggs, J (1999) *Teaching for Quality Learning at University: What the student does,* Society for Research in Higher Education (SRHE)/Open University Press, Buckingham

Biggs, J B and Collis, K F (1982) *Evaluating the Quality of Learning: The SOLO taxonomy,* Academic Press, New York

Cross, K P (1996) Improving teaching and learning through classroom assessment and classroom research, in *Improving Student Learning: Using research to improve student learning,* ed G Gibbs, Oxford Centre for Staff Development, Oxford

Dall'Alba, G (1991) Foreshadowing conceptions of teaching, *Research and Development in Higher Education,* **13,** pp 293–97

Denzin, N K and Lincoln, Y S (eds) (2000) *Handbook of Qualitative Research,* 2nd edn, Sage, Thousand Oaks, CA

Entwistle, N J and Ramsden, P (1983) *Understanding Student Learning,* Croom Helm, London

Entwistle, N J, Tait, H and McCune, V (1998) *The Approaches and Study Skills Inventory For Students* (unpublished), University of Edinburgh, Dept of Higher and Further Education

George, J and Cowan, J (1999) *A Handbook of Techniques for Formative Evaluation: Mapping the student's learning experience,* Kogan Page, London

Gibbs, G (1992a) *Improving the Quality of Student Learning,* Technical and Educational Services, Bristol

Gibbs, G (1992b) Improving the quality of student learning through course design, in *Learning to Effect,* ed R Barnett, SRHE/Open University Press, Buckingham

Gibbs, G (1994) *Improving Student Learning: Theory and practice,* Oxford Centre for Staff Development, Oxford

Gibbs, G (1996) *Improving Student Learning: Using research to improve student learning,* Oxford Centre for Staff Development, Oxford

Guba, E G and Lincoln, Y S (1989) *Fourth Generation Evaluation,* Sage, Newbury Park, CA

Kelleher, J, Sommerlad, E and Stern, E (1996) *Evaluation of the Electronic Libraries Programme: Guidelines for ELIB project evaluation,* Tavistock Institute, London

Marton, F and Säljö, R (1997) Approaches to learning, in *The Experience of Learning: Implications for teaching and learning in higher education,* 2nd edn, ed F Marton, D Hounsell and NJ Entwistle, Scottish Academic Press, Edinburgh

Marton, F, Dall'Alba, G and Beaty, E (1993) Conceptions of learning, *International Journal of Educational Research,* **19,** pp 277–300

Moon, J (1996) Generic level descriptors: their place in the standards debate, in *In Focus: Modular higher education in the UK,* Higher Education Quality Council, London

Olsson, T (2000) Qualitative aspects of teaching and assessing in the chemical engineering curriculum: applications of the SOLO taxonomy, in *Improving Student Learning Through the Disciplines,* ed C Rust, Oxford Centre for Staff and Learning Development, Oxford

Prosser, M and Trigwell, K (1999) *Understanding Learning and Teaching: The experience in higher education,* SRHE/Open University Press, Buckingham

Ramsden, P (1992) *Learning to Teach in Higher Education,* Routledge, London

Rist, R (2000) Influencing the policy process with qualitative research, in *Handbook of Qualitative Research,* 2nd edn, ed N K Denzin, and Y S Lincoln, Sage, Thousand Oaks, CA

Schwandt, T A (2000) Three epistemological stances for qualitative inquiry: interpretivism, hermeneutics, and social constructionism, in *Handbook of Qualitative Research*, 2nd edn, ed N K Denzin and Y S Lincoln, Sage, Thousand Oaks, CA

Sommerlad, E and Ramsden, C with Stern, E (2001) *Synthesis of TLTP3 Annual Reports*, Tavistock Institute, London

Study Group on the Conditions of Excellence in American Higher Education (1984) *Involvement in Learning: Realising the potential of American higher education*, National Institute of Education, Washington, DC

Tait, H, Entwistle, N and McCune, V (1998) ASSIST: a reconceptualisation of the Approaches to Study Inventory, in *Improving Student Learning: Improving students as learners*, ed C Rust, Oxford Centre for Staff and Learning Development, Oxford

Wilson, K, Lizzio, A and Ramsden, P (1997) The development, validation and application of the Course Experience Questionnaire, *Studies in Higher Education*, **22**, pp 3–25

Wisdom, J (1995) Getting and using student feedback, in *Directions in Staff Development*, ed A Brew, SRHE/Open University Press, Buckingham

Yin, R (1994) *Case Study Research: Design and methods*, Sage, Thousand Oaks, CA

Index

Tables and figures are indicated by italic page references